AF335643

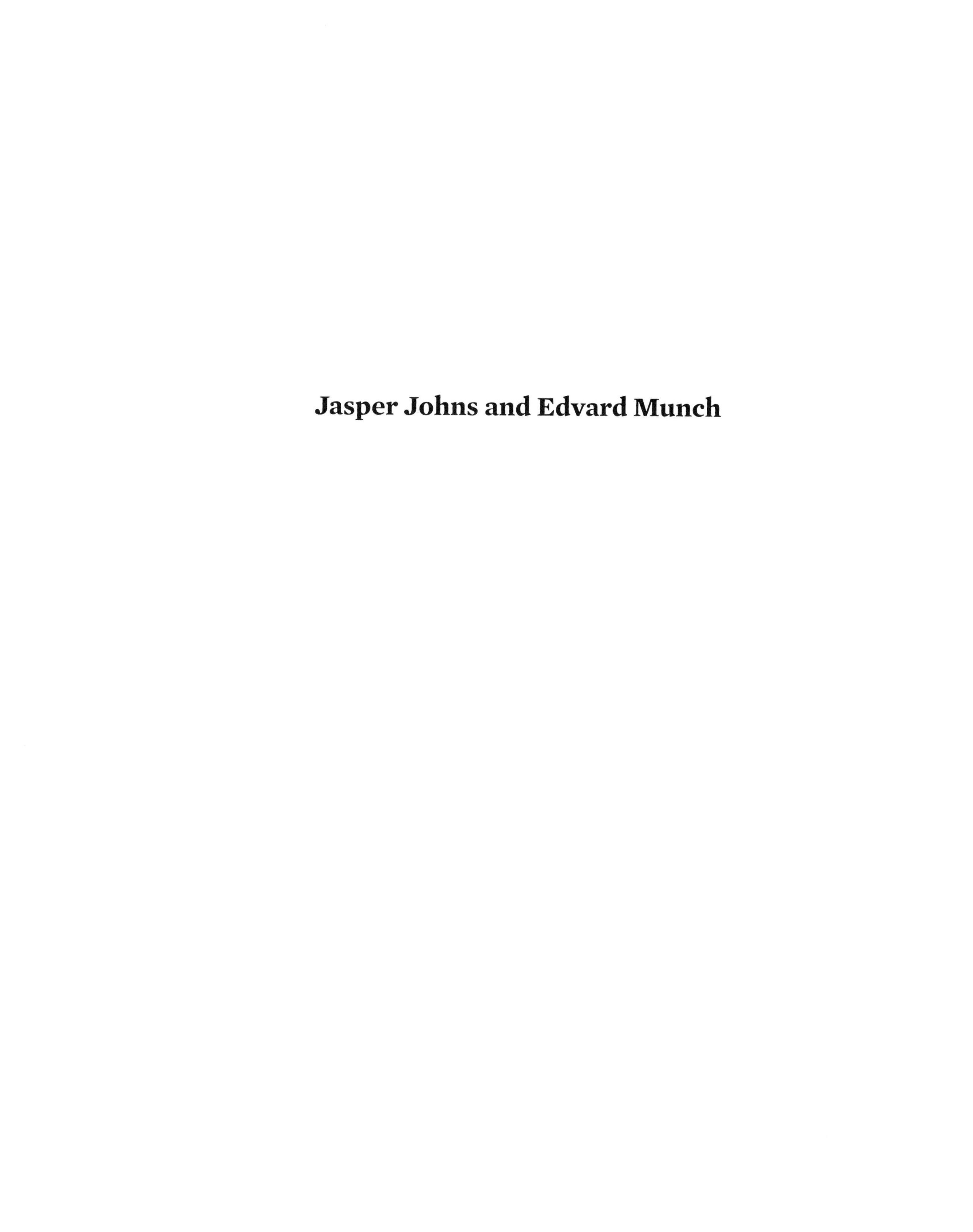

Jasper Johns and Edvard Munch

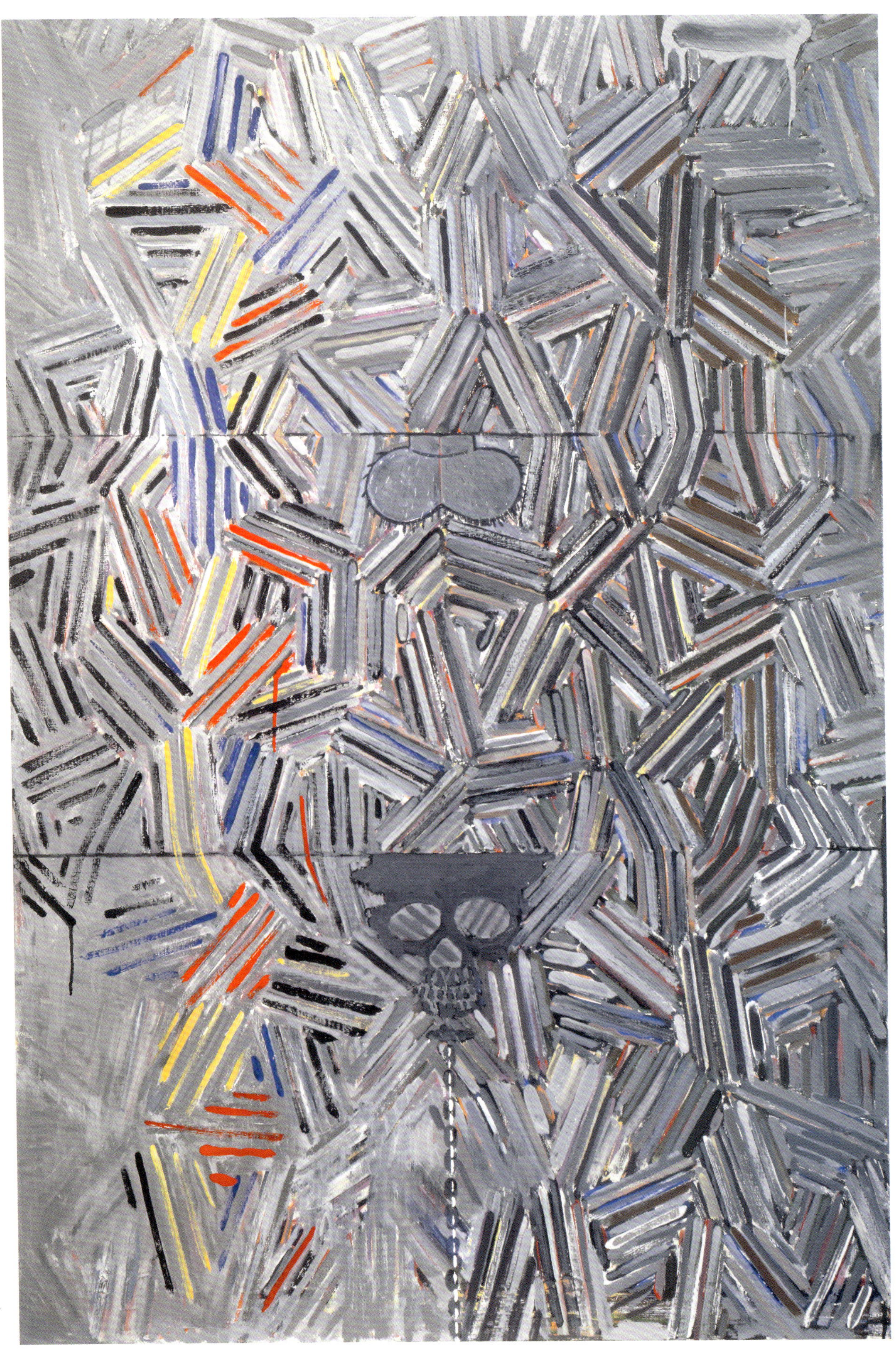

Jasper Johns and Edvard Munch

Inspiration and Transformation

John B. Ravenal

Virginia Museum of Fine Arts and Yale University Press
in partnership with the Munch Museum

Presented by

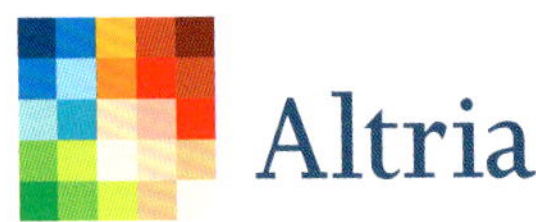

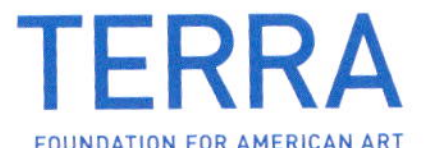

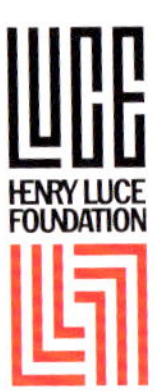

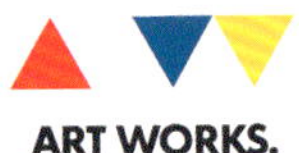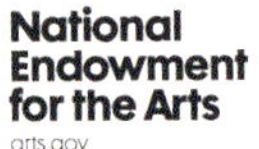
National Endowment for the Arts
ART WORKS.
arts.gov

This catalogue accompanies exhibitions at the following museums:

Munch Museum, Oslo, Norway, June 18–September 25, 2016
Virginia Museum of Fine Arts, Richmond, November 19, 2016–February 20, 2017

The exhibition was organized by the Virginia Museum of Fine Arts, in partnership with the Munch Museum.

The catalogue was co-published by the Virginia Museum of Fine Arts and Yale University Press, in partnership with the Munch Museum.

©2016 Virginia Museum of Fine Arts. All rights reserved. Except for legitimate excerpts customary in review or scholarly publications, no part of this book may be reproduced by any means without express written permission of the publisher.

Library of Congress Cataloging-in-Publication Data

Names: Ravenal, John B., 1959– author. | Johns, Jasper, 1930– | Munch, Edvard, 1863–1944. | Virginia Museum of Fine Arts, organizer, host institution. | Munch-museet (Oslo, Norway) organizer, host institution.
Title: Jasper Johns and Edvard Munch : inspiration and transformation / John B. Ravenal.
Description: Richmond, VA : Virginia Museum of Fine Arts and Yale University Press in partnership with the Munch Museum, 2016. | Includes bibliographical references and index.
Identifiers: LCCN 2016012486 | ISBN 9780300220063 (hardback : Yale) | ISBN 9788290128888 (Munch Museum)
Subjects: LCSH: Johns, Jasper, 1930– —Exhibitions. | Munch, Edvard, 1863–1944— Exhibitions. | Munch, Edvard, 1863–1944—Influence—Exhibitions. | BISAC: ART / History / Contemporary (1945–). | ART / History / Modern (late 19th Century to 1945). | ART / Individual Artists / General. | ART / Collections, Catalogs, Exhibitions / General. | ART / Criticism & Theory.
Classification: LCC N6537.J6 A4 2016 | DDC 709.2—dc23 LC record available at http://lccn.loc.gov/2016012486

Produced by the Department of Publications
Virginia Museum of Fine Arts
200 N. Boulevard, Richmond, VA 23220
vmfa.museum

Published in association with
Yale University Press
302 Temple Street, P.O. Box 209040
New Haven, CT 06520-9040
yalebooks.com/art

Rosalie West, Editor in Chief and Project Editor
Stacy Moore, Editor
Chelsea Neal, Publications Assistant
Sarah Lavicka, Chief Graphic Designer
John Hoar, Project Designer
Deborah Patton, Indexer

Composed and typeset in Mercury Text, Gotham and Avenir typefaces.
Printed by Conti Tipocolor, Florence, Italy

Front cover: Details of **Between the Clock and the Bed** by Johns (fig. 71) and **Self-Portrait between the Clock and the Bed** by Munch (fig. 75)

Frontispiece: Johns, **Tantric Detail I** (fig. 68)

Back cover: *Left,* Johns, **Savarin** (fig. 47); *right,* Munch, **Self-Portrait** (fig. 44)

Contents

Directors' Forewords

The Virginia Museum of Fine Arts is fortunate to collaborate with the Munch Museum on this once-in-a-lifetime opportunity to examine Jasper Johns alongside the very paintings and motifs by Edvard Munch that he referenced during a turning point in his work. The depth of relationship has never been explored so significantly, and so stunningly, as with the groundbreaking scholarship and presentation of these works in Oslo and in Richmond. Among notable firsts, this will be the first time in more than twenty years that all three of Johns's *Between the Clock and the Bed* paintings will be displayed together—and perhaps the only time they will ever be exhibited alongside their inspiration, Munch's *Self Portrait Between the Clock and the Bed*, as well as the actual bedspread from Munch's home.

It is a pleasure to continue collaborating with John Ravenal, our former VMFA Sydney and Frances Lewis Family Curator for Modern and Contemporary Art, on this celebrated project. Although he is now Director of the deCordova Sculpture Park and Museum, his ties to VMFA remain strong. We are further indebted to Jasper Johns, who has given his support and generously lent to the exhibition for both venues. This collaboration would not have been possible without the support of my colleague and friend, Munch Museum Director Stein Olav Henrichsen, and Chief Curator Jon-Ove Steihaug, who have shepherded this project from the beginning. We appreciate the interest shown by Consul General Elin Bergithe Rognlie, Royal Norwegian Consulate General, New York. The Terra Foundation for American Art was instrumental in facilitating this cross-cultural conversation by supporting the exhibition's presentation at both venues. Altria Group, VMFA's partner in the arts for more than fifty years, continued their legacy of support as the exhibition's presenting sponsor in Richmond. We are also grateful to the Henry Luce Foundation and the National Endowment for the Arts for their major support of this project.

The Virginia Museum is home to an exceptionally talented staff, who have ably organized the exhibition and guided its presentation at both partner institutions. Dr. Michael R. Taylor, Chief Curator and Deputy Director for Art and Education, has directed the project, supported by Courtney Burkhardt, Exhibitions Project Coordinator. Design and logistical aspects of the exhibition were overseen by Stephen Bonadies, Deputy Director for Facilities and Collections Management; finances by Hossein Sadid, Chief Financial Officer; and exhibition publication and fundraising efforts by Claudia Keenan, Deputy Director for Resources and the Visitor Experience.

We are honored to partner with the Munch Museum and Director Stein Olav Henrichsen on this exploration into the work of two renowned artists, Johns and Munch—a collaboration that advances the field of art historical scholarship, and celebrates the inspiration and transformation that engages us all in their work.

Alex Nyerges
Director
Virginia Museum of Fine Arts

This exhibition came into being on the initiative of the Virginia Museum of Fine Arts. We have had a very productive collaboration and I would like to thank Director Alex Nyerges and the VMFA's staff for their professionalism and dedication to the project. Our gratitude also goes to Curator John Ravenal, who has developed the scholarly foundation for the exhibition and written the exhibition catalogue.

This is the first exhibition that critically examines the relationship between Jasper Johns's and Edvard Munch's art as well as the first comprehensive presentation of Johns's art in Scandinavia. As John Ravenal writes here, Munch became an important source of inspiration for Johns from the 1970s and into the 1980s, a period in the latter's artistic career that was "marked by major thematic and formal shifts—including the appearance of figurative imagery, perspective, references to time and strong emotion." Munch's art thus provides access to an important phase in Johns's art, just as Johns sheds new light on Munch with his retrospective treatment of some of Munch's motifs and themes.

However, this catalogue and the related exhibition shown at the Munch Museum in Oslo and the Virginia Museum of Fine Arts in Richmond do not represent the first time that the works of Jasper Johns and Edvard Munch have been presented side by side. Munch and Johns were shown together in *Echoes of the Scream* in 2001, an exhibition that also encompassed works by artists such as Marina Abramovic, Francis Bacon, and Joseph Beuys. Munch is associated with the breakthrough of modernism in European art at the end of the nineteenth century, and he was a pioneer of the various expressionist movements of the twentieth. Johns's early work was seen as a break with the idea of a subjective and expressive idiom in favor of a more conceptual approach to painting. The fact that Johns and Munch might appear to be so different makes the underlying connections that this exhibition discloses all the more interesting.

Johns+Munch, the title of the exhibition at the Munch Museum, is the fifth in a total of six exhibitions in the museum's series *+Munch*, presented in 2015–16, in which Munch has been compared to an equal number of artists—from Vincent van Gogh and Gustav Vigeland to Asger Jorn, Jasper Johns, Robert Mapplethorpe, and Bjarne Melgaard.

I thank Idemitsu Petroleum Norge for their support of the Munch Museum's exhibition program, and the Norwegian architectural and design firm Snøhetta for an inspiring collaboration and exhibition design. I would also like to express my gratitude to all of the Munch Museum's expert employees who have contributed to realizing this unique project.

Translated from Norwegian by Francesca M. Nichols

Stein Olav Henrichsen
Director
The Munch Museum

Preface and Acknowledgments

The connection between the works of Jasper Johns and Edvard Munch arises directly from Johns's interest in Munch's work, an interest he revealed by stenciling Munch's initials on his 1981 *Savarin* print and titling a group of three late crosshatch paintings after one of Munch's late self-portraits. This publication and exhibition offer the first sustained exploration of this fascinating subject. In doing so they pursue two linked goals: to describe how and when Munch entered into Johns's work—that is, to detail the arc of inspiration and transformation; and to show that this engagement provided a catalyst for, not just a symptom of, the marked change in Johns's work during the early 1980s when he returned to recognizable imagery after a decade of abstract painting.

My interest in the subject was sparked by Johns's last great crosshatch work, *Between the Clock and the Bed*, 1982–83, given to the Virginia Museum of Fine Arts (VMFA) by Sydney and Frances Lewis. Over the course of nearly seventeen years as VMFA's Curator of Modern and Contemporary Art, I considered why Johns titled this complex abstract work after one of Munch's great meditations on human mortality. My interest in Munch had begun in my college years, around the time my mother first traveled to Oslo to research and write about his art. Finally in 2012, the time seemed right to propose a major exhibition uniting these strands by telling the story of Johns and Munch together.

The organization of this international exhibition would not have been possible without the full participation of the Munch Museum in Oslo, and I extend sincere gratitude to Stein Olav Henrichsen, Director. It has been a special pleasure to work with Jon-Ove Steihaug, Chief Curator and Director of Collections and Exhibitions, whose expertise, generosity, and enthusiasm have contributed immensely to the project. I also deeply appreciate the efforts of his colleagues at the Munch Museum, including Ute Kuhlemann Falck, Senior Curator of Prints and Drawings; Magne Bruteig, Senior Curator of Prints and Drawings; Petra Pettersen, Curator of Paintings; Knut Listerud and Espen Kregnes, Project Managers; Sivert Thue, Researcher; Trygve Lauritzen, Head of Security; Tiril Krabbesund, Registrar; Emma Chan and Erika Gohde Sandbakken, Conservators; Francesca Nobili, freelance exhibition designer; and Arne Borgan and Tor-Bjørn Adelgren, Exhibition Technicians.

No exhibition is possible without the generosity of lenders. In addition to the Munch Museum's extraordinary loan of some sixty-five works, the many other museums and private collectors who lent their works are recognized on a separate page and in the image captions. In addition, I thank the Art Institute of Chicago; Philadelphia Museum of Art; and Museum of Fine Arts, Boston.

I was fortunate to present research on the exhibition at three conferences and I thank the organizers, especially Pari Stave at The American Scandinavian Society; Birgitte Sauge, Eva Amine Wold Engeset, and Mai Britt Guleng for Munch 150 in Oslo, *Edvard Munch and/in Modernism*; and Shin-Eui Park and Jeong Eun Ho, *Munch in Seoul*, Seoul Korea, Culture & I Leaders. Many other individuals provided special assistance with research and loans, and I am pleased to acknowledge them: Katherine Alcauskas, Carlos Basualdo, Patricia Berman, Brian Berry, Roberta Bernstein, Ashley Brown, Bettina Sulser Bryant, Barbara Bertozzi Castelli, Jean-Christophe Castelli, Ellen Chaffin, Christophe Cherix, Zenia Chrysostomidis, Jay Clarke, Caroline Collier, Harry Cooper, Eileen Costello, Barbara Cura, Kathleen Curry, Lucy Dew, Stephan Diederich, Carol Eliel, Siri Engberg, Barbara Engelbach, Melissa English, Sally Epstein, Jennifer Farrell, Richard Field, Nicole Gallo, Vicki Gambill, Kate Ganz, Mark Godfrey, Bill Goldston, Larissa Goldston, Alison de Lima Greene, Suzanne Greenawalt, Jan Howard, John Ittmann, Gregory Jecmen, Rebecca Jones, Bill Katz, Sarah Kianovsky, David Kiehl, Wynn Kramarsky, Charlotte Laridon, Margo Leavin, Mary Anne Lee, Mary-Kay Lombino, Susan Lorence,

Catherine Malone, Robert Manley, Allison McLaughlin, Jen Mergel, Marisa Muller, Ingrid Moe, Dominic Molon, Bob Monk, Judith Niemyer, Annette Novelli, Gary Owen, Mark Pascale, Avril Peck, Jeanette Preston, Ashley Ragg, Morton Rapp, Charlie Ritchie, Clare Rogan, Elin Bergithe Rognlie, James Rondeau, Mark Rosenthal, Cora Rosevear, Clarence Sheffield, Jr. , Pari Stave, Ann Temkin, Reto Thüring, Ulrich Tillmann, Jacqueline Tran, David Walker, Cathleen Walther, Joni Moisant Weyl, Gerd Woll, Andrew Young, and two peer readers, who remain anonymous to me. I am pleased to thank Patricia Fidler at Yale University Press for supporting the co-publication of this book. In addition, I am grateful to Agnes Gund for her support, and to Marion Boulton Stroud, aka Kippy, for the beautiful respite she provided for research and writing at the Acadia Summer Arts Program.

At VMFA, I am grateful to many former colleagues for their contributions. Alex Nyerges, Director, was an enthusiastic supporter from the start. Robin Nicholson, former Deputy Director for Art and Education, and Sylvia Yount, former Chief Curator, helped launch the exhibition, and Michael Taylor, Chief Curator and Deputy Director for Art and Education; Lee Anne Chesterfield, Director for Museum Planning and Board Relations; and Claudia Keenan, Executive Director of the Foundation and Deputy Director for Resources and Visitor Experience, helped guide the project to completion. Courtney Burkhardt served as project coordinator with her usual good cheer, aided by Aiesha Halstead; Karen Daly as lead exhibition registrar, assisted by Kelly Burrow, superbly managed the transport of art and myriad other details; Trang Nguyen contributed her usual keen attention to detail as exhibition designer. For the production of this beautiful catalogue, I offer a special appreciation to Rosalie West, Editor in Chief, whose thorough and sensitive editing, attention to detail, and skills managing complex projects help VMFA publications adhere to the highest standards; Sarah Lavicka, Chief Graphic Designer, for her expert oversight; John Hoar,

for his elegant book design; and Howell Perkins, Manager of Photographic Resources, who obtained digital files and rights for hundreds of images. In Publications, Stacy Moore and Chelsea Neal contributed important editorial support, and valuable research assistance was provided by Maggie McClellan Albee, Reference Librarian. Allan Altholz and Pryor Green guided the marketing and communications, and Jessica Bauserman, Youth and Family Programs Educator, created innovative programming. The Advancement team, including Jillian Jones, former Manager of Individual Giving; Mary Scott Swanson, Manager of Institutional Giving; Naomi Crown, Manager of Corporate Relations; and Sharayah Cochran, Corporate and Foundation Relations Associate, secured funding. Carol Sawyer and Bruce Suffield in Paintings Conservation; Stephen Bonadies, Deputy Director for Collections and Facilities Management; and Travis Fullerton, Chief Collection Photographer, Manager of Imaging Resources, all provided needed expertise. I also benefitted from the help of Sarah Eckhardt, Associate Curator of Modern and Contemporary Art, and from interns and research assistants over several years, including Amber Esseiva, Rachel Hutcheson, Laura Keller, and especially Owen Duffy.

It is a special privilege to thank Jasper Johns. His gracious engagement with this project included lending work from his personal collection, accommodating my visits, reading the manuscript, and fielding numerous questions. I am deeply grateful for his interest and support. In addition, sincere thanks are due to the staff at the Johns Studio — Sarah Taggart, former Administrative Assistant, and Maureen Pkowski, Administrative Assistant — whose help was invaluable at every stage of the organizational process.

Love and appreciation, as ever, to Ginny, Eva, and Daniel.

John B. Ravenal
Executive Director
deCordova Sculpture Park and Museum

Lenders to the Exhibition

Nelson Blitz, Jr. and Catherine Woodard

Cleveland Museum of Art, Ohio

Gemini G.E.L., Los Angeles

Brian Goldston and Peter Balis

Larissa Goldston

Stan and Renie Helfgott

Jasper Johns

Robert and Jane Meyerhoff Collection

Julie and Edward J. Minskoff

Munch Museum, Oslo

Museum of Fine Arts, Houston

The Museum of Modern Art, New York

National Gallery of Art, Washington, DC

Marsha and Jeffrey Perelman

Ryobi Foundation

Jack Shear

Tate Gallery, London

Universal Limited Art Editions

Virginia Museum of Fine Arts, Richmond

Whitney Museum of American Art, New York

And other private collectors
who wish to remain anonymous

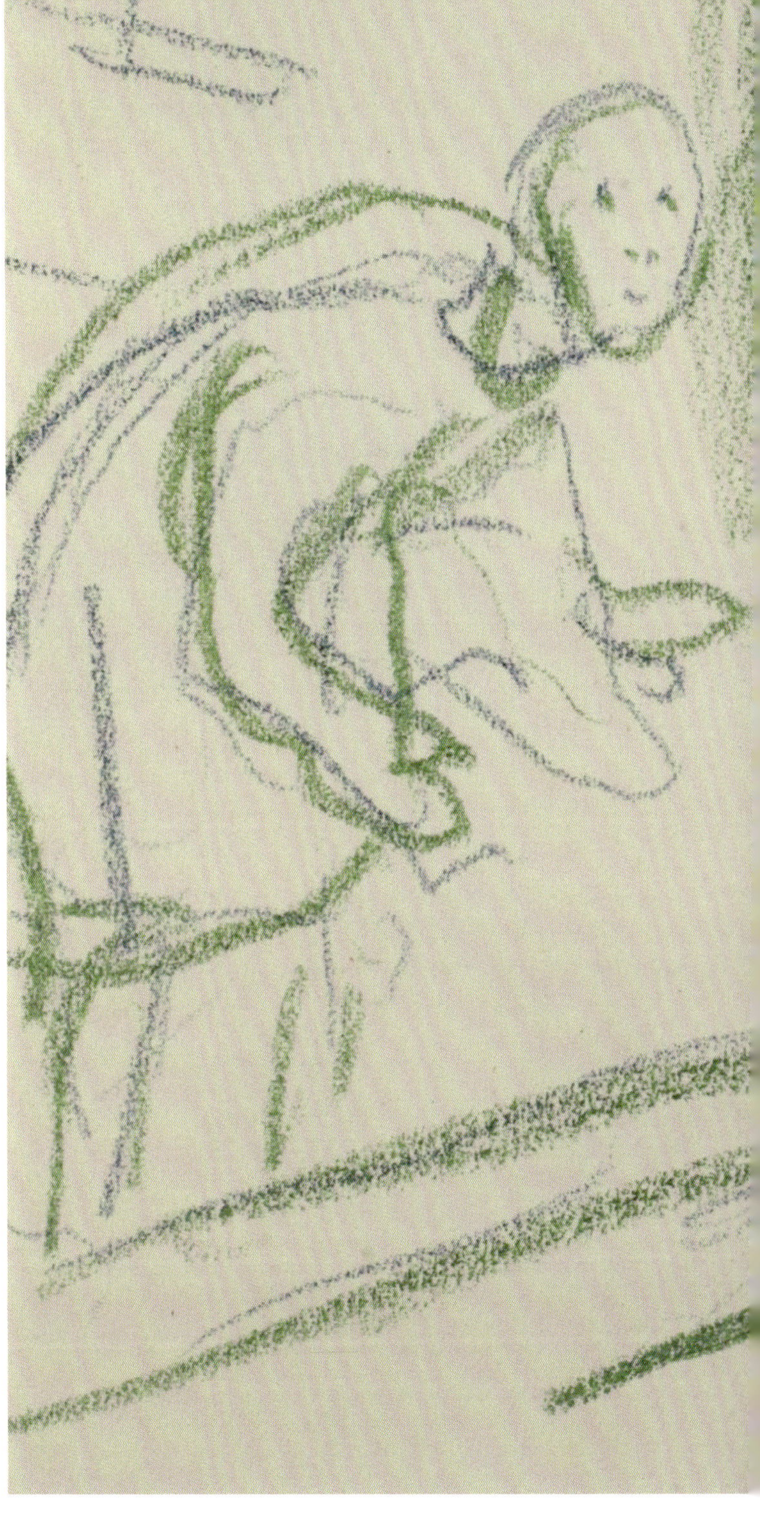

Munch, **Bent-over Man Looking at His Mirror Image**, 1919, crayon in sketchbook, 5 x 7 in. (12.8 x 17.8 cm). Munch Museum

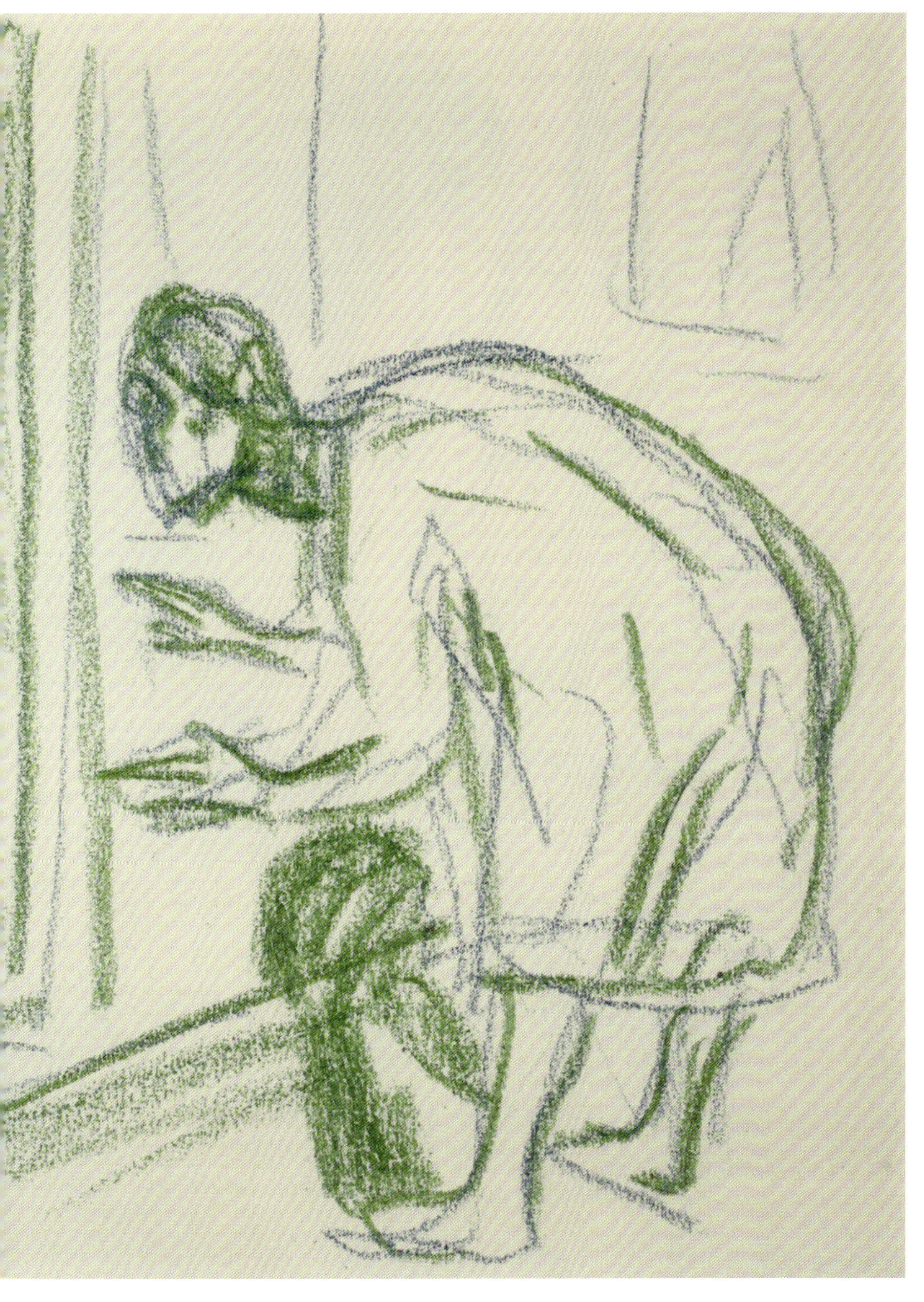

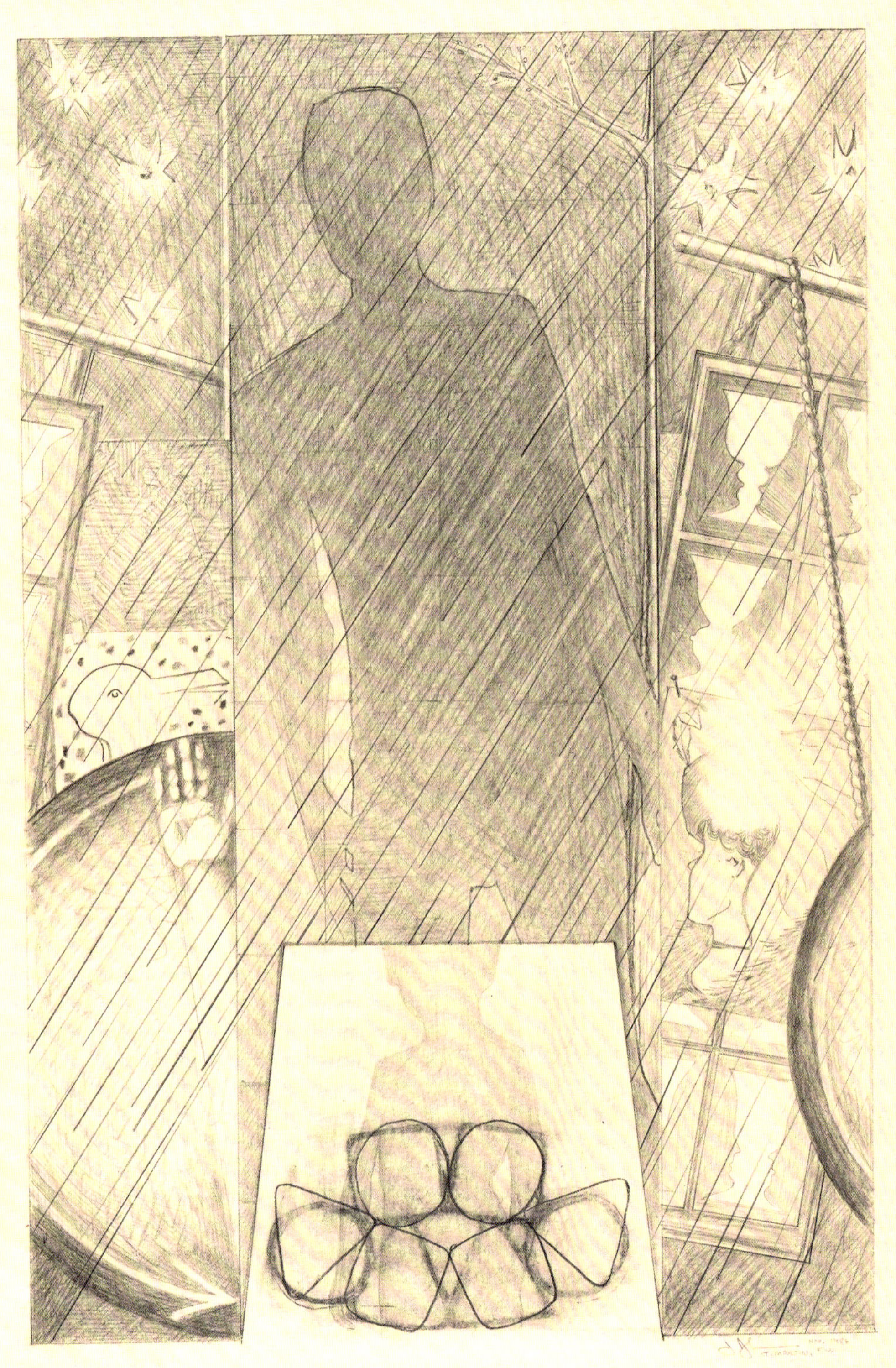

Jasper Johns and Edvard Munch
Inspiration and Transformation

Introduction

Many contemporary artists have drawn inspiration from the art and life of Norwegian Expressionist Edvard Munch (1863–1944), including Andy Warhol, Joseph Beuys, Elizabeth Murray, and Anselm Kiefer. Their adaptations from Munch's paintings and prints have functioned as a two-way lens, giving insight into their creative process while revising and revitalizing the perception of Munch's art.[1] During a crucial period midway through his career, Jasper Johns, too, looked to Munch as a source of inspiration, studying his innovative working methods as well as his signature themes of love, loss, sex, and death. Johns engaged in a dense process of absorption, quotation, repetition, and transformation to create his own images. At the same time, Munch's presence infused Johns's work with new content that allowed him to give voice to a broadened range of expression.

Johns (born 1930) has borrowed from diverse artists from the fifteenth through the twentieth century—Leonardo da Vinci, Matthias Grünewald, Paul Cézanne, Pablo Picasso, Marcel Duchamp, René Magritte—and their presence is woven throughout his work in ways both overt and hidden. Numerous scholars and critics have addressed these connections, and the explication of sources forms a substantial part of the literature on Johns's work.[2] Munch has not been excluded from this literature, but his place is usually relegated to a second tier, and accounts of the connection often hold to the same brief and, as it turns out, possibly inaccurate story.[3] This is a surprising gap, given the frequency and directness of Johns's references to Munch, which include some two dozen unique images with obvious instances of quotation and many more that build on these allusions in various ways.[4] This level of impact suggests that a revised narrative about Johns's relationship to Munch is warranted. In addition, the period of Johns's greatest interest in Munch is marked by major thematic and formal shifts—including the appearance of figurative imagery, perspective, references to time, and strong emotion—that this essay will argue are attributable in part to Munch's example.

Johns made his interest in Munch a matter of public record when he included Munch's initials in a print from 1981 and titled his last crosshatch paintings of the early 1980s after Munch's late *Self-Portrait between the Clock and the Bed,* which will be discussed below. In addition, some three decades later, Munch still appeared to be on his mind. Johns's recent series of paintings, *Regrets,* made between 2012 and 2014, are inspired by a found photograph of the British painter Lucian Freud sitting on a single bed with a geometric-patterned coverlet, his hand to his head in a gesture of despair. An interviewer asked Johns the following question: "*Regrets* brought to mind your painting *Between the Clock and the Bed* (1981)—not just the mirroring (with the crosshatches in the earlier work), but also the reference to Edvard Munch, the bed, and a kind of despair. Is there any relationship?" And Johns, in his famously laconic manner, replied, "As you have made the relationship, so have I."[5]

Even with these acknowledgments, there is no denying that Johns and Munch make strange bedfellows, and the great differences in their art may in part explain the lack of deeper attention to the connection. Johns's work of the 1950s rejected the emotional and subjective approach to making art that Munch's work helped inaugurate a half century earlier. Munch had a direct impact at the beginning of the twentieth century on German Expressionism, based in large part on his residency in Berlin from 1893 to 1908.[6] This trajectory of art as personal expression culminated several decades later in New York with Abstract Expressionism,[7] which was reaching a peak about the time Johns arrived there in the early 1950s.[8] After a short period of experimentation with gestural abstract painting, Johns rejected this approach and destroyed every example of his work in this vein that he could get his hands on. As he described in retrospect,

> I have attempted to develop my thinking in such a way that the work I've done is not me—not to confuse my feelings with what I produced. I didn't want my work to be an exposure of my feelings. Abstract Expressionism was so lively—personal identity and painting were more or less the same, and I tried to operate the same way. But I found I couldn't do anything that would be identical with my feelings. So I worked in such a way that I could say that it's not me. That accounts for the separation.[9]

To free himself from the burden of drawing on his feelings as a source of imagery, Johns used found images—"things the mind already knows," he called them, or things "taken . . . not mine."[10] These images were of a generic sort, not connected with any individual creator, and also of a functional nature. Starting in

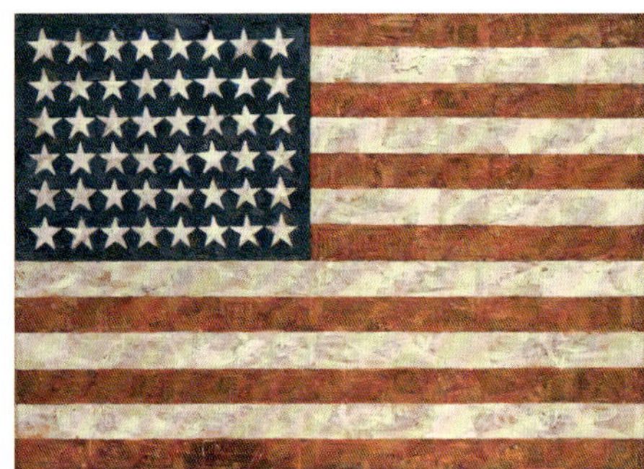

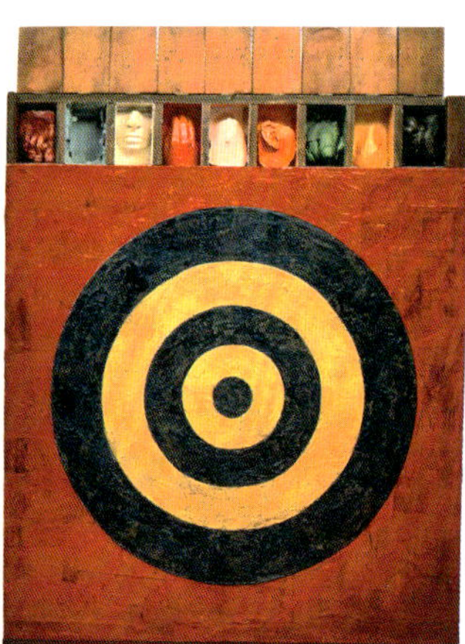

fig. 1 Johns, **Flag**, 1954–55, encaustic, oil, and collage on canvas (three panels), 42 ¼ x 60 ⅝ in. (107.3 x 153.8 cm). The Museum of Modern Art, New York, Gift of Philip Johnson in honor of Alfred H. Barr, Jr.

fig. 2 Johns, **Target with Plaster Casts**, 1955, encaustic and collage on canvas with objects, 51 x 44 x 3 ½ in. (129.5 x 111.8 x 8.8 cm). Collection of David Geffen, Los Angeles

1954 with flags (fig. 1) and targets (fig. 2), Johns then moved on to numbers, letters, and maps for the remainder of the decade.

What unites these motifs is their deliberate nonexpressiveness. They are at once familiar and overlooked—ubiquitous elements that exist close at hand and offer little resistance to the repetition, variation, and mutation Johns employed in his work. In a word, they are neutral, although as Johns wrote in a 1963 sketchbook, "'Neutral' expresses an intention."[11]

Johns's preference for found or impersonal imagery—"something that wouldn't have to carry my nature as part of its message"[12]—stands in direct contrast to Munch's approach to art. Beginning in the 1880s, in his native Norway and then in Paris and Berlin, Munch worked his way out of the naturalist mode of his teachers and mentors—artists such as Christian Krohg and Frits Thaulow—toward Symbolism and Expressionism, distorting observable reality in response to the inner pressures of memory and emotion. "My pictures are my diaries," he wrote.[13] The emotions that preoccupied Munch concerned anxiety, loneliness, jealousy, fear, and grief.

> My whole life has been spent walking by the side of a bottomless chasm, jumping from stone to stone. Sometimes I try to leave my narrow path and join the swirling mainstream of life, but I always find myself drawn inexorably back towards the chasm's edge and there I shall walk until the day I finally fall into the abyss. For as long as I can remember I have suffered from a deep feeling of anxiety which I have tried to express in my art. Without anxiety and illness I would have been like a ship without a rudder.[14]

At the same time, Munch saw his intensely personal images as addressing universal human experience. As he described, "In my art, I have tried to express my own life and its meaning. In so doing I hope that I will also help other people to understand their own lives."[15] Motivated by personal experience and often traceable to autobiographical events, Munch's work also offered a more encompassing statement about the precarious condition of the individual in modern society.

Johns's awareness of Munch can be traced back at least to 1950 when, at age twenty, he saw the artist's first retrospective exhibition in the United States, held at The Museum of Modern Art (MoMA).[16] Munch had died six years earlier at age eighty, and had left all the work in his possession—thousands of paintings, drawings, prints, photographs, and sculptures, along with lithographic stones, copperplates, woodblocks, notebooks, letters, manuscripts, and clippings—to the city of Oslo. While a dedicated Munch Museum did not open until 1963, several important retrospective exhibitions were organized in Europe and the United States after his death.[17]

It is not now known whether Johns was drawn to the 1950 exhibition because he was already aware of Munch's work or simply thought a major show at MoMA worth seeing, and the experience appears to have remained dormant until the mid-1970s.[18] Johns does not believe he saw the three subsequent solo exhibitions of Munch's work in New York over the next two decades,[19] but he would likely have been aware of them and of Munch's increasing stature among US scholars and audiences. Two print curators with whom Johns had close connections—Riva Castleman at MoMA and Richard Field, then at Wesleyan University's Davison Art Center—were each deeply familiar with the work of Johns and Munch. Castleman had organized exhibitions of both artists' work,[20] and Field had hung their work side by side in a 1975 exhibition called *Images of Death*.[21] Johns may also have known of the growing interest in Munch's work among contemporary artists, including Jim Dine, with whom he had exhibited in Pop Art and Neo-Dada exhibitions starting in the early 1960s. Dine traveled to Oslo in the mid-1970s to spend time at the Munch Museum, and his first published woodcut, *The Woodcut Bathrobe,* 1975, was directly inspired by Munch's work.[22] While Warhol's *After Munch* series of 1983 postdates most of Johns's Munch-inspired work, it also reflects the atmosphere of active interest in Munch that existed at the time among his peers.[23]

Crosshatching

The story of Johns's engagement with Munch's work deepened, paradoxically, during the ten-year period when the abstract motif of crosshatching became the exclusive subject of Johns's paintings.[24] Crosshatching first appeared in the painting *Untitled,* 1972 (fig. 3), where it fills the far left panel of a four-part work. Johns described the source for this pattern during a 1976 interview with Michael Crichton:

> I was riding in a car, going out to the Hamptons for the weekend, when a car came in the opposite direction. It was covered with these marks, but I only saw it for a moment—then it was gone—just a brief glimpse. But I immediately thought that I would use it for my next painting.[25]

Johns later added to the account: "It had all the qualities that interest me—literalness, repetitiveness, an obsessive quality, order with dumbness, and the possibility of complete lack of meaning."[26] Despite its specificity, the crosshatch story obscures as much as it reveals. No date has ever been fixed for when Johns observed the decorated car, and thus we do not know how long the motif percolated in his mind—becoming more "his" than "taken"—before he used it.[27] In addition, the serendipitous nature of the story sidesteps the fact that hatch marks and crosshatching would already have been very familiar to Johns as an acclaimed draftsman and printmaker; from the Middle Ages onward these techniques were a basic means in the graphic arts for rendering light and shade and creating the illusion of three dimensions. Seeing the pattern on the car, then, was a moment more of recognition than of discovery—that a fundamental unit of his existing artistic vocabulary could be isolated and elevated as an analog to the flags, maps, numbers, and letters he previously sourced out in the world.

At the same time, crosshatching offered Johns a way to further subdue the residual meanings that clung to these other found motifs. Crosshatching was a purer vehicle, emptied of every reference except to itself, even if sparked by a passing car. In short, it was a mark about making marks, or, as Rosalind Kraus called it, "an image of pictorial technique."[28] This extreme neutrality explains why Johns adopted crosshatching as the exclusive motif for his next decade of abstract paintings, and why, too, by the end of that time, it had become a straightjacket from which he sought to escape.

In addition to its flexibility, crosshatching also allowed Johns to further his interest in confusing the boundaries between abstraction and representation. In his flag paintings, he had extended the image to the edges of the canvas, raising the question of whether it was a flag or the image of a flag. Similarly, the crosshatch works can be seen both as abstract paintings and as highly realistic paintings of abstract patterns. In *Untitled*, 1972, he joined the crosshatch panel to two other abstract panels, both bearing a flagstone pattern—another found motif that he glimpsed from a car, this time on a wall in Harlem.[29] The fourth panel of the painting, however, stands apart, with highly realistic fragments of bodies cast in wax and nailed to wooden slats crisscrossing the back of a canvas. Johns had incorporated cast body parts in earlier work, all the way back to paintings such as *Target with Plaster Casts*, 1955 (fig. 2). But in *Untitled*, 1972, the greater realism, use of different male and female bodies, and allover dispersal rather than neat containment lend a macabre tone. At the same time, joining this panel on equal terms to the crosshatching and flagstone panels created an equivalency, suggesting that abstraction and representation are fungible categories.

Johns underscored this relativity in the 1974 print version of *Untitled*, 1972 (fig. 4). Here, beneath the immediately visible images, he blind printed—embossing and impressing with no ink—the pattern of each panel beneath the colored ink version to its right.[30] The body fragments panel, then, moves all the way around to the beginning of the sequence and appears as a ghost beneath the crosshatching (fig. 5)—thus joining extreme realism and extreme abstraction as if one and the same.

Following *Untitled*, 1972, Johns made his first painting using only crosshatching. *Scent* (fig.6) initiates the intricate compositional strategies that defined Johns's

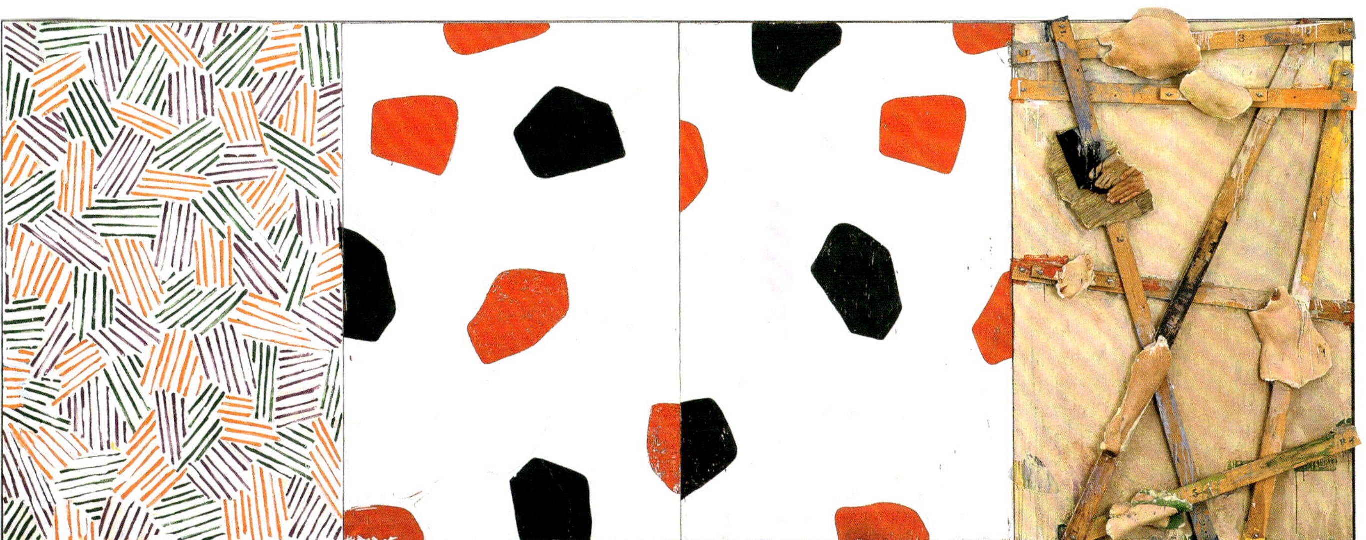

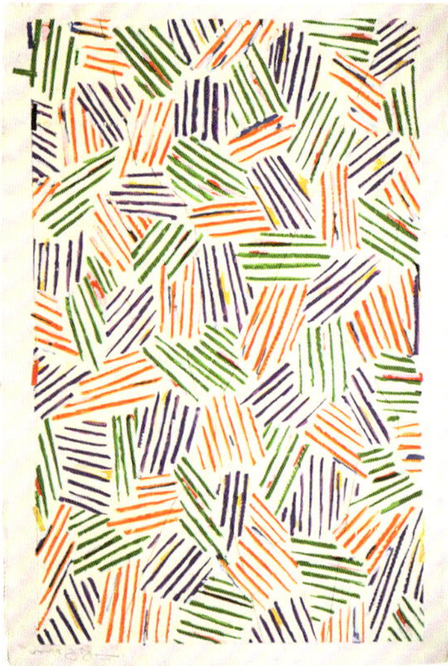 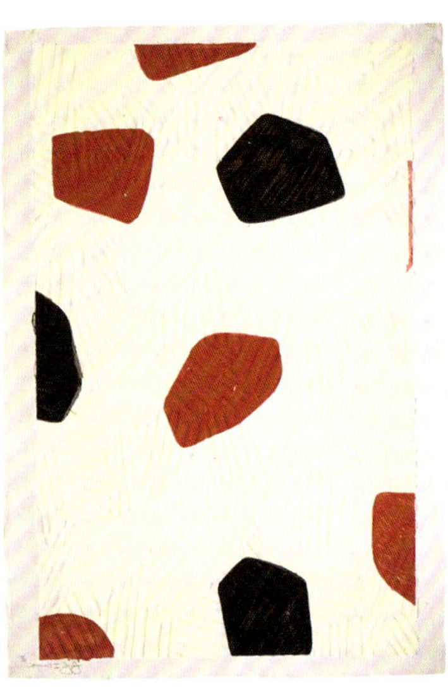 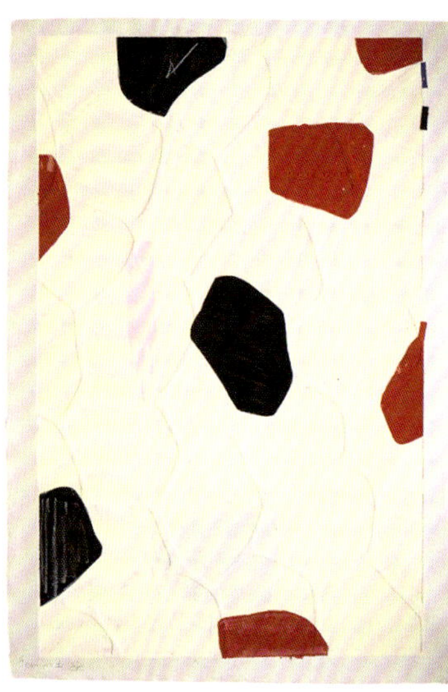 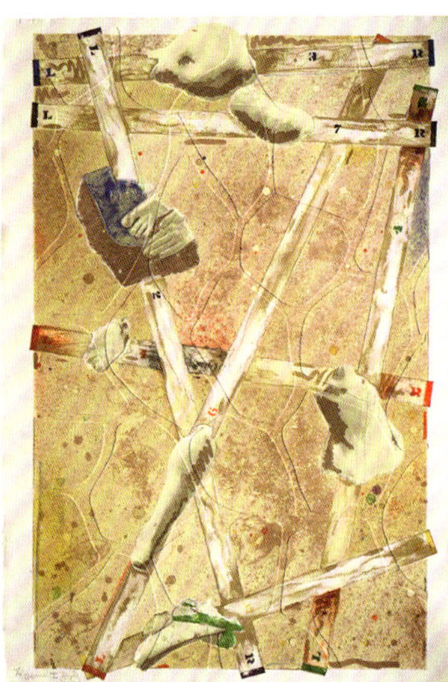

paintings for the next decade. What at first seems to be a random dispersal of bundled strokes in secondary colors—green, orange, and purple—is soon understood as a precise arrangement in which no areas of the same color are placed side by side. In addition, the allover field actually comprises three adjoining panels, each further divided by faint lines into three vertical strips. Finally, the far left and far right strips are identical, and the strips on either side of the two internal panel divisions are identical, leaving only the middle strips of each panel as unique—an arrangement that maps as ABC, CDE, EFA.[31]

In a print version of *Scent* (fig. 7), Johns combined lithography, linocut, and woodcut to parallel his use of both encaustic and oil in the painting. The print mirrors the painting's composition in an elaborate joining of "hand-drawn, traced, and possibly mechanically repeated"[32] crosshatching, creating a pattern that appears as "coded sequences across the image."[33]

The title of the painting and print echo a 1955 painting by Jackson Pollock, possibly his last, and draws a parallel with Pollock's method of covering the canvas with an allover pattern.[34] At the same time, Johns's ordered strokes offer a measured and impersonal alternative to Pollock's spontaneous drips and pours, and raise the larger question of how artists position themselves in relation to art of the past. The painting's association with Pollock allowed Johns to both address and reject the notions of a signature stroke and individual expression. This ambivalence arises in the play between the image and the title, creating a tension between Johns's impulse to jettison anything that is not strictly "his" and his strong inclination to embed references to art of the past within his work. This dynamic of simultaneously incorporating and distancing also pertains to Johns's relationship to Munch. Kraus summarized this attitude as ironic and extended Johns's web of references to Monet's fields of shimmering color and Picasso's strong hatching in early and late Cubism. The crux of the attitude, as she saw it, is in collapsing or negating past distinctions within the new system or "performative voice" of Johns's

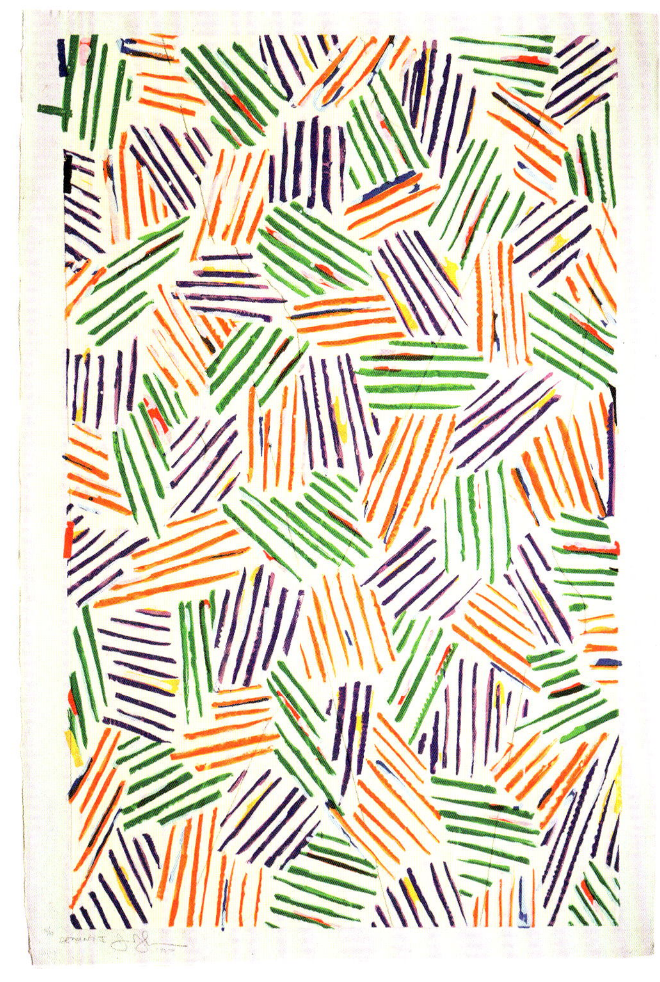

fig. 4 Johns, **Four Panels from Untitled 1972**, 1974, lithographs with embossing, 40 x 28 ½ in. (101.6 x 72.4 cm) each. Courtesy of Gemini G.E.L., Los Angeles

fig. 5 Johns, **Four Panels from Untitled 1972** (detail), 1974

fig. 6 Johns, **Scent**, 1973–74, oil and encaustic on canvas (three panels), 72 x 126 ¼ in. (182.9 x 320.6 cm). Ludwig Forum for International Art, Aachen, collection of Peter and Irene Ludwig

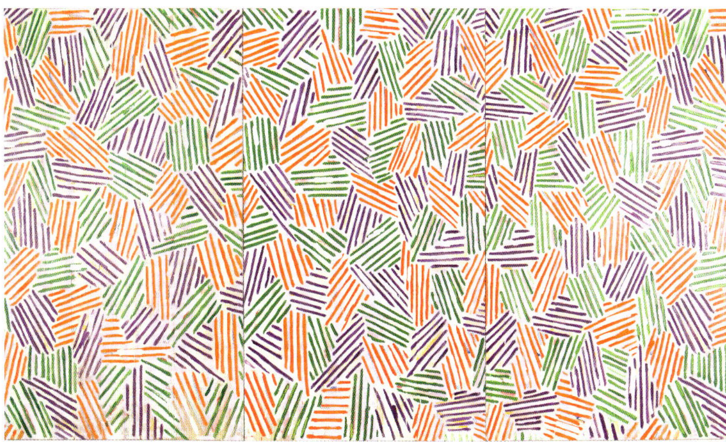

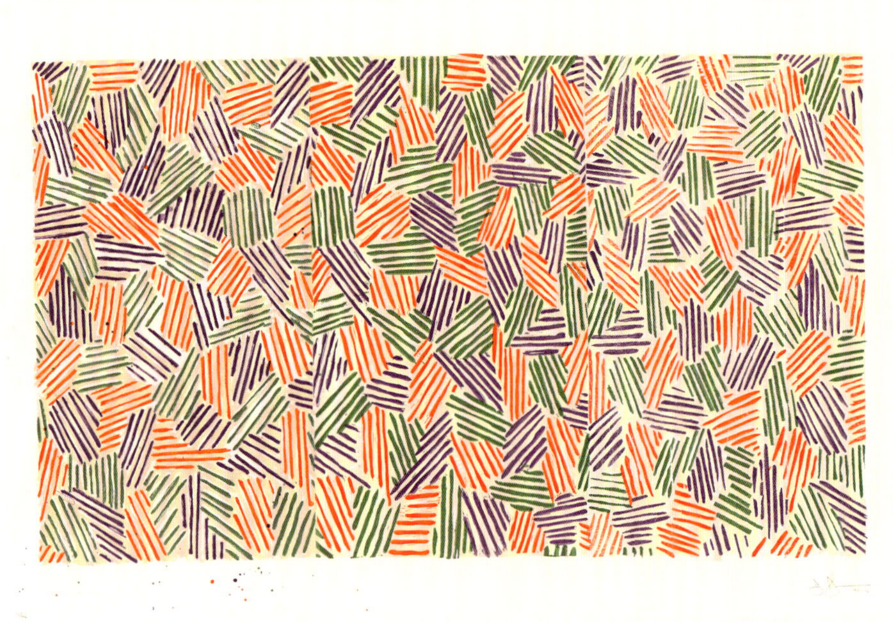

fig. 7 Johns, **Scent**, 1976, lithograph, linocut, and woodcut, 31 ½ x 47 in. (79.4 x 119.4 cm). Ryobi Foundation

paintings.[35] It is an endgame that, curiously, arose at the beginning of Johns's decade of crosshatching and perhaps explains his willingness just a few years later to look at Munch, an artist whose practice seemed so diametrically opposed to his own, but whose work would soon offer a way out of this apparent impasse.

In the crosshatch paintings that followed *Scent,* Johns explored ever more complex variations on continuity and discontinuity, mirroring and reversal. The *Corpse and Mirror* series refers to the *Exquisite Corpse* of Surrealism, familiar to many as a game in which children create a hybrid creature by taking turns drawing and then hiding the different parts of a body by folding the paper until the drawing is finished. In *Corpse and Mirror II* (fig. 8), Johns referred to the folds by dividing the left side of the painting into three stacked panels, each painted without referring to the others except at the seams. The right side mirrors the left, with important distinctions: the real horizontal panel divisions from the left are only painted on the right; the hatches are blurred; and intrusions, such as a ring at the far edge resembling the bottom of a paint can, draw attention to the surface—altogether marking it as a "reflection." A closely related work on paper from the following year explores this dynamic further in grisaille (fig 9).

Mirroring existed in Johns's work almost from the beginning,[36] but with the crosshatch works, it became a principal motif, inspired in part by Johns's deep involvement with printmaking, where reversals are an inherent part of the process. The complex layerings in the *Corpse and Mirror* works, as in *Scent* and *Untitled*, 1972, advance an apparent contradiction in which a quasimechanical pattern, apparently lacking personal expression, creates a field where the subtlest variations contain multiple implications. In addition, as will be discussed below, they show Johns loading the abstract pattern of crosshatching from the start with the capacity for literary, symbolic, and figurative allusion.

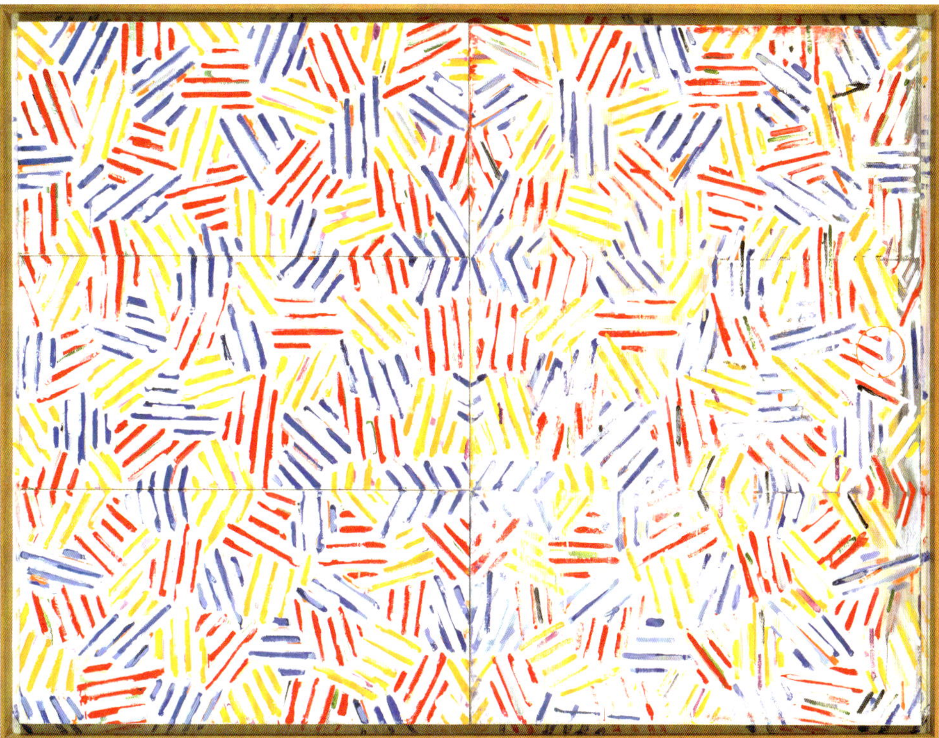

fig. 8 Johns, **Corpse and Mirror II**, 1974–75, oil on canvas (four panels), with painted frame, 57 ⅞ x 75 ¼ in. (147 x 191.1 cm). Collection of the artist

fig. 9 Johns, **Corpse and Mirror**, 1975–76, watercolor on paper, 20 x 28 in. (50.8 x 71.1 cm). Private collection

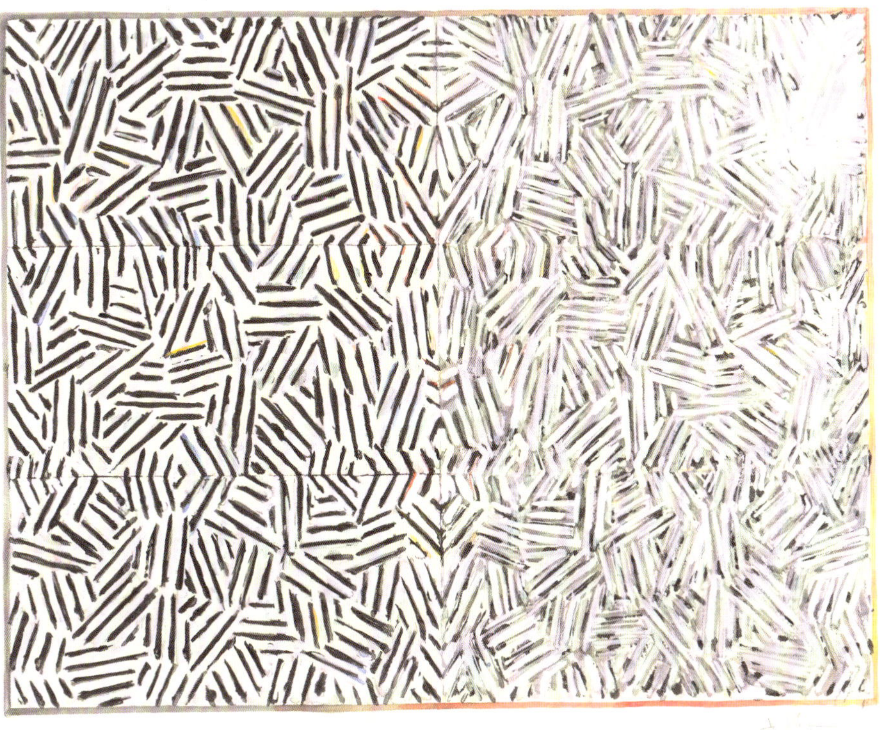

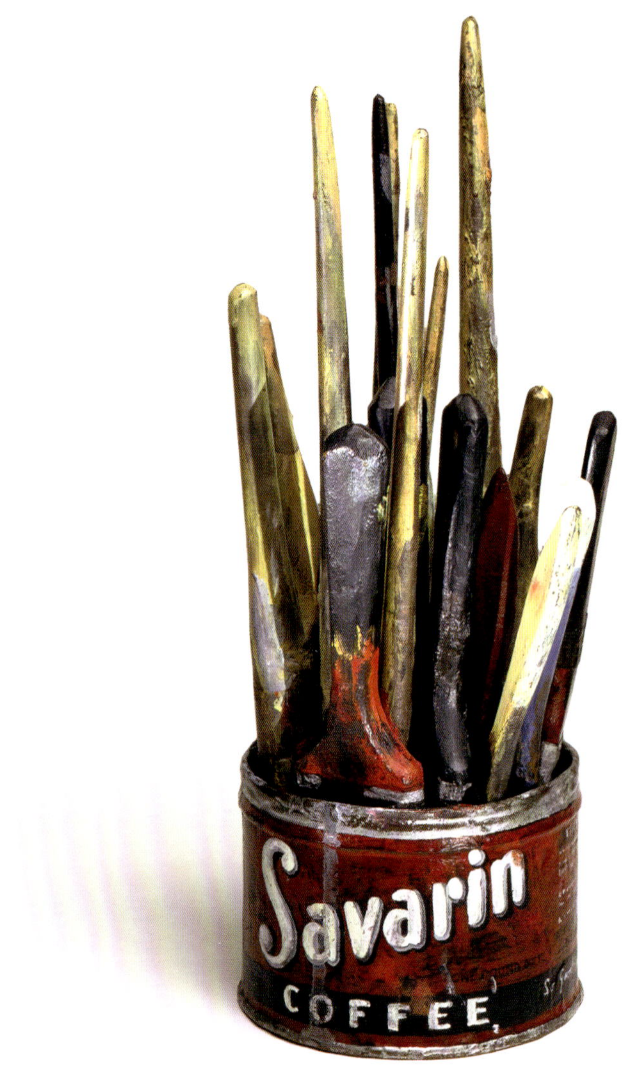

fig. 10 Johns, **Painted Bronze**, 1960, oil on bronze, 13 ½ x 8 in. (34.3 x 20.3 cm). Kravis Collection, promised gift to The Museum of Modern Art, New York

Savarin Can and Brushes

In the early 1980s, Johns's decade of crosshatching culminated in some of his most prominent references to Munch. But several years earlier, it was crosshatching combined with another, very different motif that created the first opportunity for Munch's presence to surface in his work. The motif is the Savarin coffee can with upside-down paintbrushes. It first appeared in 1960 in *Painted Bronze* (fig. 10), one of a group of sculptures that Johns based on common household items: flashlights, lightbulbs, toothbrushes, eyeglasses, and ale cans.[37] At the same time, *Painted Bronze* stands apart from the everyday subjects of these other sculptures, and from the found motifs of Johns's paintings and prints up to this time. As a representation of something closely tied to Johns's studio—an empty coffee can in which brushes

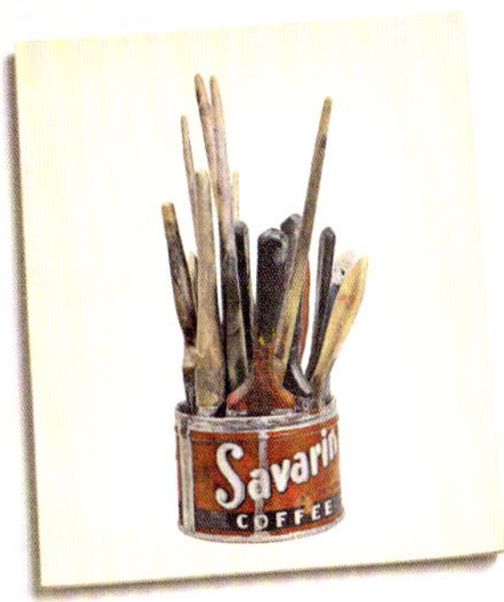

fig. 11 **Jasper Johns**, 1964, exhibition catalogue, Jewish Museum

could soak in solvent—the can and brushes transcend the anonymity of the found object. They are specifically Johns's tools, creating an identity that he underscores through highly detailed painting of their surfaces,[38] even including his fingerprints on the brush handles and can. Johns's next use of the Savarin can motif retains the personal connection while also pushing it in the opposite direction, toward an emblematic function. In 1964, he chose to feature *Painted Bronze* on the cover of the catalogue for his survey exhibition at the Jewish Museum in New York (fig. 11).[39] Silhouetted against an empty white ground—all text is on the back—the sculpture is at once an example of Johns's work, an affirmation of artistic identity, and a stand-in for the artist on the occasion of his first solo museum show.[40]

Johns had begun making lithographs in 1960 at the experimental print workshop Universal Limited Art Editions (ULAE) on Long Island. He took up etching in 1966[41] and used his own sculptures as subjects, continuing his practice of representing earlier motifs in new media and contexts. In 1968 ULAE published his first series, *1st Etchings*. One of them (fig. 12), offers a quick sketch of *Painted Bronze* seen from slightly above and sitting on a shallow surface. The can label is shown backward as Johns chose not to adjust for the reversal that ensued during printing. Below the

fig. 12 Johns, **1st Etchings (Savarin)**, 1968, intaglio, 25 x 20 in. (63.5 x 50.8 cm). Ryobi Foundation

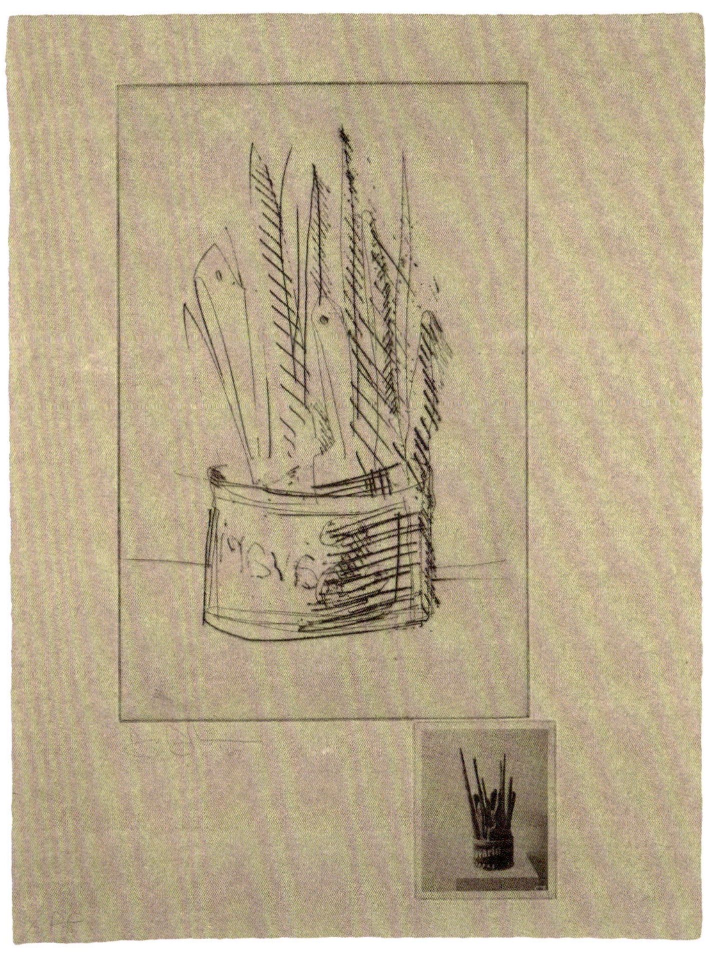

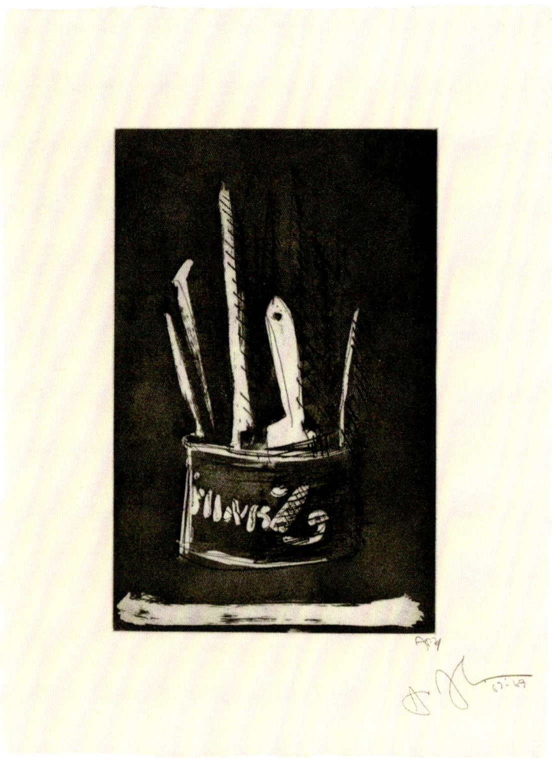

fig. 13 Johns, **1st Etchings, 2nd State (Savarin)**, 1968, intaglio, 25⁵⁄₁₆ x 19⁹⁄₁₆ in. (65.4 x 48.9 cm). Ryobi Foundation

fig. 14 Johns, **Savarin**, 1977, lithograph, 48 x 32 in. (121.9 x 81.3 cm). Courtesy Universal Limited Art Editions

print is a small photoengraved halftone image based on a snapshot of the sculpture placed on a pedestal. The small image is the basis for the hand-drawn one above; the reversal of the label in the etching underscores the distinction between the photograph and the print—between source and interpretation.[42]

In a related print published the following year in the portfolio *1st Etchings, 2nd State* (fig. 13)—the sculpture appears alone, centered on the sheet. An inky aquatint wash laid over the etched drawing lends a brooding tone. A white mark across the bottom suggests a stroke made by one of the brushes, perhaps an ironic nod to Abstract Expressionism's valorization of unique gesture. Comparison with the photograph in the previous image shows that the stroke is also the inverse of the dark front of the pedestal; it marks a vertical plane whose sides are now cropped by the tighter focus. This stroke also foreshadows the predella-like space that will appear at the bottom of the later *Savarin* prints. Moreover, its bone-white presence offers an uncanny harbinger of the skeleton arm that will appear beneath the can ten years later and announce Johns's first overt reference to Munch.[43]

A gradual sequence of incremental moves led up to this moment. In 1977, the Whitney Museum of American Art organized a survey exhibition of Johns's work.[44] Johns's involvement extended to designing a poster (fig. 14) and the catalogue cover (fig. 19). In both of these designs he combined something old and something new, as befits a retrospective, placing *Painted Bronze* from 1960 against a crosshatch pattern

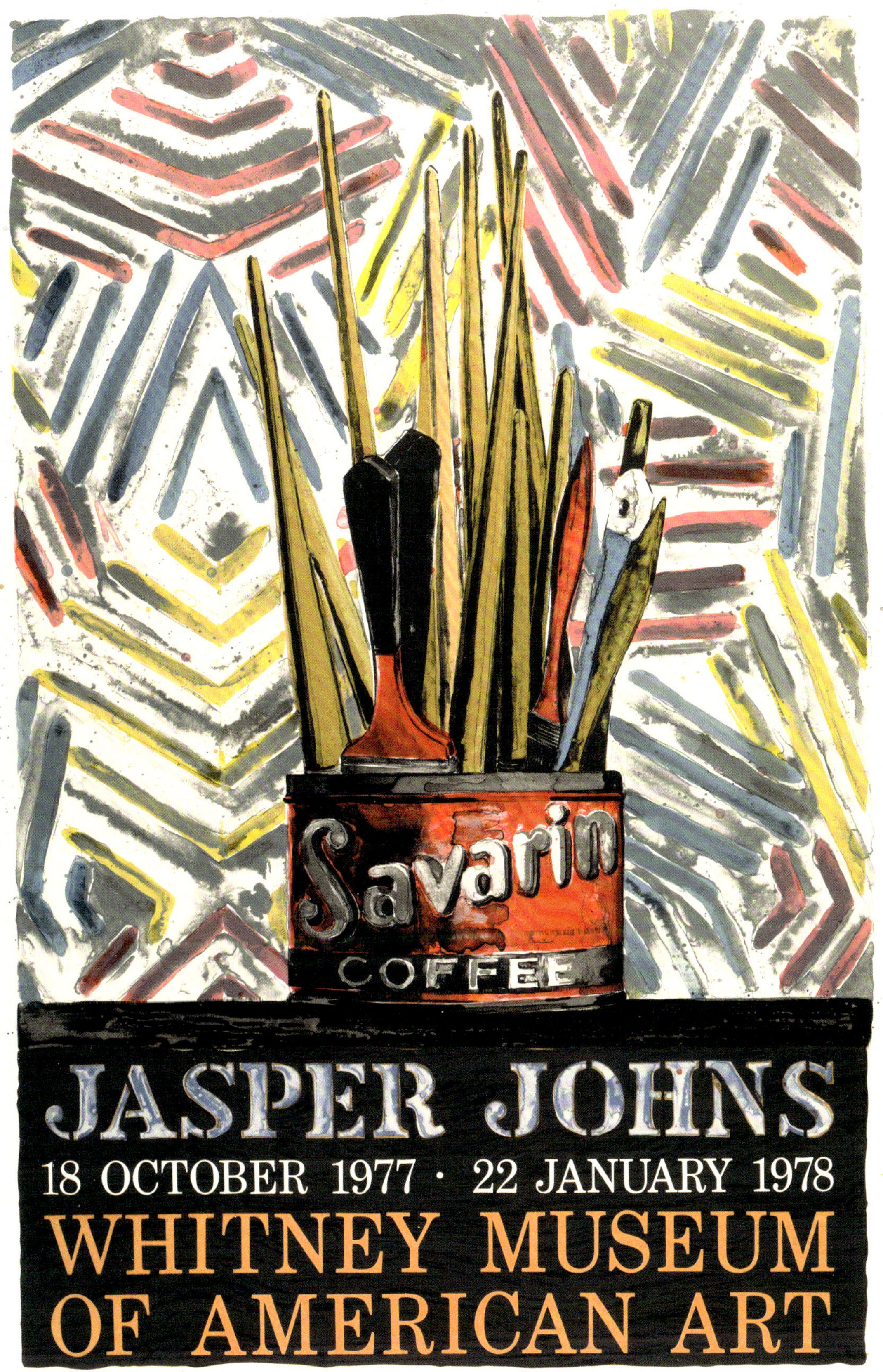

Savarin
COFFEE
JASPER JOHNS
18 OCTOBER 1977 · 22 JANUARY 1978
WHITNEY MUSEUM
OF AMERICAN ART

representing his work at the time of the exhibition. The pairing also reflects Johns's work in multiple media, offering a painting and a sculpture represented by a print. In the poster, the Savarin can appears from a new angle, at approximately eye level. It sits on a thin dark ledge, projecting slightly forward into space instead of back on the flat surface as in the 1968 etchings. The ledge may be the front of a table seen head-on, given the can's elevated position, but there are no more clues. Exhibition text appears below, in a vertical plane whose darkness suggests continuity with the thin ledge above it, but is revealed on closer looking to be printed from a separate plate.

The Whitney poster echoes the Jewish Museum catalogue cover. Again, at a moment of high visibility, it offers an emblem of a painter's studio practice as a surrogate for the artist. Johns has described his use of the sculpture in this context as a deliberate advertisement for himself,[45] which explains its larger-than-life size, unusual for found motifs in his work. The notion of the can and brushes as an advertisement echoes old-fashioned shop signs displaying tradesmen's emblems. It is also the same logic behind centuries of self-portraits in which artists from Rembrandt to Van Gogh to Frida Kahlo show themselves with brushes and palettes in hand to underscore their identity, as did Munch in several of his self-portraits, including a 1904 full-length painting (fig. 15) and a photograph from the following year that he staged to closely resemble it (fig. 16). In both cases, the brushes serve as the only means of identifying the well-dressed subject as an artist.

In two drawings on translucent plastic made just before the Whitney poster, Johns can be seen considering variations on the pairing of the Savarin can sculpture and the crosshatch pattern, as if studying solutions to a problem—or searching for ways to make the problem more complex. A precisely rendered pencil and crayon drawing (fig. 17)[46] includes a blush of red on the letter *S*, referring to the color of the can, which appears to sit on the same thin ledge as in the Whitney poster. A dark line running around the perimeter of the drawing, however, cuts in immediately beneath the can and suggests that the "ledge" may be outside of the space of the can, part of a frame rather than an independent horizontal surface. The crosshatch pattern is also reminiscent of the Whitney poster, although it is sparser and fainter, and the cluster of lines beside the brush handles on the far right differ in orientation. A blank area at the left of the drawing seems an odd intrusion into the pattern, but comparison with the *Corpse and Mirror* works shows that the vertical line between this empty area and the crosshatching occurs at the same place as the seam in the paintings, and that the horizontal line near the lower left—which carries over faintly to the lower right—repeats another of the divisions in the paintings.[47]

An ink drawing (fig. 18) shows the sculpture lit from the right and casting a shadow on the flat surface underneath. The strong crosshatch pattern here extends across the entire surface, in its own way emphasizing the seam to the left of the sculpture that connects to the *Corpse and Mirror* works.

Johns is thought to have eschewed perspective until it returned in the early 1980s, and his work has regularly been described as completely flat and aligned with the actual surface.[48] The Savarin prints and drawings, however, show him considering illusionistic space—albeit shallow—several years earlier, as he shifted

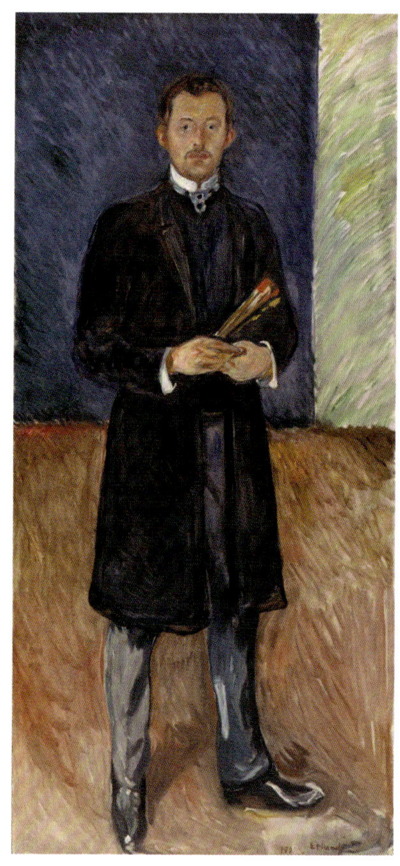

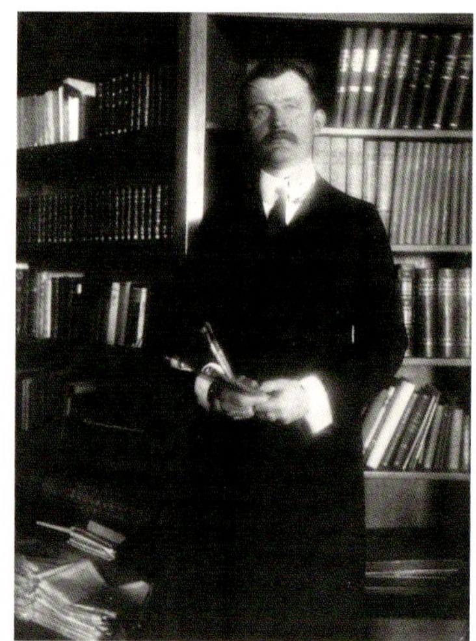

the vantage point of the can and pushed it forward and back in relation to the table or ledge and the painting behind it. At the same time, Johns continued to pose questions about the nature of the objects represented. Is this an image of a real can and brushes or of the trompe l'oeil *Painted Bronze*—that is, a representation or a representation of a representation?[49] And is the crosshatching a detail of a painting hanging on a wall or just a pattern filling a background? In any case, in each scenario, the sense of an object in real space persists—a still life comprising early and late examples of Johns's work in different media. And by this time, the Savarin can was firmly established as a motif that represented Johns publicly—a stand-in that was treated differently than his other motifs by always appearing whole and frontally, like a portrait. It is this deployment of the can and brush motif that, with just a small move, allowed it to connect with Munch.

fig. 15 Munch, **Self-Portrait with Brushes**, 1904, oil on canvas, 77 ½ x 35 ¾ in. (197 x 91 cm). Munch Museum

fig. 16 **Munch in Herbert Esche's library, Chemnitz**, 1905, unknown photographer. Munch Museum Archives

fig. 17 Johns, **Savarin**, 1977, graphite pencil and crayon on plastic, 37 x 32 ¼ in. (94 x 81.9 cm). Private collection, New York

fig. 18 Johns, **Savarin**, 1977, ink on plastic, 36 ¼ x 26 ⅛ in. (92.1 x 66.4 cm). The Museum of Modern Art, New York, Gift of the Lauder Foundation

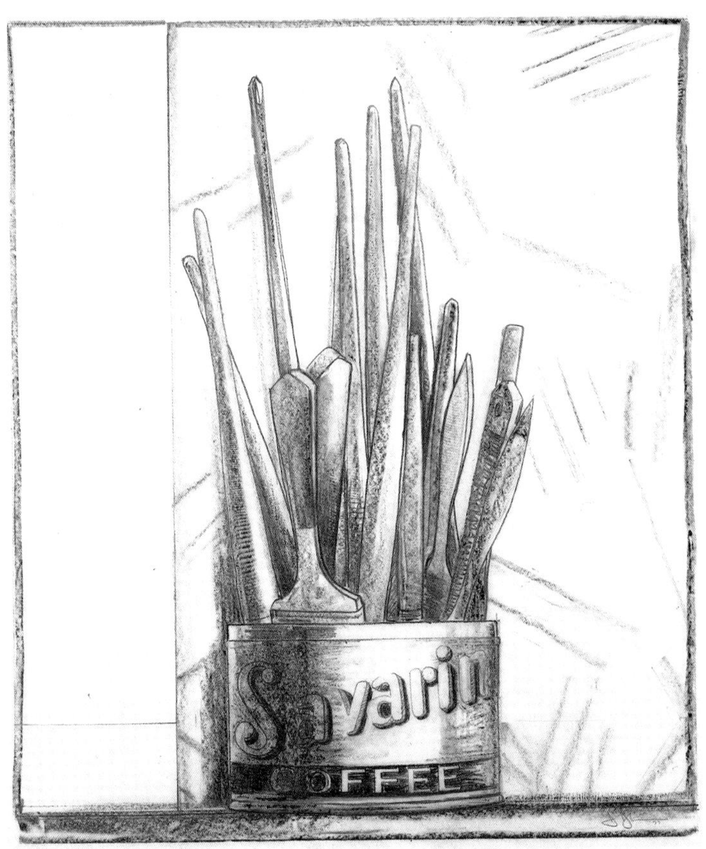

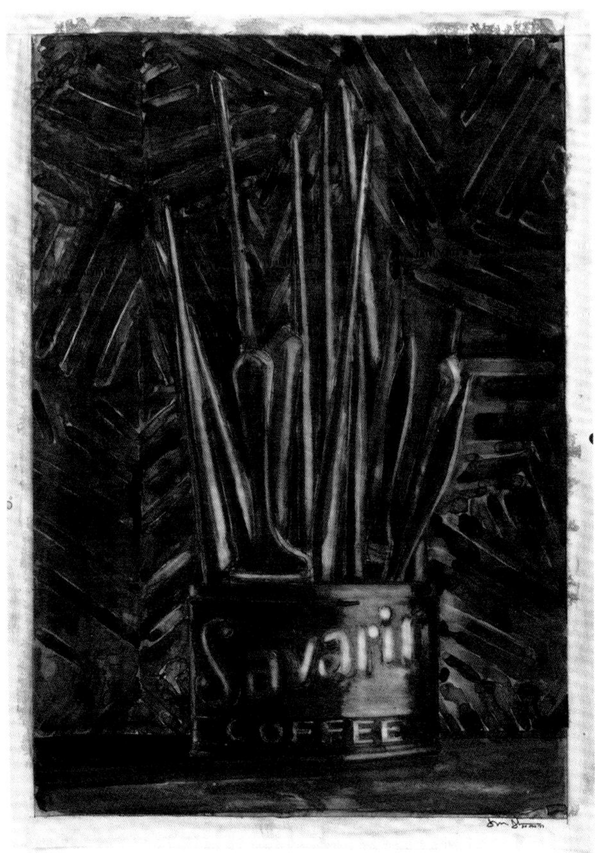

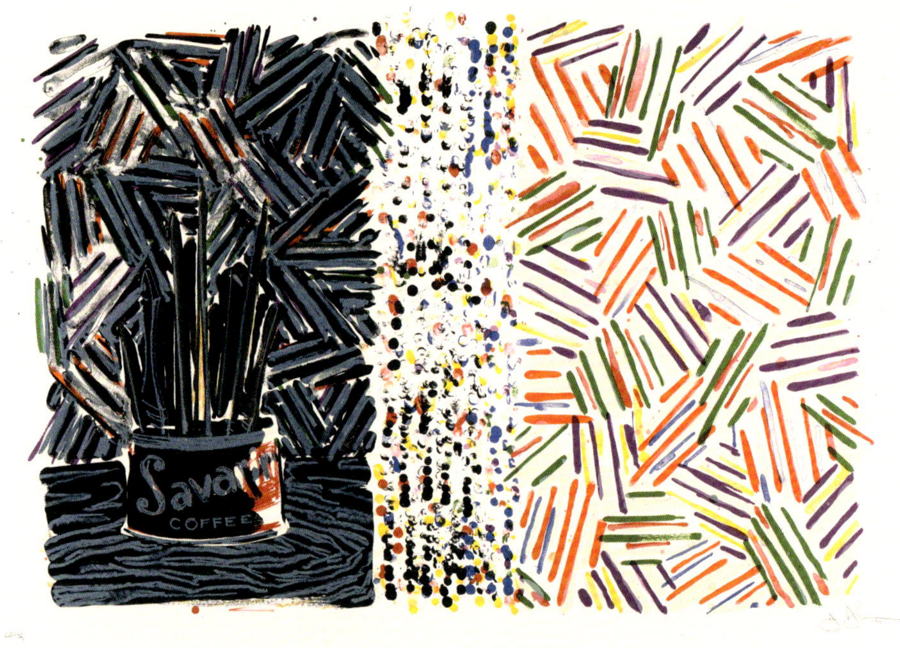

fig. 19 Johns, **Untitled**, 1977, lithograph, 27 ½ x 40 in. (69.9 x 101.6 cm). Collection of Stan and Renie Helfgott

fig. 20 Johns, **Savarin**, 1977, lithograph, 45 x 35 in. (114.3 x 88.9 cm). Collection of Brian Goldston and Peter Balis

Wood Grain

Obscured behind the text of the Whitney exhibition poster is a faint wood-grain pattern.[50] It is a folksy touch that reinforces the sense of a tradesman's sign, and thus Johns as a quintessentially American painter showing his work—plying his trade—at a quintessentially American museum (the first dedicated to the work of living American artists). In combination with the Savarin can motif, wood grain also appears to have offered another step toward Munch on what is arguably a conscious although not yet explicit level.

The design for the Whitney exhibition catalogue (fig. 19) added another variation to the wood-grain motif. While the right side, which became the front cover, sports only a colorful crosshatch pattern, the left side, or back cover, echoes the poster by including the can and brushes in front of the hatch marks.[51] But now the scene is cast in shadow and the can sits back surrounded by a pattern of loose wood grain that resembles rippling water. This image tempts one to read the wood grain in the poster, too, as a table, but the use of the separate plates counters this, and Johns's next move underscored the distinction. In *Savarin* (fig. 20), he created another lithograph of approximately the same size as the poster,[52] with the can sitting forward on the ledge. This time, however, Johns eliminated the entire text panel beneath and replaced it with a shorter panel exclusively of wood grain. The grain faces directly out, emphasizing the verticality of the plane, which recalls the front side of the pedestal in the small photoengraved image from *1st Etchings,* 1968 (fig. 12). But now this zone is established as fully independent, an area that can contain varied content, from exhibition copy to a strong wood-grain pattern.

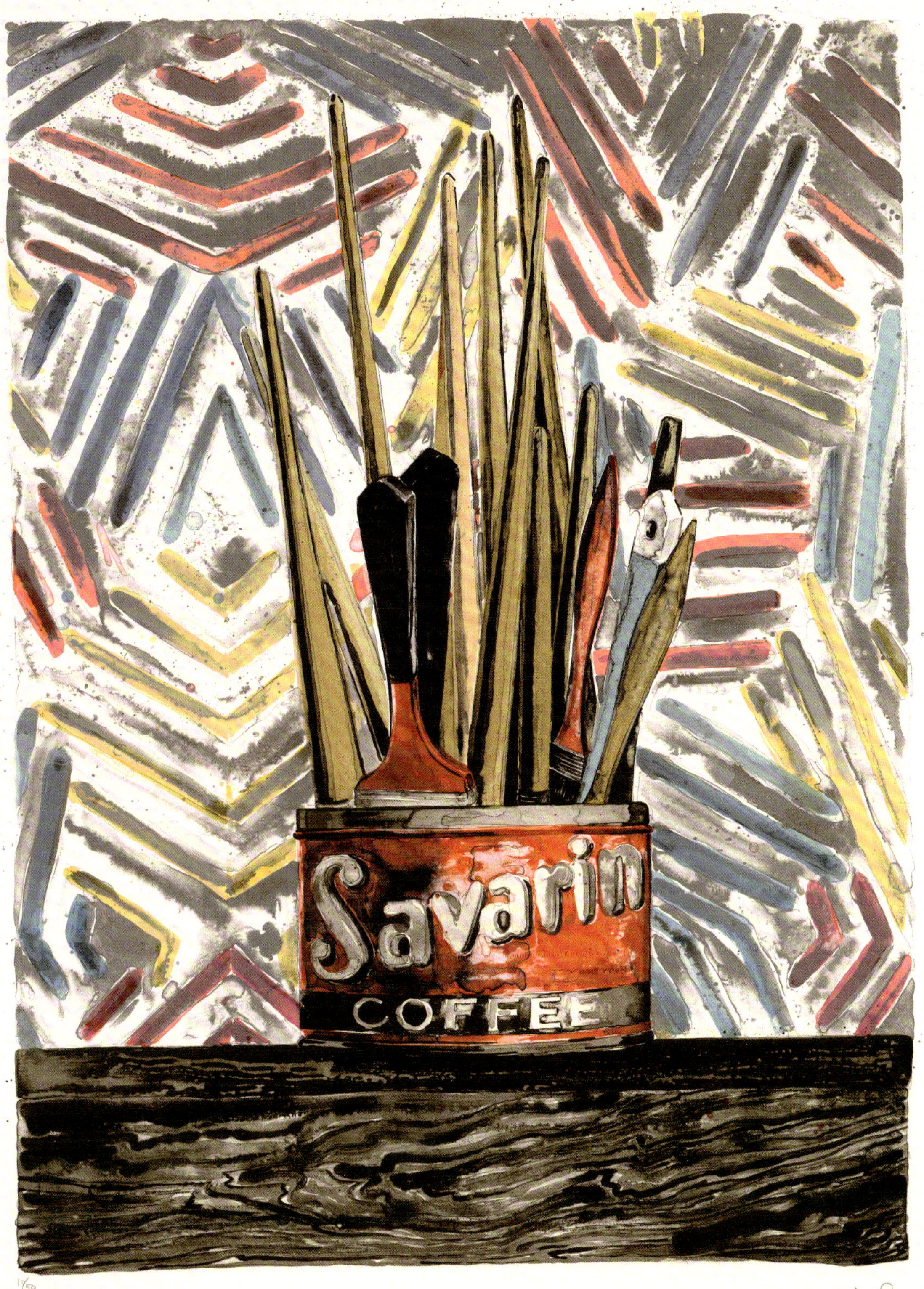

Savarin
COFFEE

The representation of wood grain had first appeared some years earlier in Johns's work, albeit in a minor role, in the same painting that introduced crosshatching, the four-paneled *Untitled*, 1972 (fig. 3).[53] Affixed to a real wood slat, one of the wax fragments in the far right panel shows part of a hand, foot, and sock placed on a section of faux wooden floor. Johns hand-painted the wax floor's pattern into the mold before casting it (fig. 21).[54] Johns again offered a representation of wood grain four years later in *Foirades/Fizzles*, the deluxe artist's book that pairs texts by Samuel Beckett with prints by Johns.[55] Johns based all the images for this publication on *Untitled*, 1972, and included one related to the hand, foot, and sock fragment (fig. 22).[56]

The very ubiquity of wood grain may explain why it has eluded serious discussion in the Johns literature. However, wood grain displays the same "literalness, repetitiveness, and obsessive quality" that he valued in his other motifs and meshes perfectly with his appropriation of neutral patterns from his immediate environment. In keeping with the discovery narratives about the flag, flagstone, and crosshatch motifs, it is possible, even, to speculate that a specific experience may also lie behind the appearance of wood grain in the *Savarin* prints—such as working on a table with a pronounced wood-grain pattern (fig. 24) while he was using an offset lithographic press at ULAE to make the Whitney poster and related works (fig.23).[57]

Unusual for Johns, he drew his wood-grain pattern by hand[58] and, in doing so, introduced an exaggerated, cartoonish quality (fig. 25). This exaggeration, along with the foregrounding of the pattern, arguably signals Johns's dawning awareness of Munch. Johns and Munch are among the great painters of Western art—including Rembrandt, Goya, and Picasso—who are equally known for their prints,

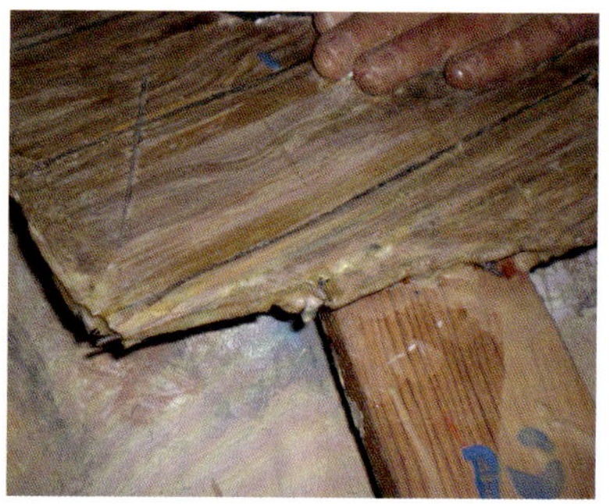

fig. 21 Johns, **Untitled** (detail), 1972. Museum Ludwig, Cologne

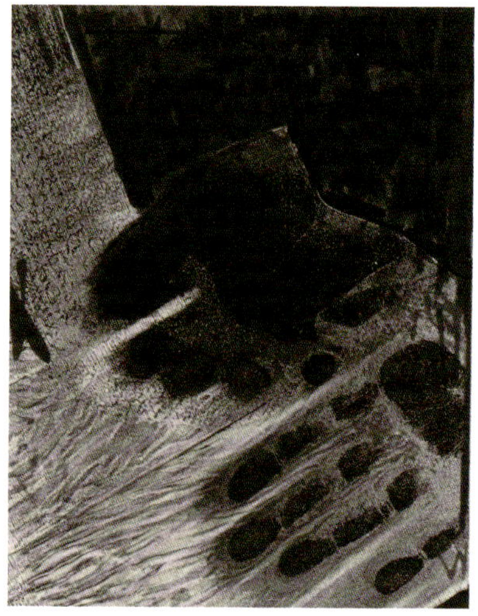

fig. 22 Johns, from **Foirades/Fizzles**, 1976, intaglio, 13 x 10 in. (33 x 25.4 cm).

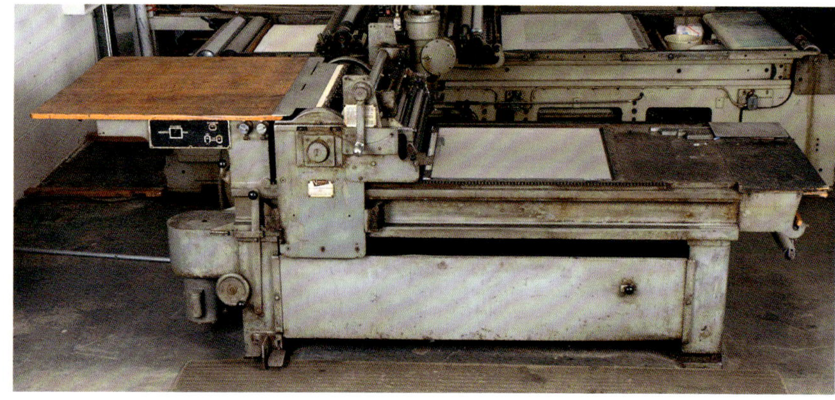

fig. 23 Letterpress at ULAE

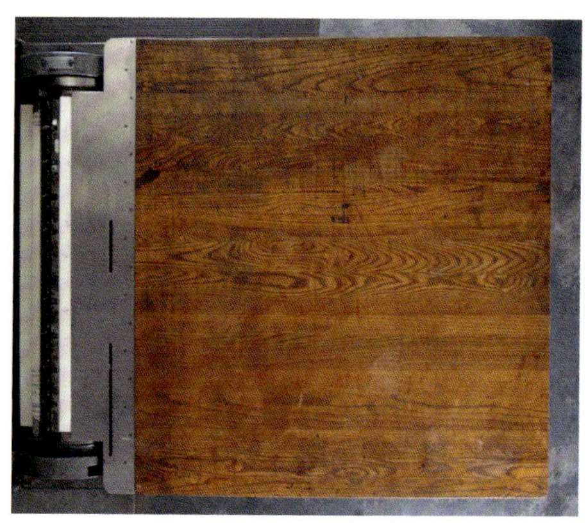

fig. 24 Detail of letterpress at ULAE

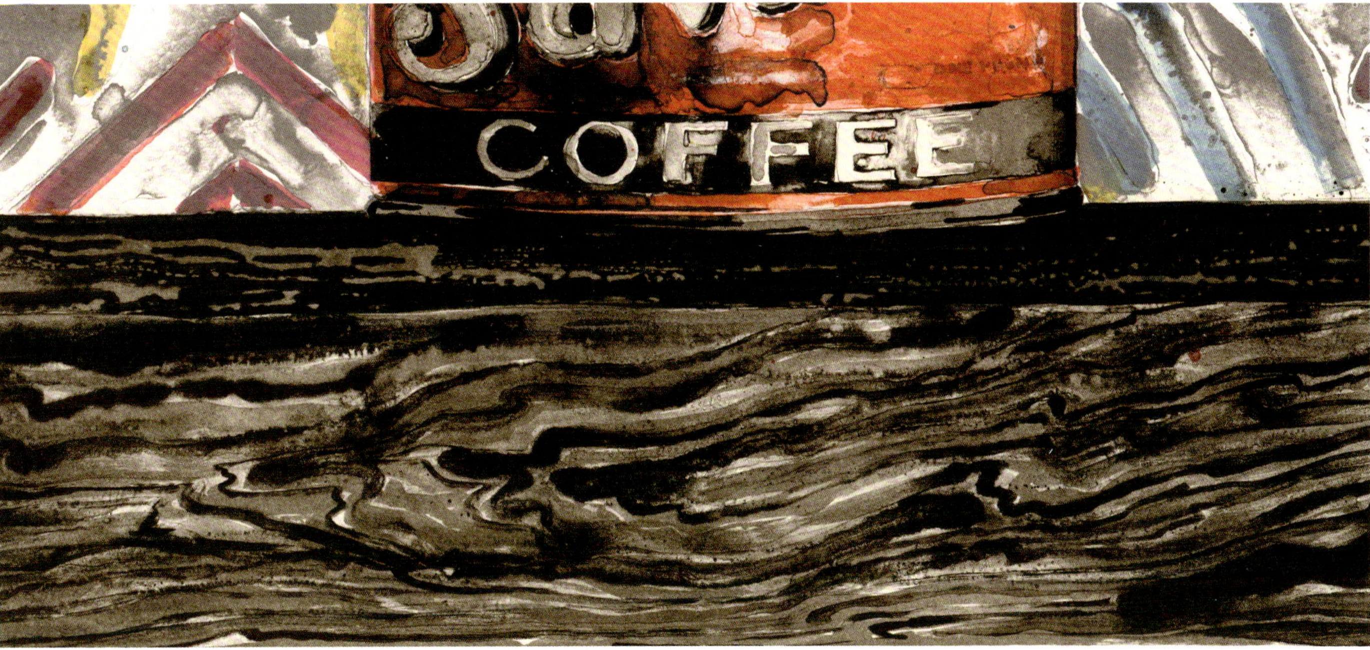

fig. 25 Johns, **Savarin** (detail), 1977

and both are among the most innovative printmakers of the twentieth century. At a time of intense exploration of various print media, it makes sense that Johns would have had Munch's distinctive use of woodcut and lithography in mind. Johns has acknowledged this recognition, even if he does not recall consciously thinking about Munch's prints while making the Savarin prints.

> If you're thinking about Munch, you can't ignore the effect of seeing, say, the woodblock prints that are printed in so many different ways as technical exercises. . . . Certainly I remember knowing his use of these things in varied ways, putting them together in various ways, with various colors and such things as that. How you draw on what your experiences have been is very difficult to state. When you do something, you are not much of the time referring to all the possibilities with which what you are doing can be associated.[59]

In addition, the European-born founder of ULAE, Tatyana Grosman, was deeply aware of Munch's achievements and may have drawn Johns's attention to the valuable technical lessons available in his experimental printmaking.[60] Such a message would have been reinforced by his friendships with the print curators mentioned earlier: Riva Castleman, who took Johns to art dealers around this time

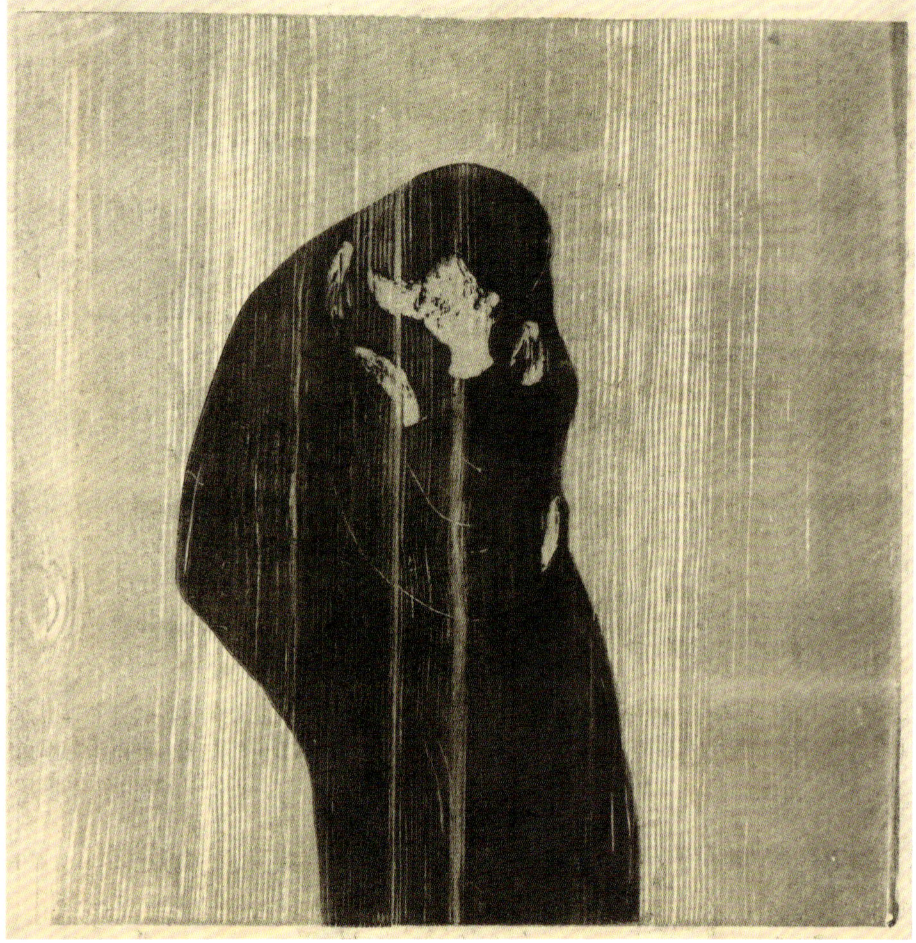

fig. 26 Munch, **The Kiss III**, 1898, woodcut, 24 ⅞ x 21 ⅞ in. (63.3 x 55.5 cm). Munch Museum

fig. 27 Munch, **The Kiss IV**, 1902, woodcut, 22 ¾ x 22 ¾ in. (58 x 58 cm). Munch Museum

to buy a version of Munch's 1895 *Self-Portrait* (fig. 46), and Richard Field, who had spoken with Johns not long before about the parallels between his *Skin with O'Hara Poem,* 1965 (fig. 35), and the Munch *Self-Portrait,* which he had installed together in the Wesleyan exhibition.[61]

Overdetermination is a hallmark of Johns's work, and to try to reduce his imagery to a single source is a fool's errand. It is entirely possible that he had other artistic uses of wood grain in mind, including Cubist collage, Magritte paintings from the late 1920s, and trompe l'oeil paintings by nineteenth-century Americans William Michael Harnett and John Frederick Peto, each of which he has referred to in other works. But to these potential sources of inspiration should be joined Munch's innovative woodcuts, which incorporated strong wood-grain pattern as part of the image. For *The Kiss* series, Munch used a jigsaw to cut out the central figures from a block, like a puzzle piece. He then inked another piece of wood

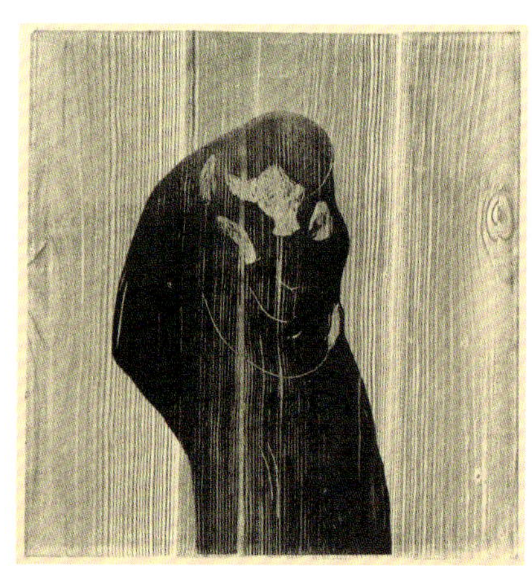

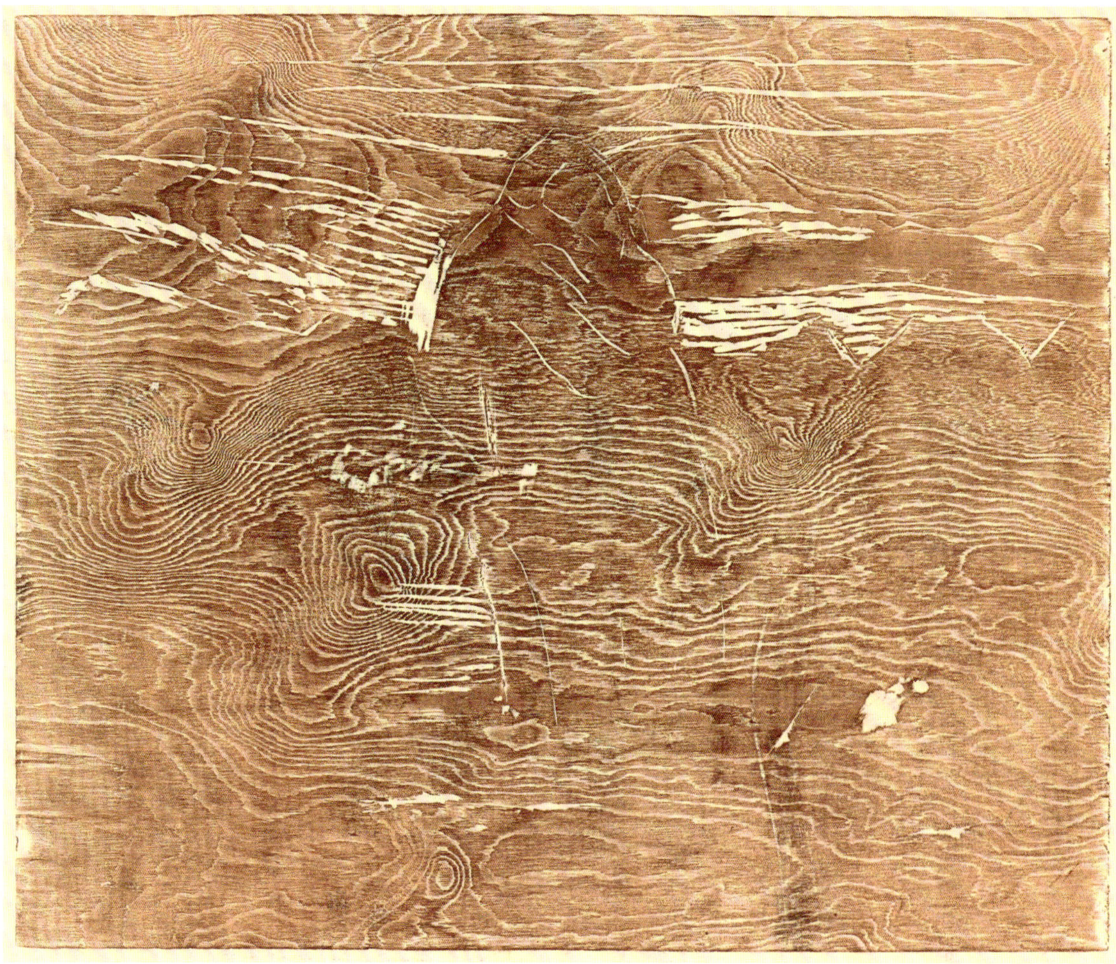

with a bold grain, printed it as a continuous ground, and printed the figures over it. Different versions of the print made in 1898 and 1902 show Munch experimenting with variations in pattern, color, and placement (figs. 26 and 27).[62]

Munch returned to the theme of *The Kiss*, and to strong wood grain, some forty years later for his final woodcut print (fig. 28). Now the couple appears outdoors. Just a few marks outline their forms as they dissolve into a dynamic plywood-patterned landscape with lightly incised mountains and clouds in the background.

Munch's most famous image, *The Scream*, exists in multiple versions and media, and its intense linear patterning may also have contributed to Johns's interest in wood grain. Munch made the first work in 1893 (fig. 29) and produced three more unique versions — variously using paint, crayon, and pastel—as well as a lithograph.

The Scream is a powerful, visionary image of isolation, despair, and fear based on an actual experience. Walking one evening with friends along an elevated path beside a fjord, Munch watched the setting sun turn the sky blood red, triggering the sensation of hearing "a huge extraordinary scream pass through nature."[63] *The Scream* underscores this existential tension by setting the rhythmic, undulating patterns of the sky and fjord against the powerful, straight lines of the path and railing, which recede sharply into space. In the lithographic version (fig. 30), Munch replaced the painting's harsh color contrasts with simple black and white, relying on strong line to convey the force of the figure's existential cry. Ute Kuhlemann Falck relates that almost from the beginning this print was mistaken for a woodcut. She describes this and related lithographs from the same time, including *Angst* (fig. 31), which exists in monochrome and two-color versions, as displaying a "black line woodcut aesthetic."[64] Interestingly, *The Scream* lithograph appeared a year before Munch began making actual woodcuts. Falck places the lithograph in the context of a reviving interest in traditional woodcut technique among European artists from the 1860s on, and she feels Munch consciously transferred some of the simple reductive power of historic and popular woodcuts to lithography, including the lack of shading and strong contrast of black and white.

While wood grain in Johns's work may have been an analog for crosshatching—dumb, neutral, obsessive—in its first prominent appearance, when it came out from behind the text in the Whitney poster, Johns played it up—drawing it freehand

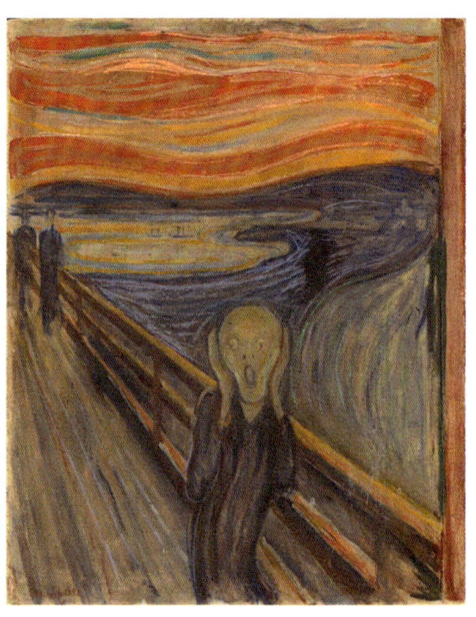

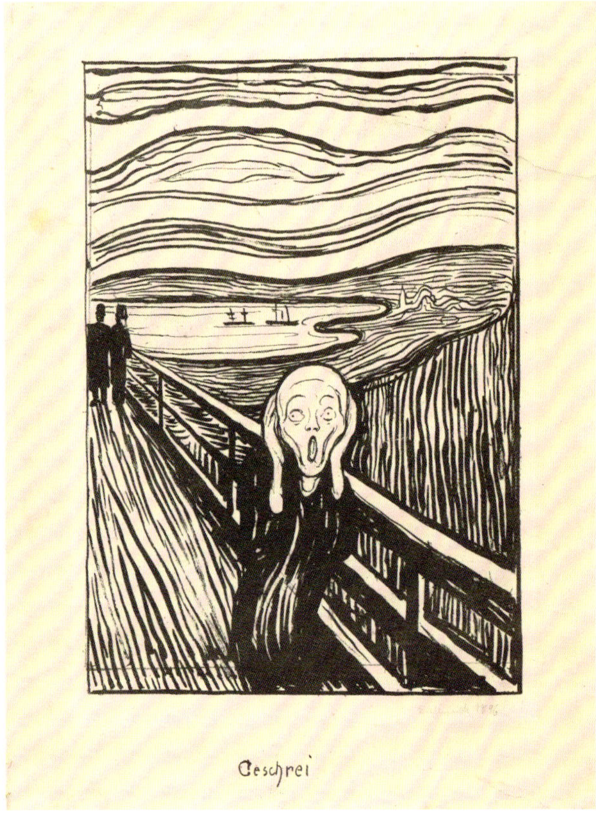

fig. 29 Munch, **The Scream**, 1893, tempera and crayon on unprimed cardboard, 35¾ x 28⅞ in. (91 x 74 cm). National Museum of Art, Architecture and Design, Oslo

fig. 30 Munch, **The Scream**, 1895, lithograph, 18⅜ x 13⅝ in. (46.5 x 34.5 cm). Munch Museum

fig. 31 Munch, **Angst**, 1896, lithograph, 22 ½ x 16⅞ in. (57.2 X 43 cm). Munch Museum

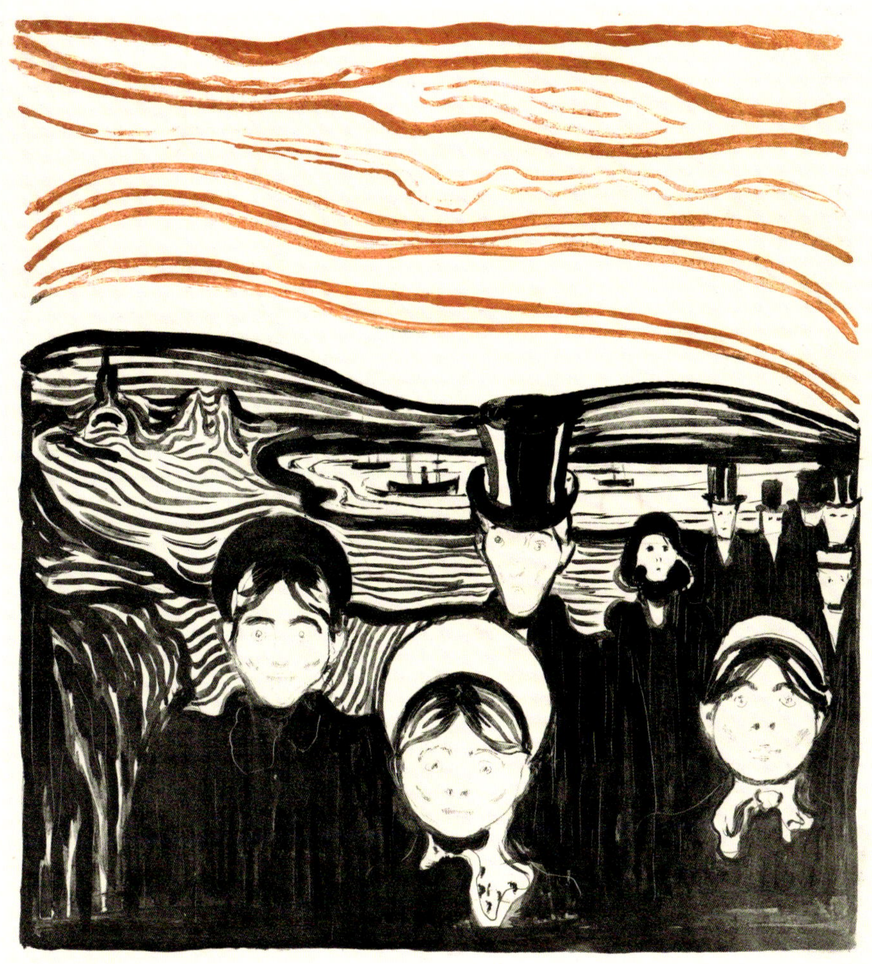

and investing it with some of the exaggeration of Munch's arabesque lines. In addition, Johns's images of wood grain traversed the ambiguous terrain explored by Munch, referring to the pattern of wood grain and the aesthetic of woodcut through the medium of lithography. Commenting on images of *The Scream* and *The Kiss*, Johns said, "And you don't really know what the connection between [the pattern in the lithograph] and the wood grain [in *The Kiss*] is, you don't know which comes first in his mind. Whether this is because he's been working with the wood or whether he's attracted to the wood because it has these forms."[65] Johns's interest in this ambiguity offers another connection with Munch, beyond a shared motif to questions of representation and illusion. In the same way that the neutral pattern of crosshatching allowed Johns to incorporate references to Picasso and Pollock, the humble pattern of wood grain seems to have been an early vehicle for incorporating references to Munch—perhaps not consciously at first, but before long openly, as subsequent moves over the next few years confirmed.

Handprints and Armprints

At the same time that he was making the Whitney poster and related prints, and also exploring wood grain as an expressive device, Johns became aware of the similarity between crosshatching and handprints. Several paintings and drawings of 1977 and 1978 were the first to suggest the parallel, and with the addition of a human hand, they changed the meaning of what had previously passed for a neutral and anonymous pattern. They also furthered the evolution toward more recognizable citations of Munch.

In an untitled ink drawing from 1977 (fig. 33), Johns replaced the bundled parallel strokes behind the Savarin can with imprints of his right hand,[66] a dramatic gesture that raised the level of personal expression in his work.[67] The following year, in an untitled acrylic work on paper (fig. 34), he used his fingers to create the bundled lines. In addition to showing visible fingerprints, the hatch marks approximate the length of fingers so that each bundle of lines resembles a hand.[68] In a painting from the same year, *Céline* (fig. 32), Johns pushed the analogy further by interweaving the handprints and hatch marks. A motif he had valued precisely for its impersonal, even mechanical, qualities now appears equivalent to and interchangeable with its opposite: individual gesture and human touch.

These instances were not the first time hand- and armprints had appeared in Johns's work. In 1962, he pressed his oiled hands and face against paper and rubbed the surface with charcoal to create *Study for Skin I–IV*. One of these drawings led to the print *Skin with O'Hara Poem* (fig. 35), in which the artist appears desperate to escape the shallow space of the work.[69] In a group of paintings and prints from 1962 and 1963, including *Hatteras* (fig. 36), armprints are the central motif, suggesting variously a leap into space, a cry for help, and futile, repetitive circling.[70] A single

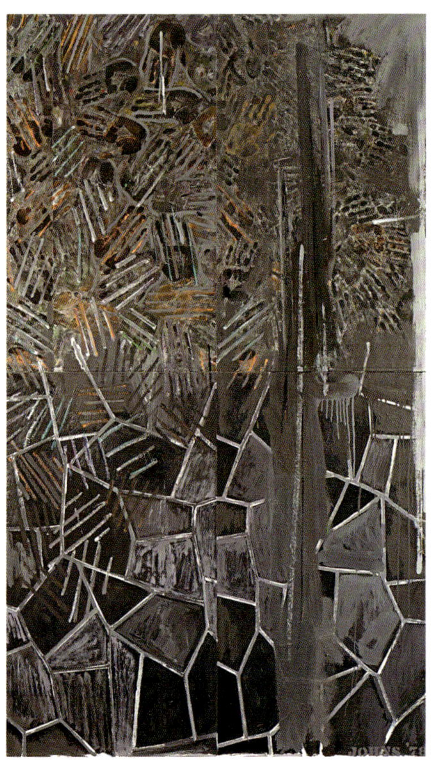

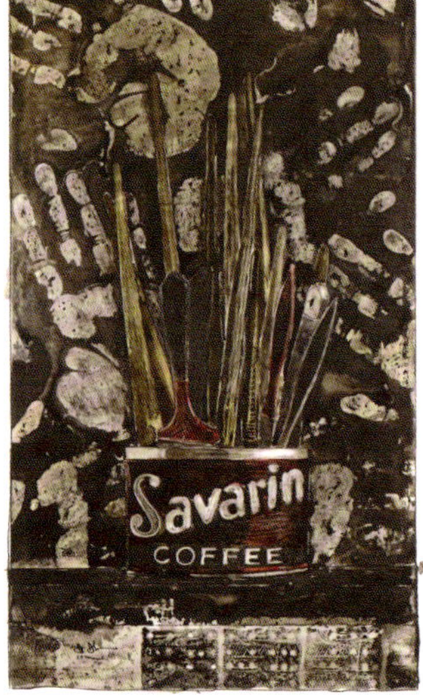

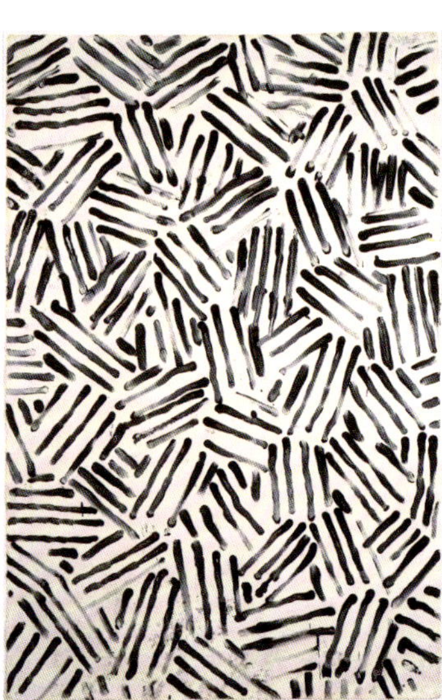

fig. 32 Johns, **Céline**, 1978, oil on canvas (two panels), 85 ⅝ x 48 ¾ in. (217.5 x 124 cm). Kunstmuseum Basel, Switzerland

fig. 33 Johns, **Untitled**, 1977, ink, watercolor, and crayon on plastic, 21 x 14 in. (53.3 x 35.5 cm). Collection of Margo Leavin, Los Angeles

fig. 34 Johns, **Untitled**, 1978, acrylic on paper, 43 ¾ x 29 in. (111.1 x 73.7 cm). Private collection

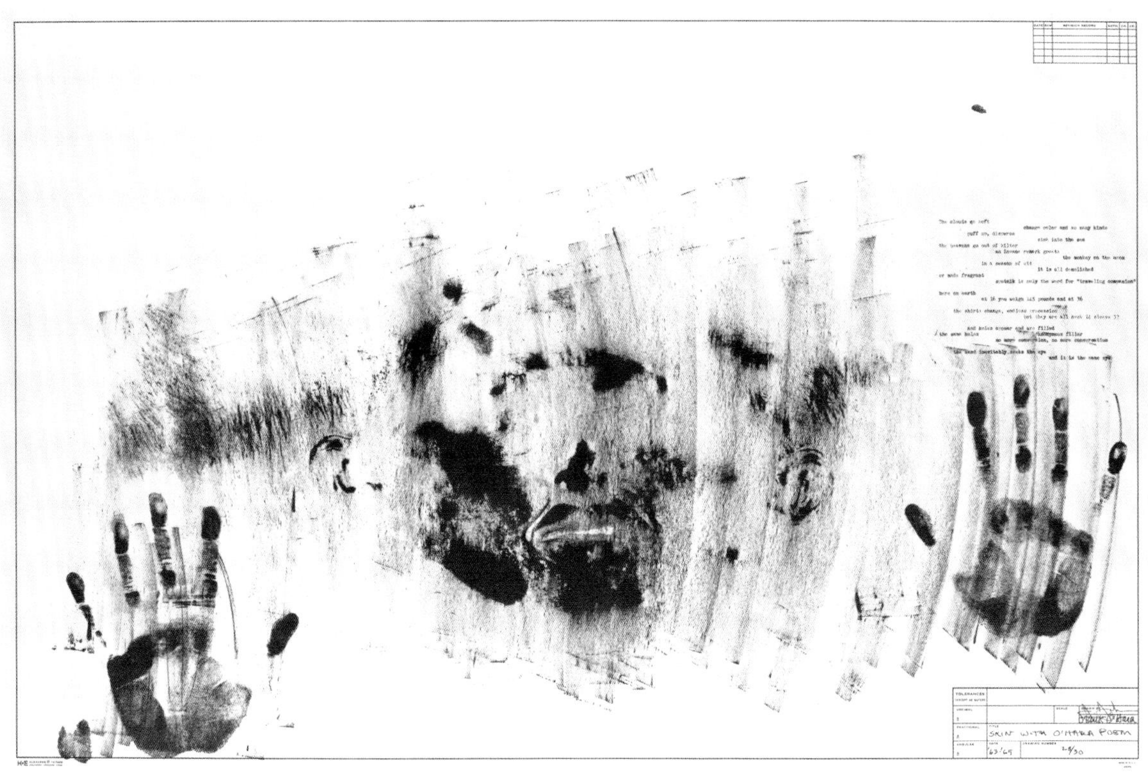

fig. 35 Johns, **Skin with O'Hara Poem**, 1965, lithograph, 22 x 34 in. (55.9 x 86.4 cm). Ryobi Foundation

fig. 36 Johns, **Hatteras**, 1963, lithograph, 41 x 29 in. (104.1 x 73.7 cm). Ryobi Foundation.

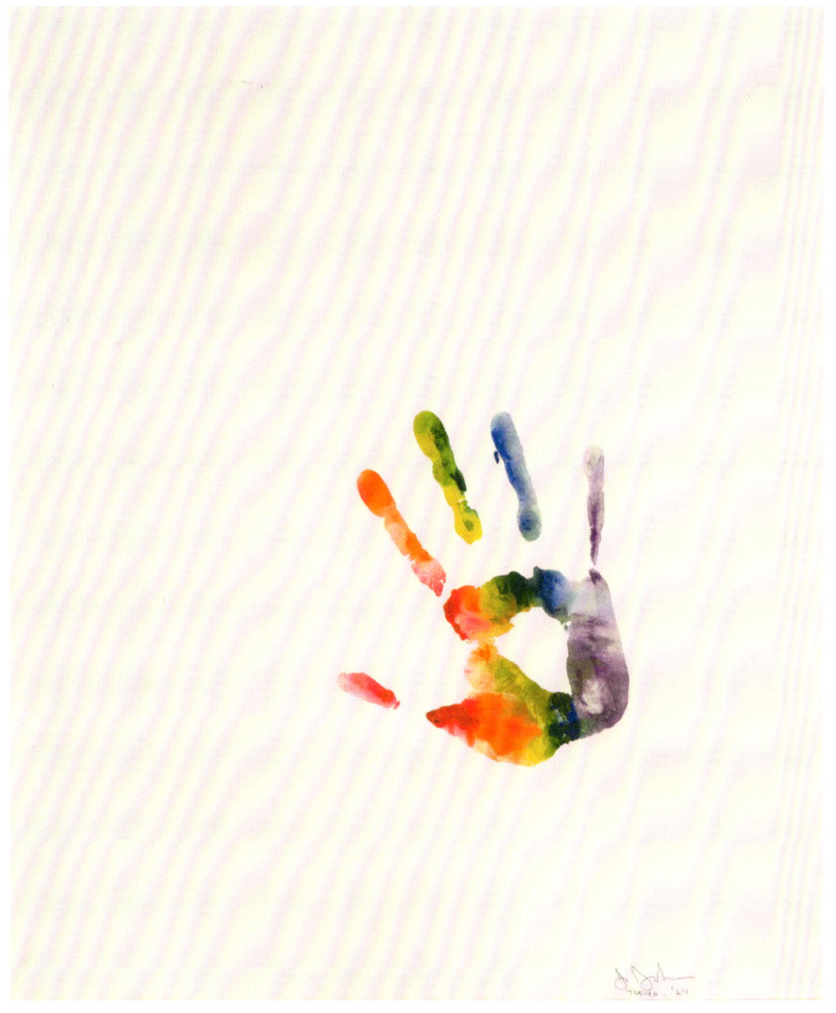

fig. 37 Johns, **Handprint**, 1964, oil on paper, 20 ⁵⁄₁₆ x 17 ¼ in. (51.6 x 43.8 cm). Collection of Jack Shear

multicolored handprint on paper from this time (fig. 37)—at once primitive, childlike, and artful—succinctly and cheerfully proclaims the symbolic potency of the hand.[71]

Shortly after reintroducing handprints into his work in 1977, Johns went on to make several more print variations with the Savarin can, including a set of six lithographs made at ULAE in 1978 and 1979 that extend the personal and expressive content of the motif and link it ever more closely to Munch. *Savarin 2 (Wash and Line)* (fig. 38) presents the can against dark aquatint, recalling *1st Etchings, 2nd State (Savarin)* (fig. 13) from ten years earlier. Now, however, the can sits on a narrow white ledge at the eye-level placement of the Whitney poster, and a dark swath beneath echoes the placement of the wood plank from *Savarin*, 1977 (fig. 20). *Savarin 3 (Red)* (fig. 39) replaces the black ground with red and inserts Johns's fingerprints throughout, notably filling the area beneath the can with full-finger impressions. *Savarin 4 (Oval)* (fig. 40) vignettes the can in a

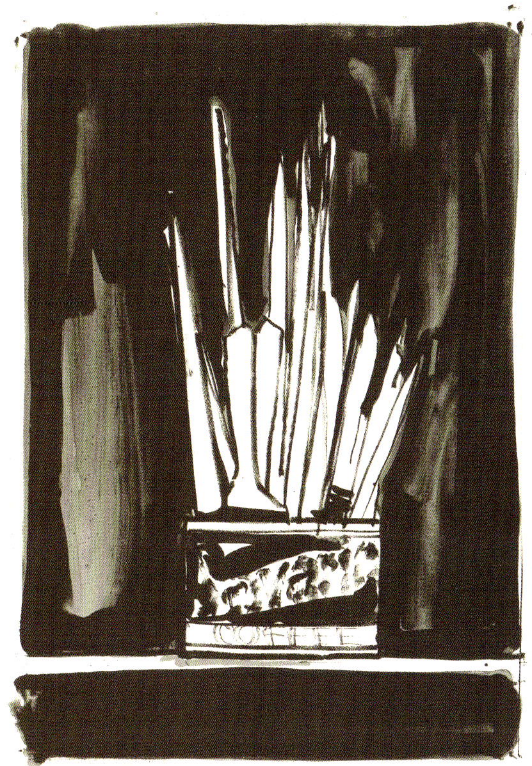

fig. 38 Johns, **Savarin 2 (Wash and Line)**, 1978, lithograph, 26 x 20½ in. (66 x 52.1 cm). Collection of Larissa Goldston

fig. 39 Johns, **Savarin 3 (Red)**, 1978, lithograph, 26 1/16 x 20 1/16 in. (66 x 52.1 cm). Collection of Brian Goldston and Peter Balis

fig. 40 Johns, **Savarin 4 (Oval)**, 1978, lithograph, 26 x 20½ in. (66 x 52.1 cm). Collection of Brian Goldston and Peter Balis

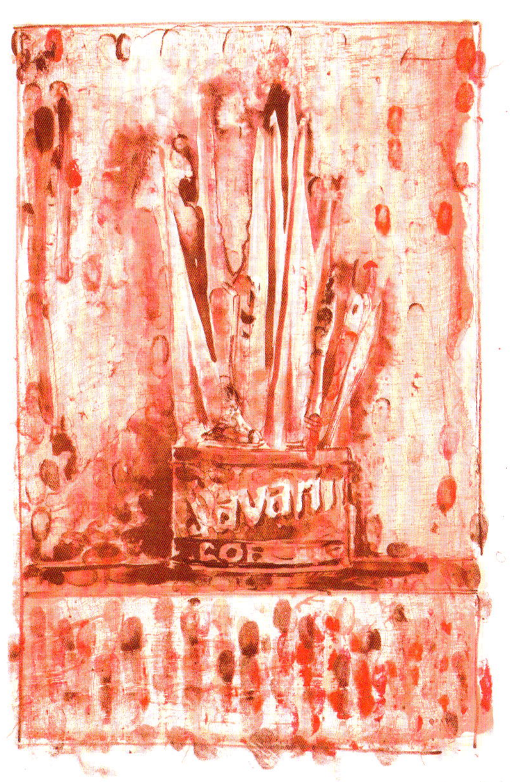

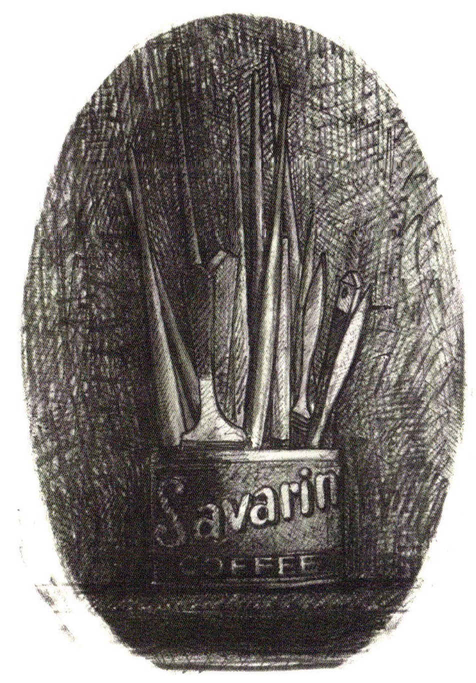

traditional portrait format, underscoring the can and brushes as a surrogate for the artist. Scratchy crosshatching in the background recalls etching, another example of Johns's interest in the ambiguity of print techniques. *Savarin 5 (Corpse and Mirror)* (fig. 41) positions the can against a distinctive crosshatch background, linked by the title to the *Corpse and Mirror* paintings. The same narrow ledge from the other prints in the series appears beneath the can, but here it is defined by a strong wood-grain pattern that, although compressed, appears to recede in space so that the can seems to sit back on the surface rather than project over the edge.

In Johns's next variations on the Savarin can, a set of four monotypes from 1978, the moment finally arrived when Munch emerged fully into the open. Johns made these new prints using impressions from plates that had remained unused or uneditioned from the prior group of six lithographs. He combined these with painterly improvisations that he printed as monotypes. Two of these four *Savarin* monotypes include the startling image of a bony arm below the can (figs. 42 and 43), an explicit citation that changes the reading of all related Savarin works. The motif recalls Johns's arm- and handprints from the 1960s but differs crucially in

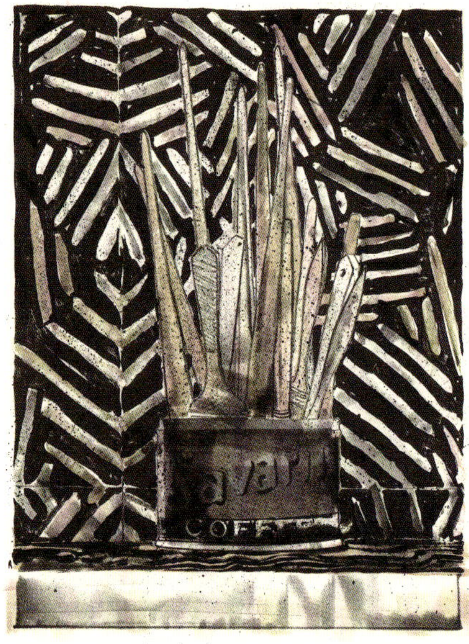

fig. 41 Johns, **Savarin 5 (Corpse and Mirror)**, 1978, lithograph, 26 x 20 ½ in. (66 x 52.1 cm). Collection of Brian Goldston and Peter Balis

fig. 42 Johns, **Savarin**, 1978, monotype, 27 ¼ x 19 ⅝ in. (69.2 x 49.8 cm). Collection of the artist

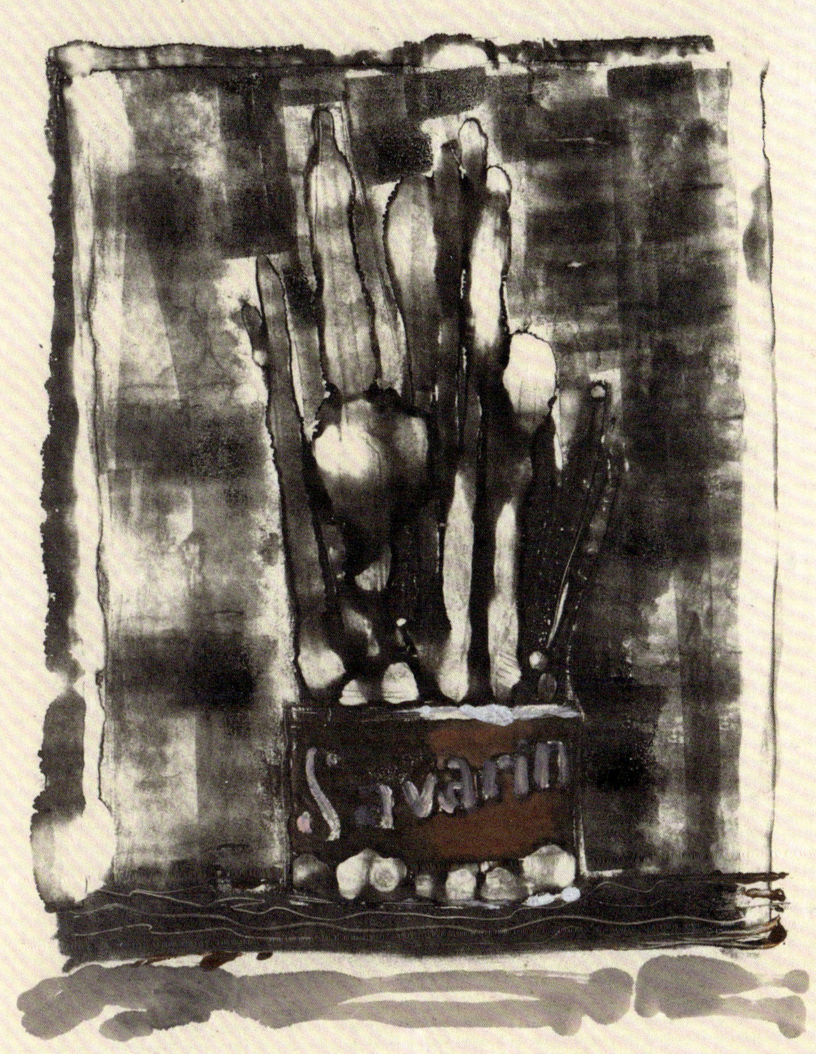

Savarin

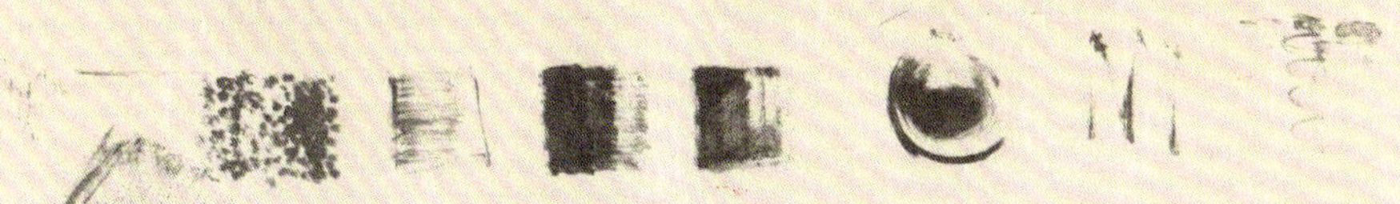

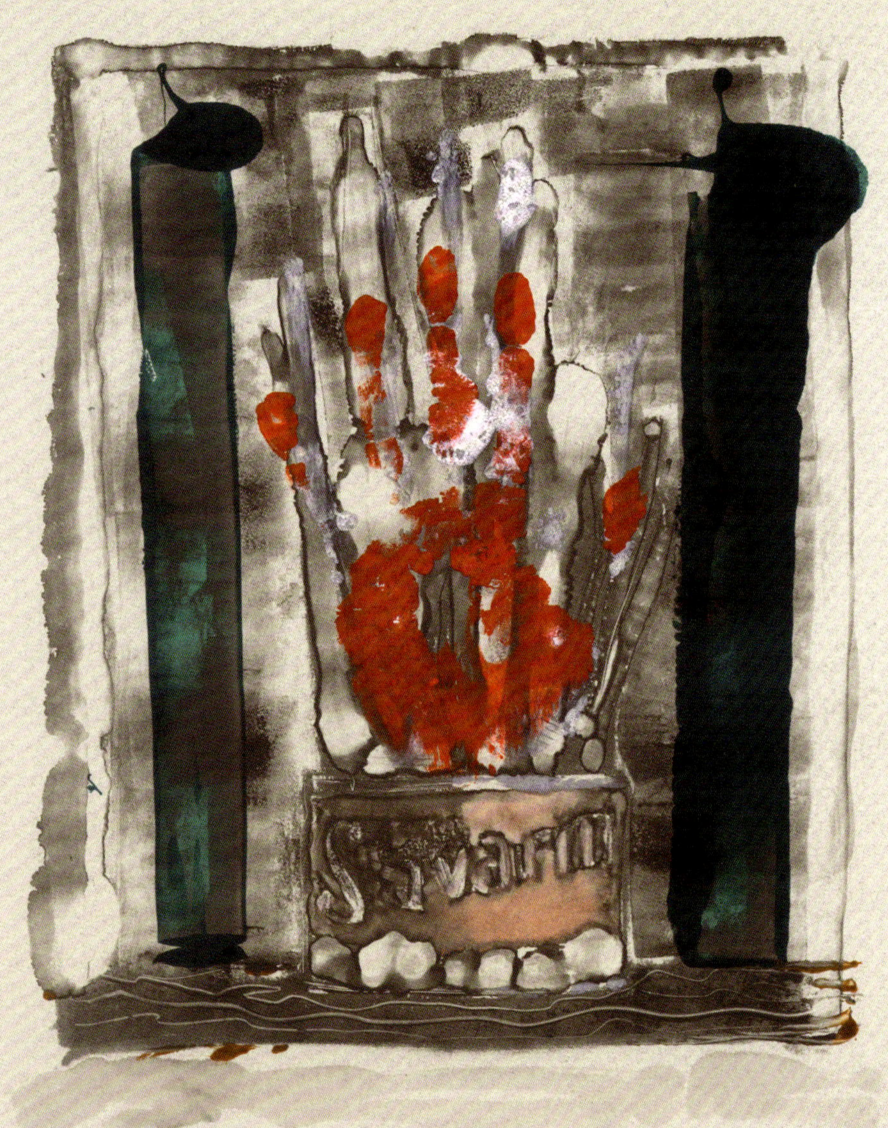

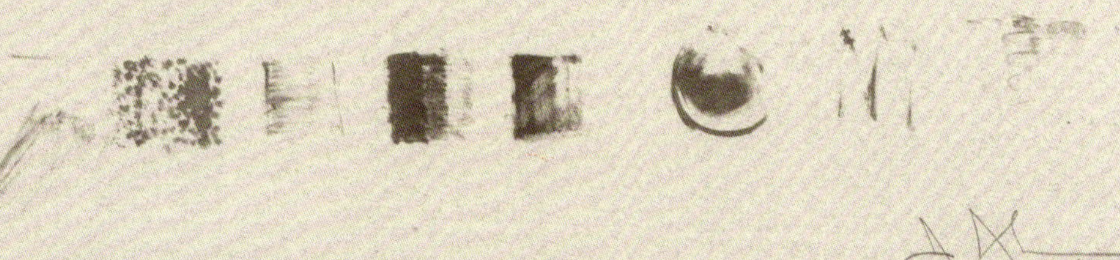

B/13 1/2

being skeletal. Previous armprints, however dark or desperate in their implications, always conveyed the sense of being live agents, part of a body standing for the whole. The skeleton arms, however, are drawn, not imprinted,[72] and they refer directly to Munch's 1895 lithographic *Self-Portrait*.

One of Munch's first prints of any type, this lithograph exists in three states. A first state with a loose brushy background (fig. 44) shows the head connected to the body and the bones placed where the artist's arm might have rested, recalling traditional portraits and self-portraits such as those by Dürer and Rembrandt. In the final state, black ink has obliterated all details, leaving the spectral head floating in a dark void (fig. 45).

fig. 43 Johns, **Savarin**, 1978, monotype, 26 x 21 ½ in. (66 x 54.6 cm). Private collection

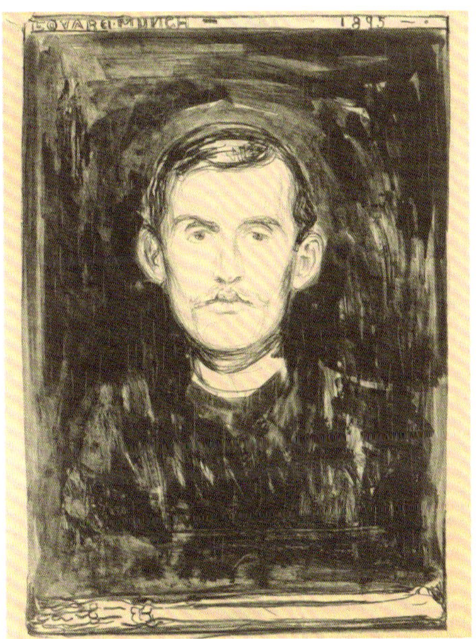

fig. 44 Munch, **Self-Portrait**, 1895, lithograph, 18 x 14 ½ in. (45.8 x 36.8 cm). Munch Museum

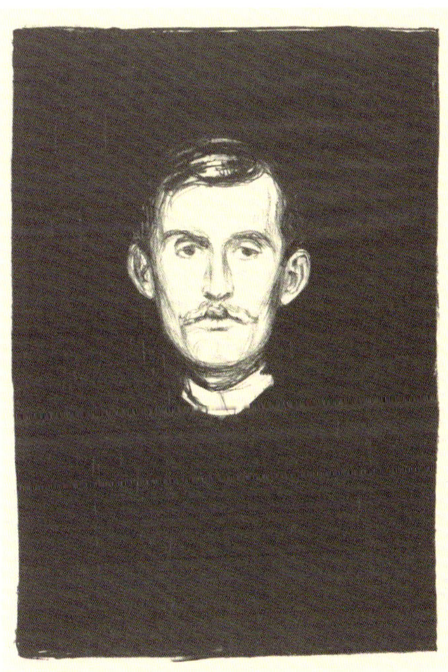

fig. 45 Munch, **Self-Portrait**, 1895, lithograph, 25 ¼ x 19 ½ in. (64 x 49.5 cm). Munch Museum

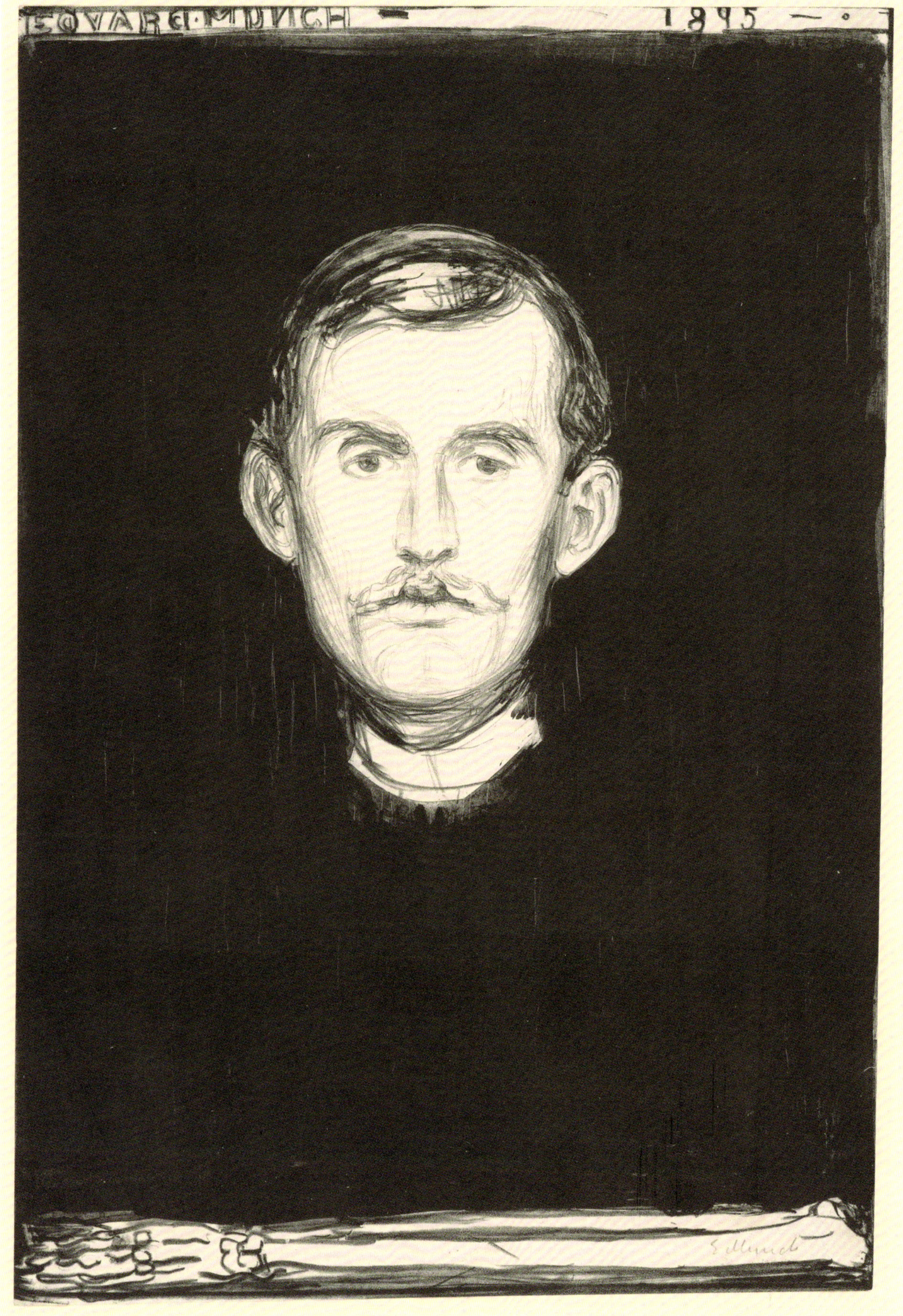

EDVARD·MUNCH
1895
E Munch

It is the state between these two that has become one of Munch's most iconic images (fig. 46). Here the strong contrast of light and dark lends greater prominence to both head and arm. The isolation of these two elements removes them further from each other in space and time, the arm now suggesting a relic of the person above. The inscription-like lettering at the top underscores the memorial tone and the uneasy tension between art and death that is staged below, with the stilled arm conveying intense anxiety about the demise of the artist's creative capacity.[73]

Johns may have recognized in Munch's famous self-portrait a perfect vehicle to reflect on his own feelings in the immediate aftermath of his Whitney retrospective, which had closed in January 1978, exactly the time he made the two monotypes containing the bony arm.[74] Having already incorporated wood-grain patterning into his work (which reappears in both of the monotypes, loosely scratched beneath the can), Johns now incorporated Munch's skeleton arm, adopting the motif in combination with his surrogate self-portrait of the Savarin can and brushes to produce his own meditation on creativity, anxiety, and public exposure.

Another aspect of these monotypes extends this connection further. In the print with the darker arm (fig. 42), the brush handles have a liquid, bulbous quality. Johns may have seen the resemblance to fingers, and in the next print—lighter because it is a second pull from the same painting on Plexiglas—he added a bold handprint. The hand both reaches for and merges with the brushes, recalling the hand and hatch mark analogy of the previous year. The blood-red color implies danger, even violence, especially in relation to the skeleton arm.[75]

In late 1978 or early 1979, Johns visited the National Gallery of Art in Washington, DC, to see *Edvard Munch: Symbols & Images*, the most comprehensive exhibition of the Norwegian artist's work to date in the United States.[76] Munch's 1895 *Self-Portrait* was included, along with 245 other paintings, prints, drawings, watercolors, woodblocks, and illustrated manuscripts. Now, twenty-eight years after his first experience at MoMA, Johns once again had the opportunity to study in person the full spectrum of Munch's career in all media. One would expect the two *Savarin* monotypes with skeleton arms to result from this visit, but they were published in May 1978, some six to ten months before Johns traveled to Washington. Rather than another story of fortuitous discovery, the connection of the Savarin prints with Munch's self-portrait lithograph is better understood as the outcome of numerous incremental steps over a decade and as part of the larger, evolving narrative of Johns's deepening interest in Munch's work. The National Gallery exhibition offered Johns a way to affirm his engagement with Munch, and by the time of his next significant step with the Savarin can two years later, he was ready to acknowledge this connection in a highly public manner.

Johns made this next *Savarin* print (fig. 47) in two phases. He began with an extra plate created for the 1977 Whitney poster but never used. This plate provided the occasional thin dark lines that match the crosshatch pattern of the 1977 drawing (fig. 18), confirming Johns's recollection that the drawing was used for this print.[77] The repurposed plate also includes the shadow along the can's left edge, the thin ledge underneath it, and the faint black lines that occur throughout

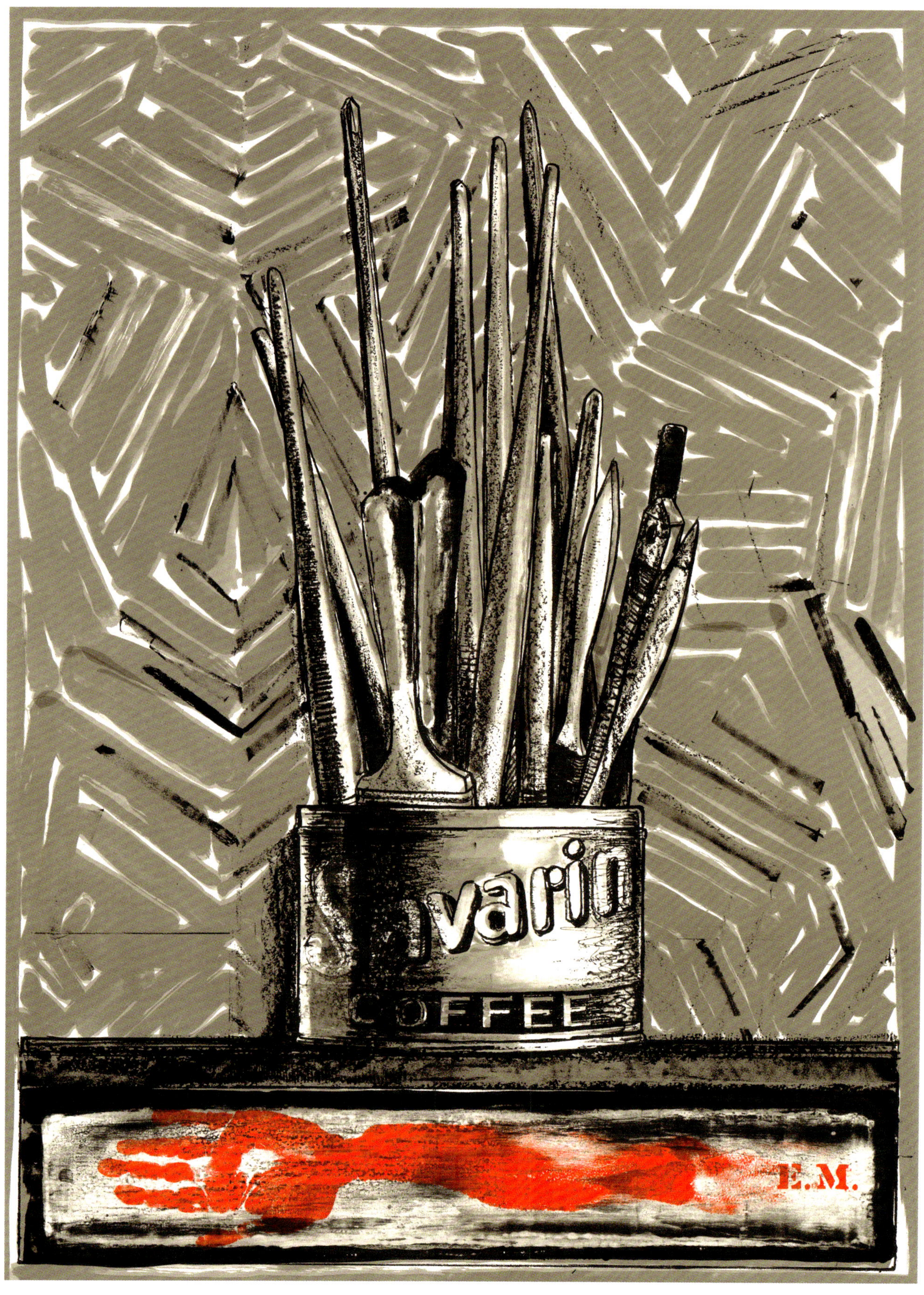

varin
COFFEE
E.M.

the background of the drawing, including the horizontal lines at the left and right of the can. The soft gray tones and the red arm were added in 1981, as were some of the darker crosshatchings.

The red arm builds on the skeleton arms of the 1978 monotypes and their references to Munch's 1895 *Self-Portrait*. But it returns to Johns's 1960s practice of imprinting his own arm. Nonetheless, it is more detached from the body than those earlier armprints and no longer suggests the capacity for action. It tapers on the right, its end decisively capped by Munch's initials, "E.M."[78] The overt nature of this homage tempts one to ask whether the arm belongs to Johns, in providing the imprint, or Munch, given the initials. The use of stenciling for the initials—a common practice in Johns's work—echoes the stencil-like lettering at the top of Munch's self-portrait. Curiously, Munch reversed several of his letters, a detail that may not have been lost on Johns, given the centrality of reversals and mirroring in his work. Taken a step further, a reversal of the initials in Johns's work would spell "ME," making another statement of connection between the two artists.[79] The space in which the arm rests—previously reserved for exhibition details and wood grain and made to seem somewhat continuous with the ledge just beneath the can—is here turned into a box by a thick black line. It lends a reliquary feel that reinforces the image of *Painted Bronze* as a surrogate self-portrait and suggests commentary similar to Munch's self-portrait: the artist's arm has become an emblem of stilled agency. The memorializing quality is reinforced now that the color has been drained from the image above, replaced by a play of light and shadow on the handles that emphasizes the fact that the brushes have been plunged head down into the can.

Late Crosshatching: Sex, Death, and the Cycle of Life

Despite the presence of the Savarin can and other recognizable imagery in Johns's drawings and prints of the 1970s, the exclusive focus of his paintings during this period was the nonrepresentational motif of crosshatching. This highly flexible vehicle had provided a means for Johns to probe a broad range of allusions and associations—in the process allowing him to create some of the defining abstract paintings of postwar art. But by the late 1970s, crosshatching had become a limitation that Johns seemed increasingly in need of violating. Crichton recognized the potential for this problem as early as 1976:

> For the moment Johns has settled into a series of paintings which elaborate on patterns of cross-hatching. He has already begun to complicate these patterns in difficult ways; one senses that eventually he will have exhausted the potential for the mathematical manipulation of the image, or that his complexities will have passed beyond the ability of anyone else to see what he has done. That will no doubt provoke another crisis in his career, another endpoint from which he must begin anew.[80]

At the time of Johns's 1996 retrospective at MoMA, Kirk Varnedoe, looking back at his late crosshatching, summarized the difficulty: "the motif's kaleidoscopic dynamism is locking up in these paintings, with intensifying rigidity and constriction."[81] Johns's response was to push in two opposing directions at once, sometimes within the same work: on the one hand, exploring even greater formal complexity and, on the other, incorporating recognizable—and highly charged—imagery.

In *Usuyuki* (fig. 48), Johns leaned toward the former through an elaborate mathematical plan of repeating subsections. He envisioned the painting moving through time and space, with two systems of marks spiraling in opposite directions "in an intangible and barely intuited rhythmic pattern."[82] At the same time, Johns inflected this "fugue-like complexity"[83] with allusions to sadness and the brevity of life through his title: *Usuyuki* refers to both the Japanese word for falling snow and a Kabuki play about the melancholy relationship between an aging man and a beautiful young geisha he desires but can no longer possess.[84]

In a painting from the following year, *Cicada* (fig. 49), Johns introduced the theme of regeneration and life cycles while still remaining squarely within the language of abstraction. Here a central core of primary-color hatches seems to emerge from a surrounding field of secondary-color marks, as if shedding a husk. The reference is to the insect, which leaves its underground home every two to seventeen years, depending on the species, to discard its exoskeleton and emerge as a winged adult for a brief mating season before dying. The title of the work appears

fig. 48 Johns, **Usuyuki**, 1977–78, encaustic and collage on canvas (three panels), 35 ¹⁄₁₆ x 57 ⅜ in. (89.2 x 145.8 cm), framed. The Cleveland Museum of Art, Leonard C. Hanna, Jr. Fund

fig. 49 Johns, **Cicada**, 1979, oil on canvas, 48 x 36 in. (121.9 x 91.4 cm). The Museum of Fine Arts, Houston, Museum purchase funded by the Caroline Wiess Law Accessions Endowment Fund

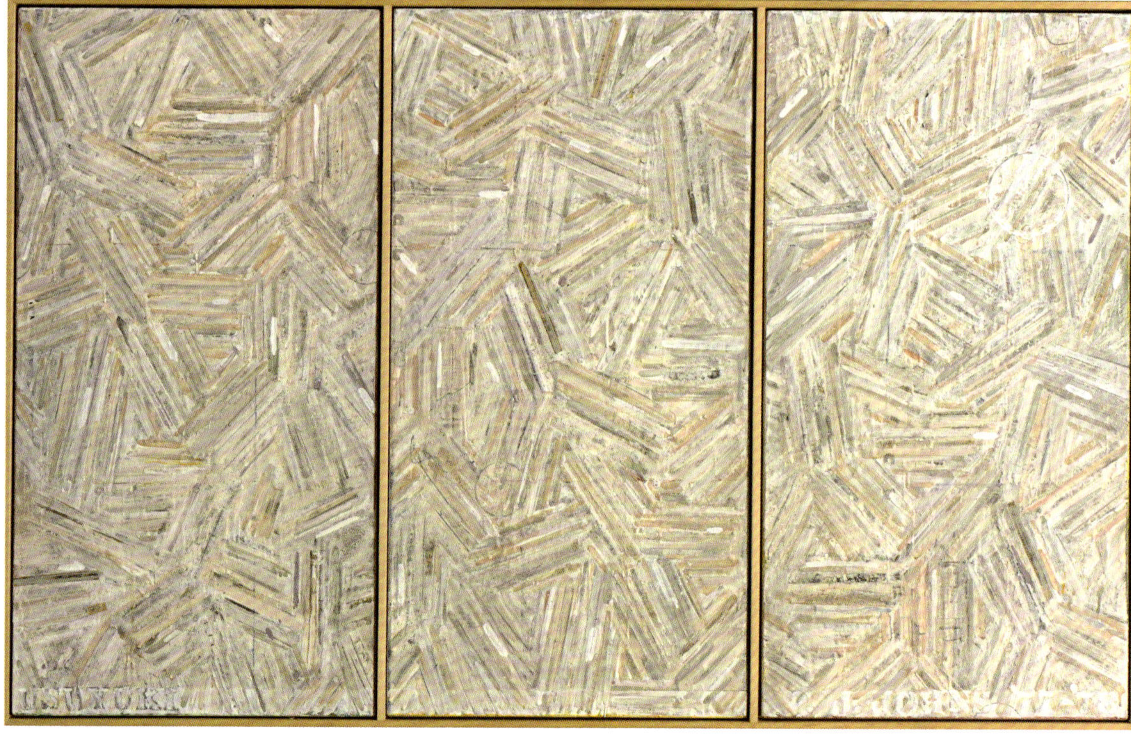

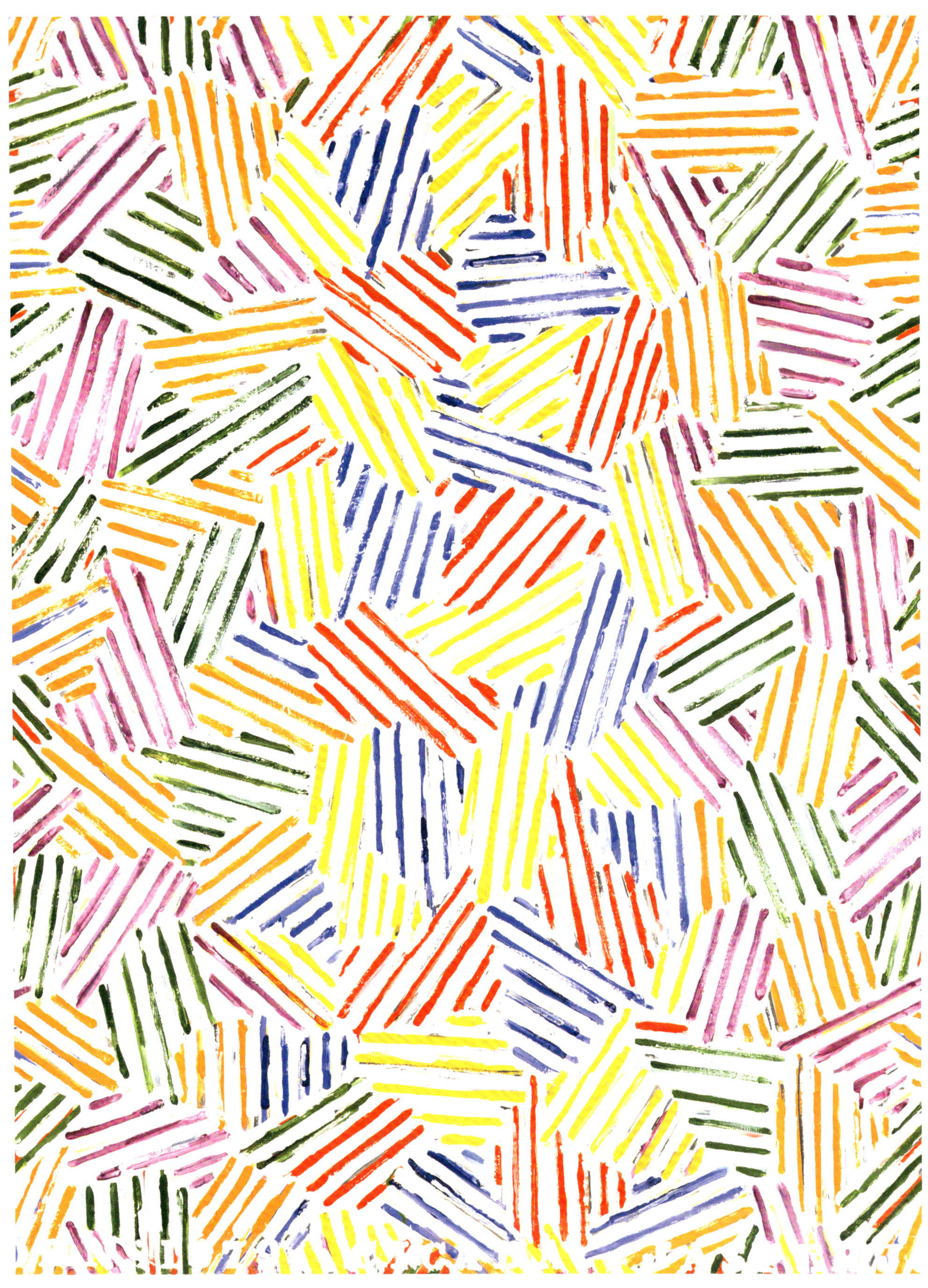

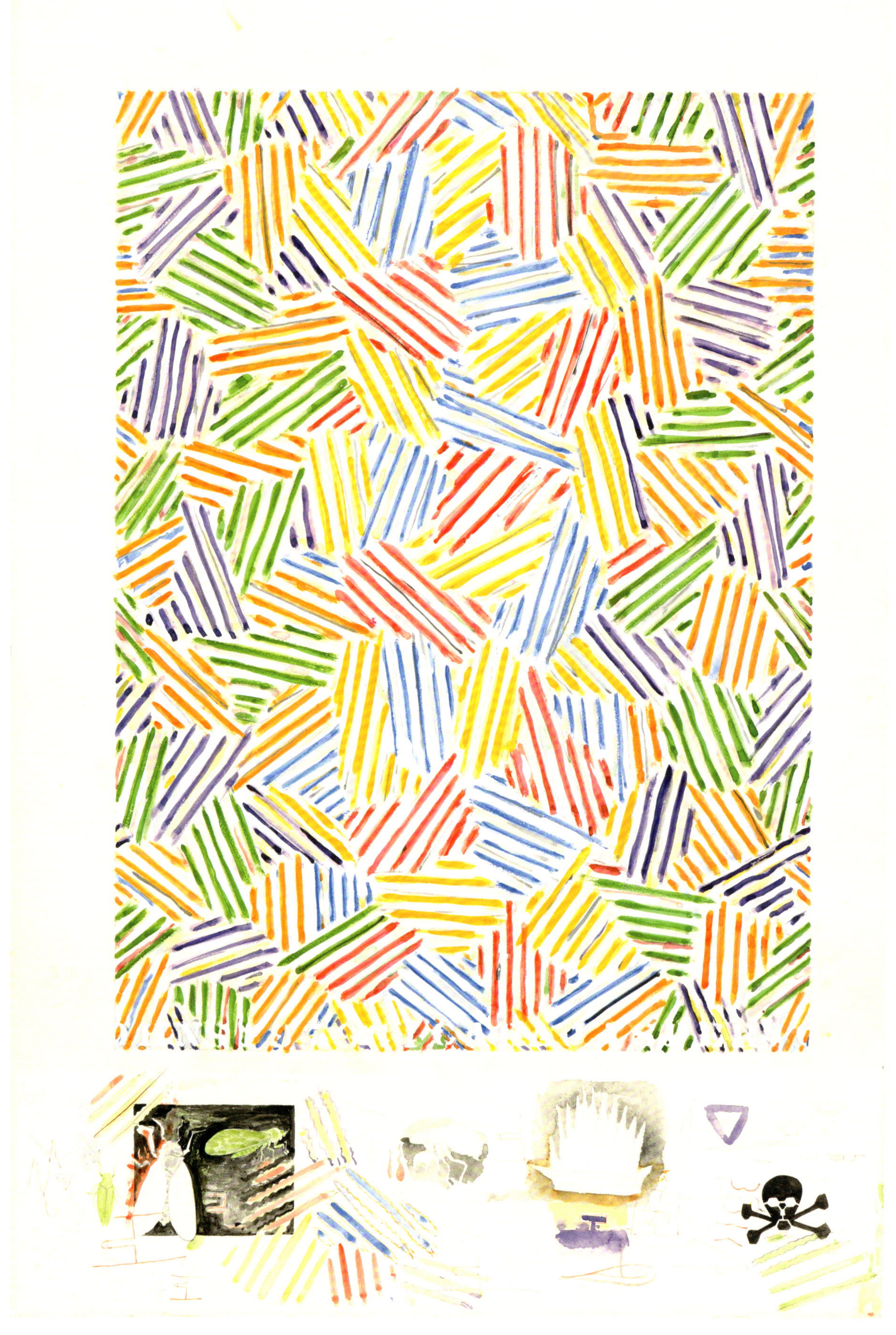

prominently stenciled at the bottom center, reinforcing the connection between the abstract pattern and the theme of metamorphosis.

In a drawing made several months later and also titled *Cicada* (fig. 50), Johns pulled back the curtain on his thought process. Here, beneath the same composition as the painting, he included a horizontal band filled with sketches and notations of the sort normally reserved for his private notebooks. There is no coherent narrative to these psychologically and emotionally loaded images, but taken together, they offer a revealing glimpse of Johns's working method as he evolved new imagery related to themes of sex, death, and regeneration. These include cicadas seen from overhead and the side; skulls in frontal and side views; geometric or stylized symbols for sexual intercourse and genitalia; spermatozoa; a lamplike form with flames representing a cremation pyre; and beneath it a lingam (phallus) set in a yoni (vulva), beside which appears the text "Pope Prays at Auschwitz: 'Only Peace.' "[85]

Characteristically, Johns borrowed most of the images from preexisting sources, including an entomological text and a *New York Times* headline about Pope John Paul II's visit to the death camp in 1979. Another source was a well-illustrated book on Tantric art from Johns's library.[86] While Munch does not appear to be a direct source for the imagery, the proximity of life and death are among his most enduring themes, and one is reminded of Johns's reference to Munch's skeleton arm the previous year and his visit to the Munch exhibition in Washington just a few months before he made the *Cicada* drawing.[87] In addition, the unusual decision to feature marginalia—the scribbles, comments, and illuminations traditionally seen in the margins of biblical manuscripts—as a prominent part of the finished work may relate to several of Munch's early paintings and prints, which would have been on view in the exhibition.

fig. 50 Johns, **Cicada**, 1979, watercolor, graphite pencil, and crayon on paper, 43 x 28¾ in. (109.2 x 73 cm). The Museum of Fine Arts, Houston, Museum purchase funded by the Caroline Wiess Law Accessions Endowment Fund

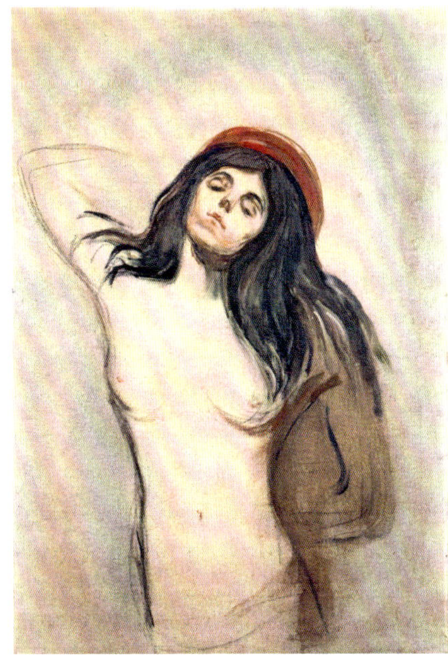

fig. 51 Munch, **Madonna**, 1895–97?, oil on canvas, 39¾ x 27¾ in. (101 x 70.5 cm). Collection of Nelson Blitz, Jr. and Catherine Woodard

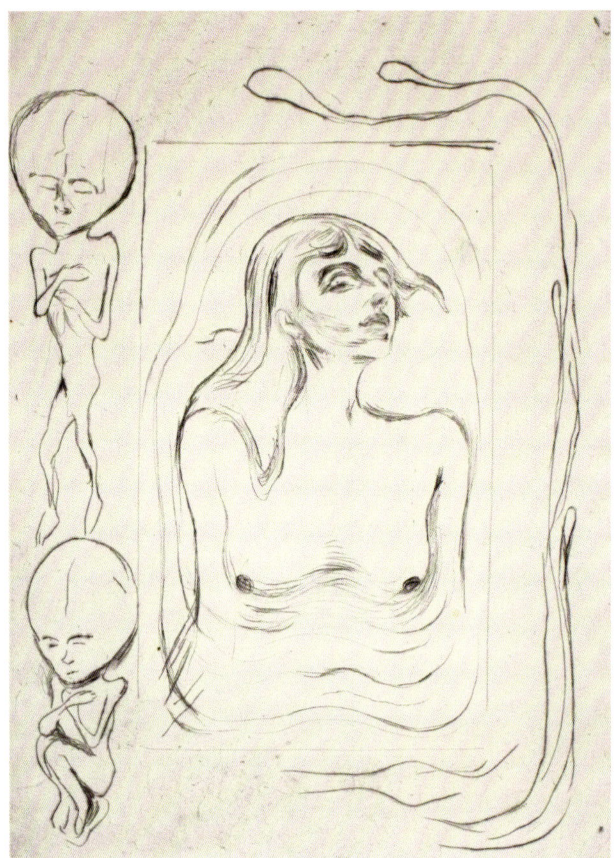

fig. 52 Munch, **Madonna**, 1894, drypoint,
25 ⅞ x 19 ¾ in. (65.9 x 50 cm). Munch Museum

One of Munch's *Madonna* paintings, from 1895–97, presents a sexualized female nude not yet surrounded by other imagery (fig. 51).[88] The figure's simultaneous exposure and withdrawal—into herself and into a haze of thinly brushed paint—suggest the self-abandonment and absorption into another being one feels during a moment of ecstasy, while also conveying a sense of moral and physical decay. Munch described the image as

> the interval when the whole world stopped in its course—Your face holds all the beauty of the kingdom of earth—Your lips, crimson as the ripening fruit, part as in pain—The smile of a corpse—Now life shakes the hand of death— the chain is forged which binds the thousand generations that are dead to the thousand generations yet to come.[89]

In print versions of *Madonna* from around the same time, Munch made the tension between love and loss more obvious by adding images in the margin. In one of his very first prints, an intaglio from 1894 (fig. 52), he surrounded the figure with large fetuses and sperm. In a lithograph from the following year, printed both in black and white (fig. 53) and in color (fig. 54), Munch again framed the figure with sperm and a fetus, now more mummy-like. In combination with the woman's darker, closed eyes and deathly pallor, these perimeter images further the equation

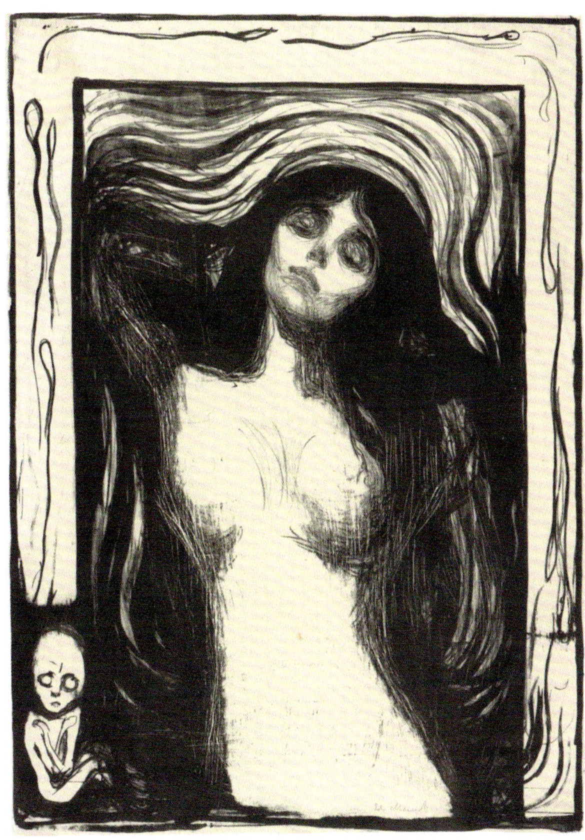

fig. 53 Munch, **Madonna**, 1895/1902, lithograph, 23 ⅝ x 17 ⅜ in. (60.4 x 44 cm). Munch Museum

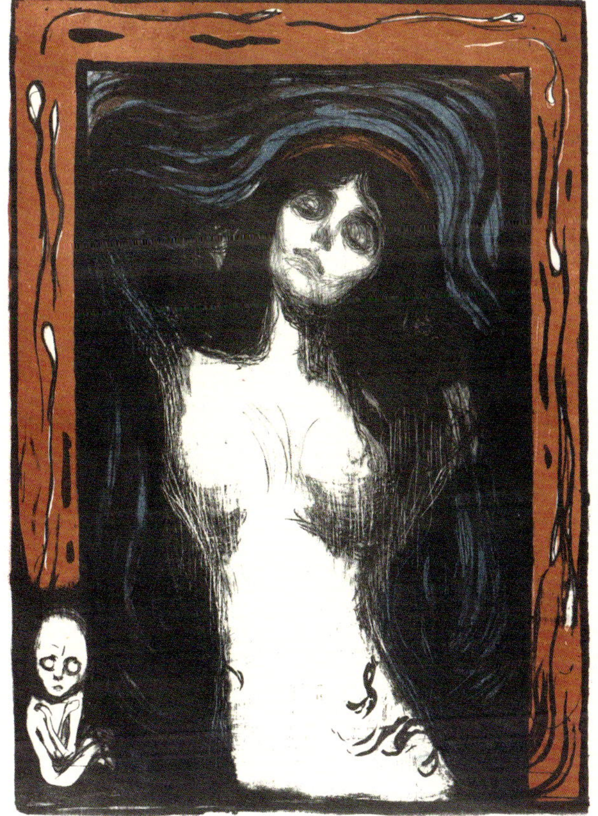

fig. 54 Munch, **Madonna**, 1895/1902, lithograph, 31 ½ x 23 ⅝ in. (80 x 60.2 cm). Munch Museum

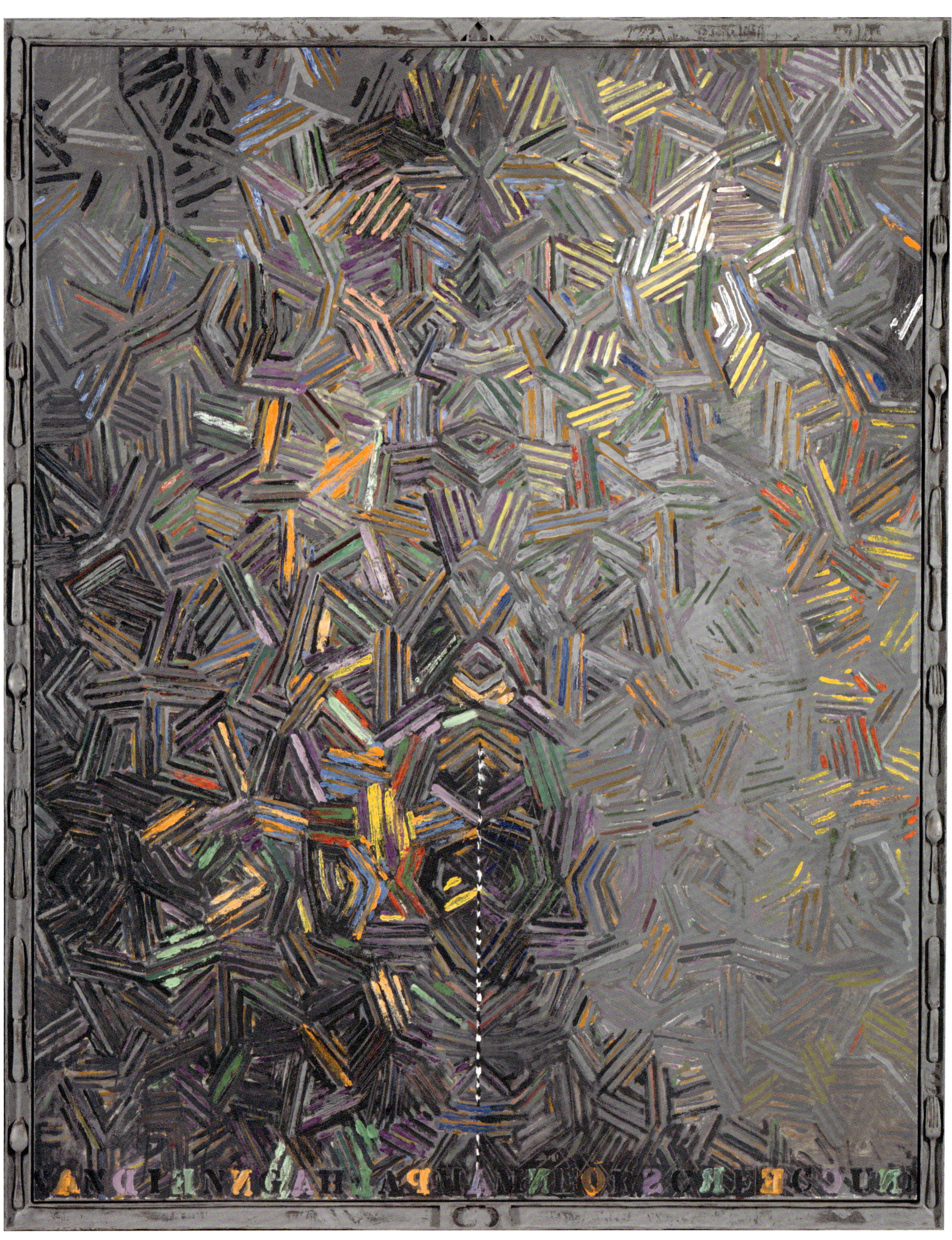

of ecstasy or satiation with a living death, reinforcing the notion of creation and destruction as inseparable partners linked in an endless cycle.

Johns's use of marginalia had a casual appearance in the *Cicada* drawing, but it assumed a more studied and deliberate role in his next painting, *Dancers on a Plane*, 1980 (fig. 55).[90] Here a painted bronze frame, cast from Johns's design, includes two highly stylized Tantric sexual images. At the bottom center, an oval shape represents testicles; at the top center a vertical shaft between two triangles represents a phallus and vagina. Johns enhanced the legibility of these symbols in a 1982 drawing made after the paintings (fig.56). (Although certainly unknown to Johns at the time,[91] an anomalous drawing in Munch's oeuvre, a detailed, mandala-like study of a vulva [fig. 57], makes a fascinating comparison with these stylized genitalia and those at the bottom of the *Cicada* drawing. The vulva

fig. 55 Johns, **Dancers on a Plane**, 1980, oil on canvas with bronze frame, 78 ⅜ x 63 ¾ in. (200 x 162 cm), framed. Tate London: Purchased 1981

fig. 56 Johns, **Dancers on a Plane**, 1982, graphite wash on paper, 35 x 27 in. (88.9 x 68.6 cm). Kravis Collection

fig. 57 Munch, **Sketch of a Vulva**, ca. 1915–30?, charcoal and pencil on paper, 21 ½ x 26 ⅝ in. (53.7 x 67.6 cm). Munch Museum

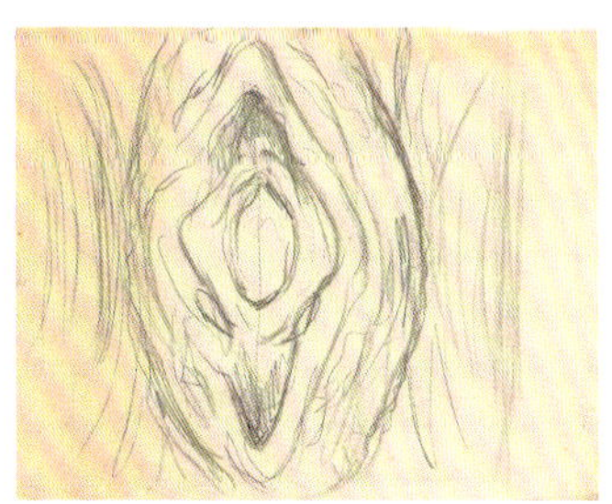

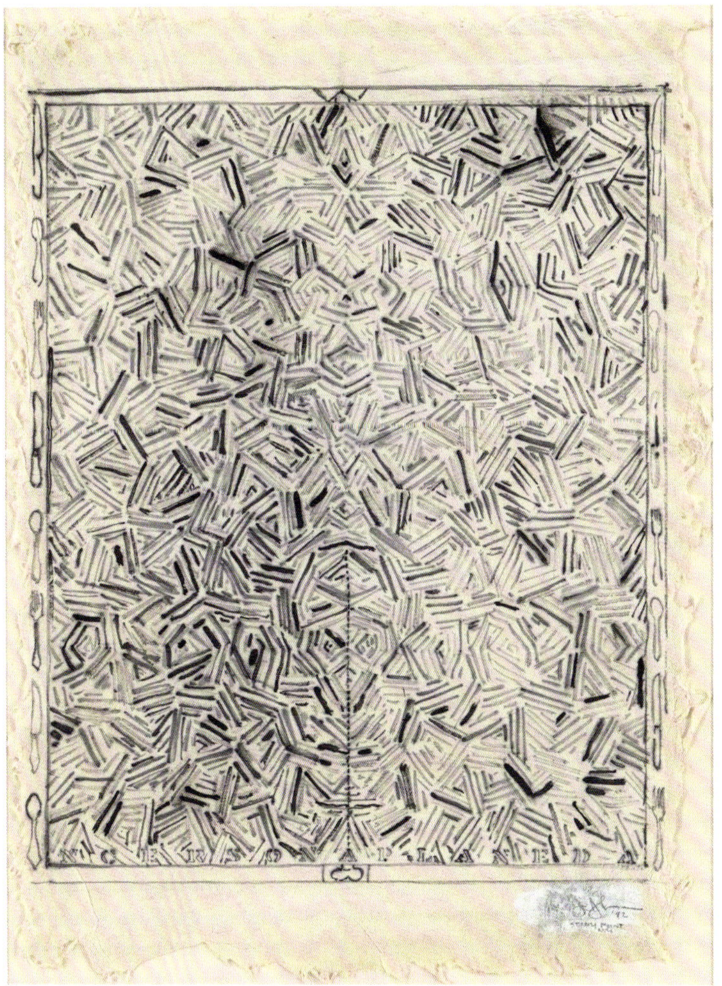

drawing shows that Munch was thinking along similar lines of stylized genitalia as symbolic imagery.)

In addition to the sexual symbols at the top and bottom, the frame of *Dancers* includes casts of spoons, knives, and forks running up and down the sides. These humble utensils had appeared periodically in Johns's work. The actual spoon and fork hanging together off the surface of the painting *In Memory of My Feelings— Frank O'Hara* (fig. 58) take on a somber reflective quality when linked with O'Hara's poem of the same title addressing the passage of time.[92] Several years later, Johns chose a place setting with knife, fork, and spoon (fig. 59) as his contribution to a book published the year after O'Hara's premature death. In doing so, he underscored the simple act of eating—consumption and digestion—as a metaphor for larger themes of mortality. When asked about the function of the utensils in these works, Johns replied, "My associations, if you want them, are cutting, measuring, mixing, blending, consuming—creation and destruction moderated by ritualized manners."[93] The cutlery around *Dancers* builds on these associations, particularly in connection with the painting's central image (discussed below). Their resemblance to the sperm and fetus surrounding Munch's *Madonna* is formal and at the same time signals a shared embrace of fundamental themes of life and death.

A late self-portrait by Munch adds an interesting twist to this symbolism. Munch shows himself seated before a large cod's head, his knife and fork held in midair as if prepared for delicate surgery (fig. 60).[94] The cod's bleached, skull-like appearance contrasts with Munch's sanguine skin tone, although they share bald pates and pronounced eye sockets. Munch appears poised to conquer death by

fig. 58 Johns, **In Memory of My Feelings—Frank O'Hara**, 1961, oil on canvas with objects, 40 ¼ x 60 x 2 ⅞ in. (102.2 x 152.4 x 7.3 cm). Museum of Contemporary Art Chicago, Partial gift of Apollo Plastics Corporation, courtesy of Stefan T. Edlis and H. Gael Neeson

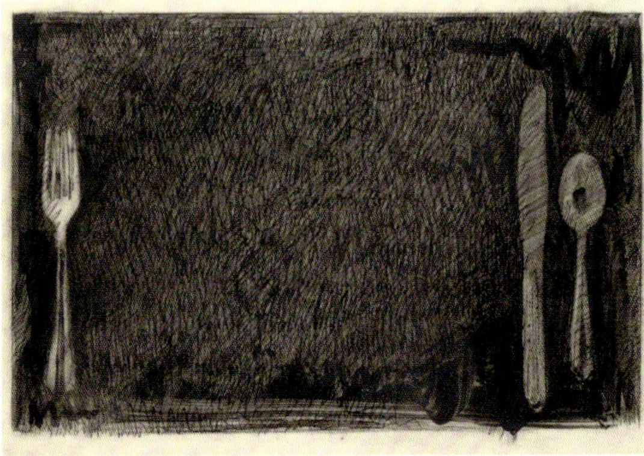

fig. 59 Johns, **Illustration for the book "In Memory of My Feelings," by Frank O'Hara**, 1967, graphite and gouache on acetate, 12 ⁷⁄₁₆ x 19 in. (31.6 x 48.2 cm). The Museum of Modern Art, New York, Gift of the Artist

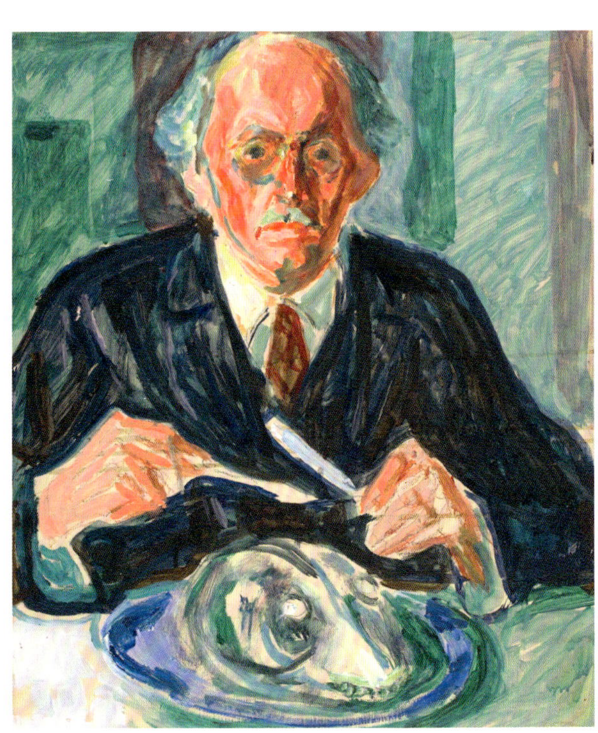

fig. 60 Munch, **Self-Portrait, with a Cod's Head on a Plate**, 1940–42, oil on wooden panel, 21 ⅝ x 17 ⅞ in. (55 x 45.5 cm). Munch Museum

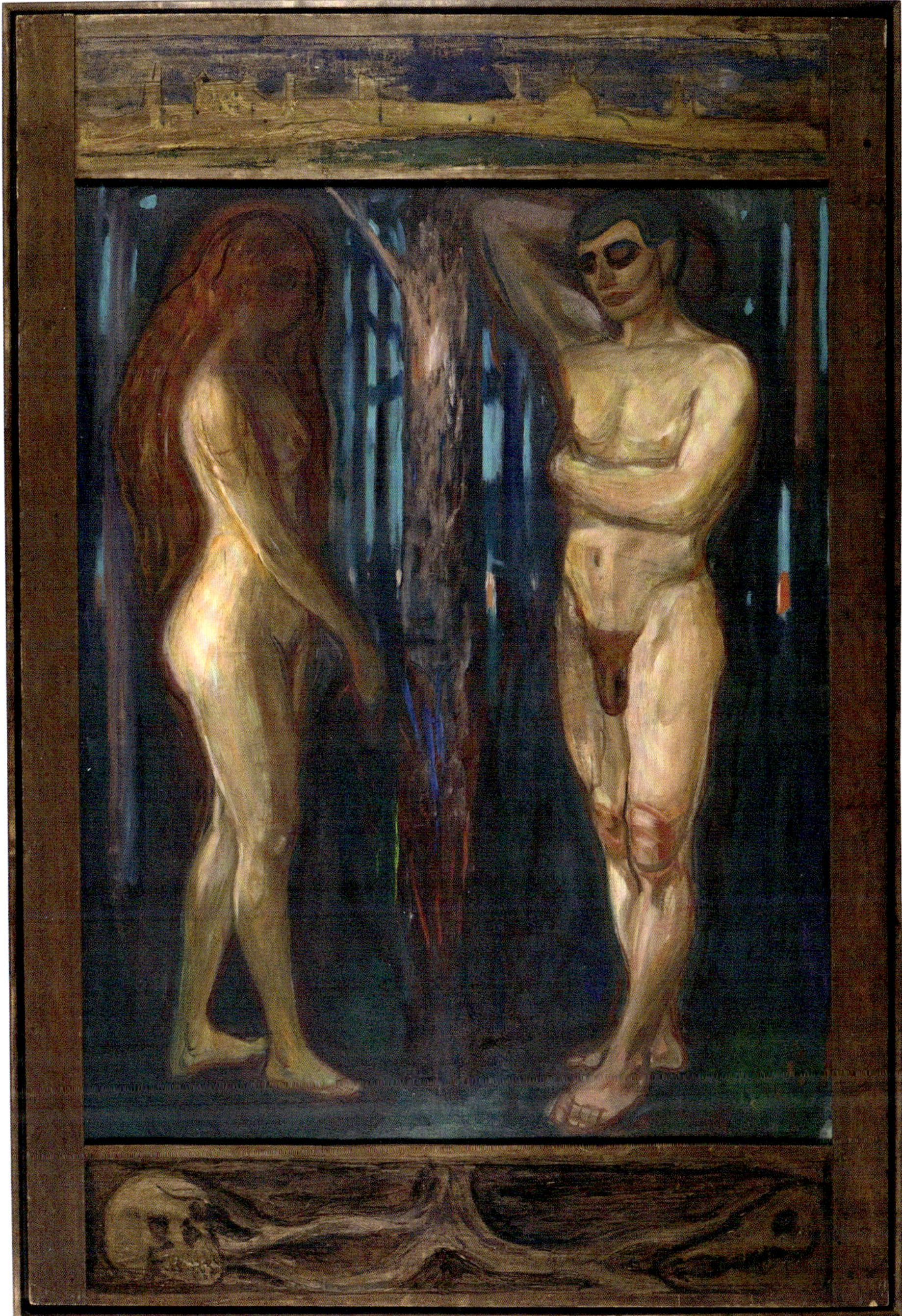

fig. 61 Munch, **Metabolism**, 1898–99, oil on canvas with carved wooden frame, 68⅞ x 56⁵⁄₁₆ in. (175 x 143 cm), painting dimensions. Munch Museum

consuming it—a bold image of human digestion as a metaphor for the metabolic cycle as a whole.

The theme of metabolism runs deeply through Munch's work. It is the title of a large painting (fig. 61) that he considered the centerpiece of his grand, multipart cycle called the *Frieze of Life*. He first exhibited the work with the title *Adam and Eve*. Two years later, he changed it to *Life and Death* and then, in 1914, added *Metabolism*.[95] Munch described it as "a picture of life as well as of death . . . that shows the wood feeding off the dead and the city growing up behind the trees. It is a picture of the powerful constructive forces of life."[96] Originally, an embryo appeared in the center of the image, contained within a small shrub, before Munch replaced it with the central tree trunk. The carved wooden frame—a further parallel with Johns's cast bronze frame—includes human and animal skulls feeding the roots of the tree, which carries energy to the city above.[97]

Munch explored the concept and process of metabolism further in numerous prints and drawings in which human bodies decaying beneath the ground nourish life above (figs. 62 and 63). "Flowers will grow up from my rotting corpse and I will live on in those blooms," he stated. "Death is the beginning of life, the beginning of a new crystallization."[98] Munch understood the process of metabolism as a powerful force, in a biological and spiritual sense, uniting both humans and nature as well as creation and destruction in an eternal rhythm.

Johns's exploration of this perpetual cycle on the frame of *Dancers on a Plane* is reinforced by the imagery within. On one level, the painting celebrates Johns's friend and collaborator Merce Cunningham, whose name appears at the bottom in letters alternating with the work's title. Johns's thirteen-year position as artistic advisor to the Cunningham Dance Company had ended the year he made the painting, and the

fig. 62 Munch, **Life and Death**, 1902 (?), etching, 11 ⅜ x 10 ¼ in. (28.6 x 26 cm). Munch Museum

fig. 63 Munch, **Metabolism**, 1916, lithograph, 31 ⅝ x 22 ¾ in. (80.6 x 57.9 cm). Munch Museum

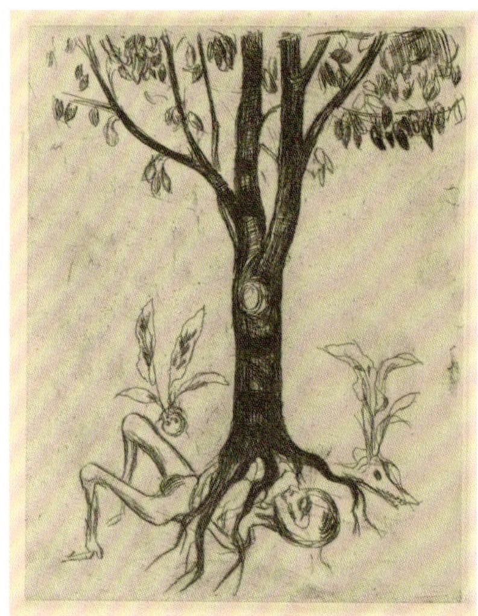

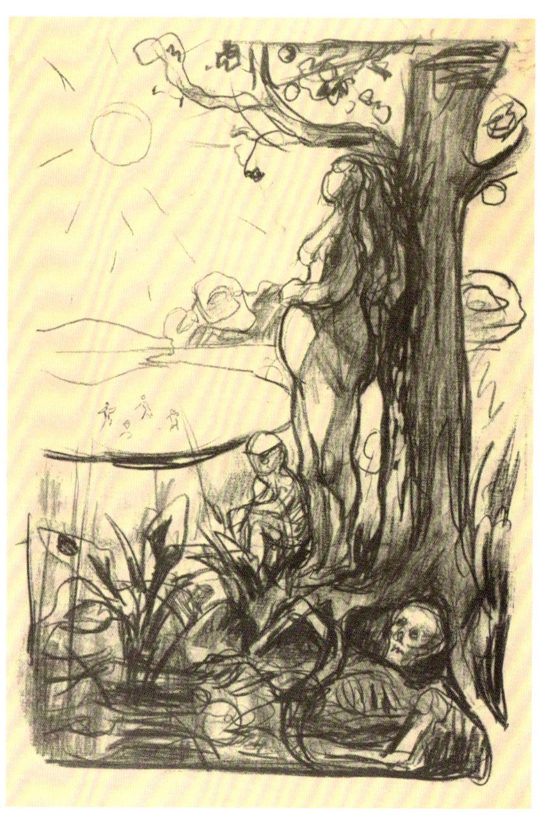

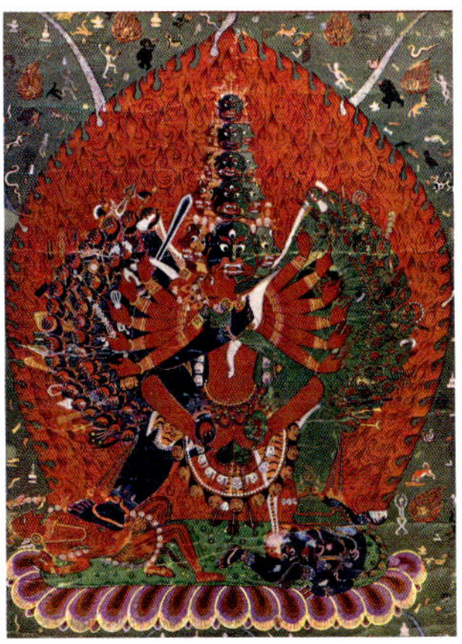

fig. 64 **The Mystical Form of Samvara with Seventy-Four Arms Embracing his Sakti with Twelve Arms**, 17th century, Nepalese, gouache on cloth, 28 x 19 in. (71.1 x 48.3 cm). Formerly collection of Ajit Mookerjee, present location unknown

dancers in the title may also extend to the members of the Cunningham troupe.[99] Johns layered the image with further allusions by reference to the same book on Tantric art that lies behind *Cicada*, in this case looking to an image of the Buddhist deity Samvara joined with his beloved consort in an ecstatic dance of procreation and self-abandonment (fig. 64).[100]

Johns described the Tantric image as "the interpenetration of destructive and creative forces."[101] His painting refers to it in the dotted line running up the center from the bottom, which echoes the fringe of Samvara's girdle, and in the stylized skull emerging from the crosshatch pattern part way up the same line, which echoes the garlands of skulls and freshly severed heads hanging from Samvara's waist. The emphasis on a central core with an active surrounding pattern also suggests the figure of Samvara with his multiple arms and frenzied coupling.

Dance, then, functions in this work as a highly fraught meeting point for sex and death—as it does in some of Munch's best-known reflections on the nature of human experience. Munch made several versions of his *Death and the Maiden*, extending an established subgenre of the medieval and Renaissance allegorical motif of the *Dance of Death*. A print from 1894 (fig. 65) shows a naked female

fig. 65 Munch, **Death and the Maiden**, 1894, drypoint, 20 ⅛ x 13 ¾ in. (51 x 35 cm). Munch Museum

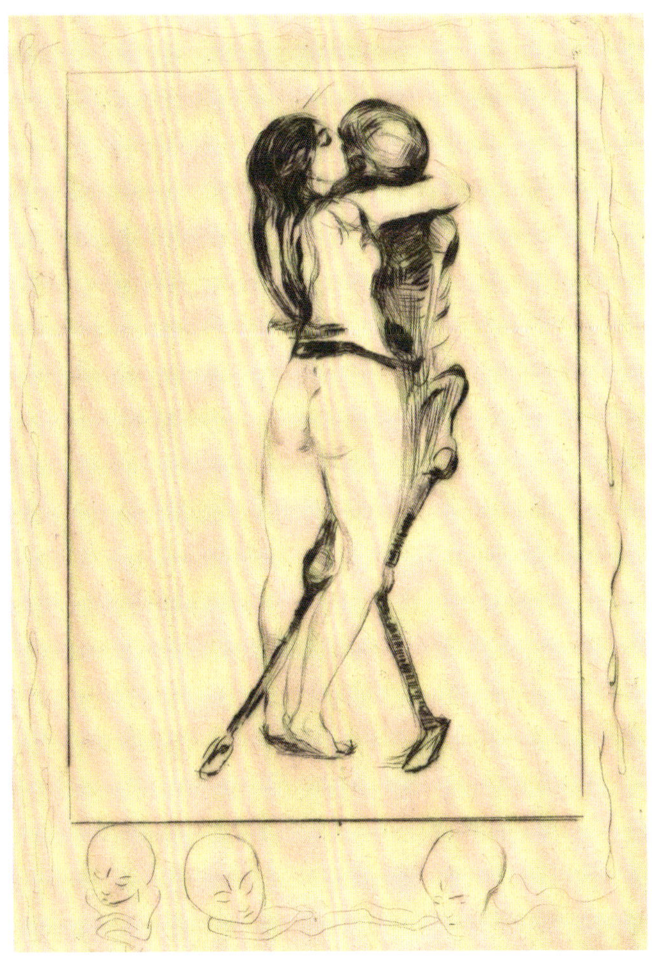

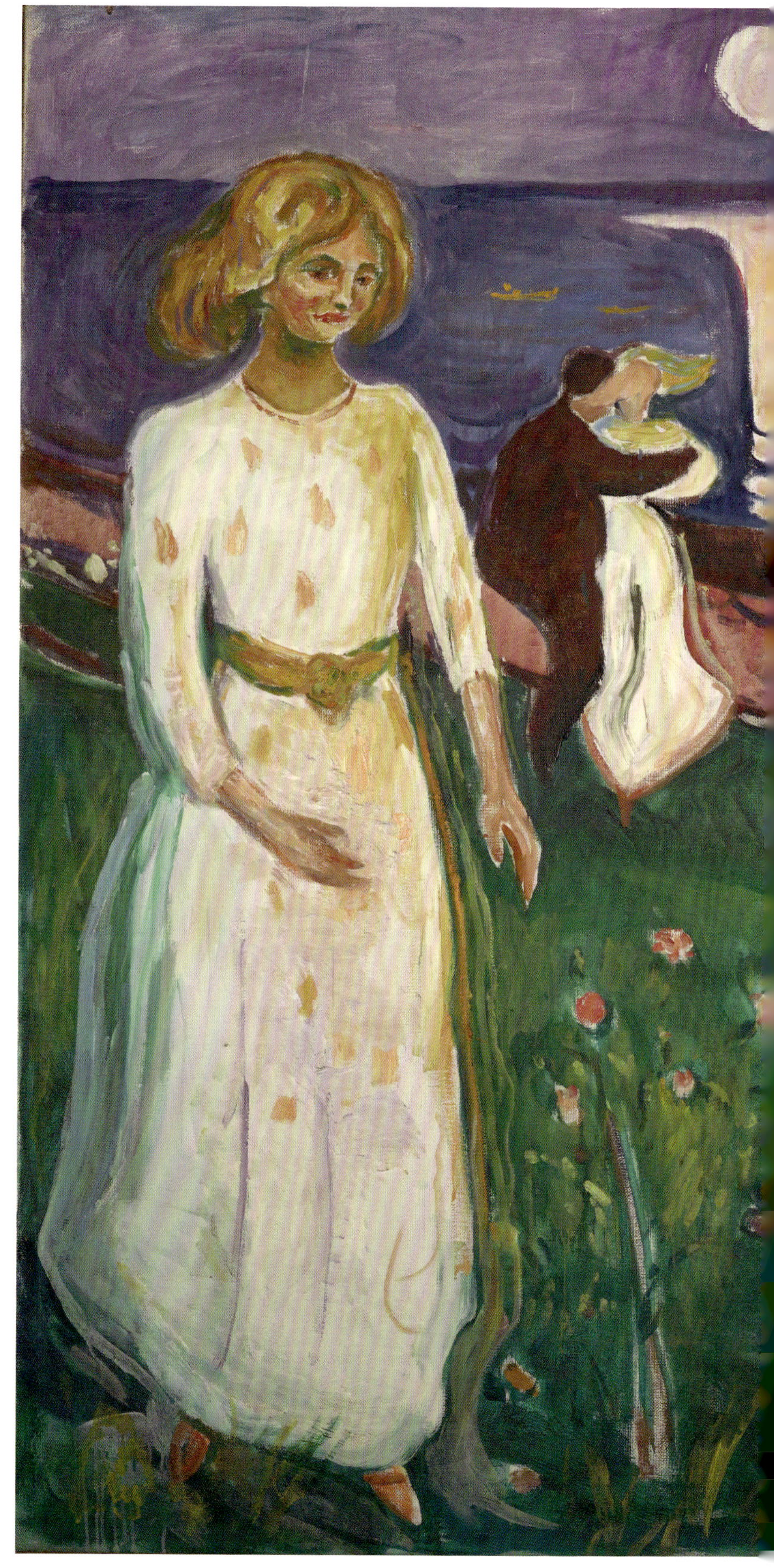

fig. 66 Munch, **The Dance of Life**, 1925, oil on canvas, 56 ¼ x 81 ⅞ in. (143 x 208 cm). Munch Museum

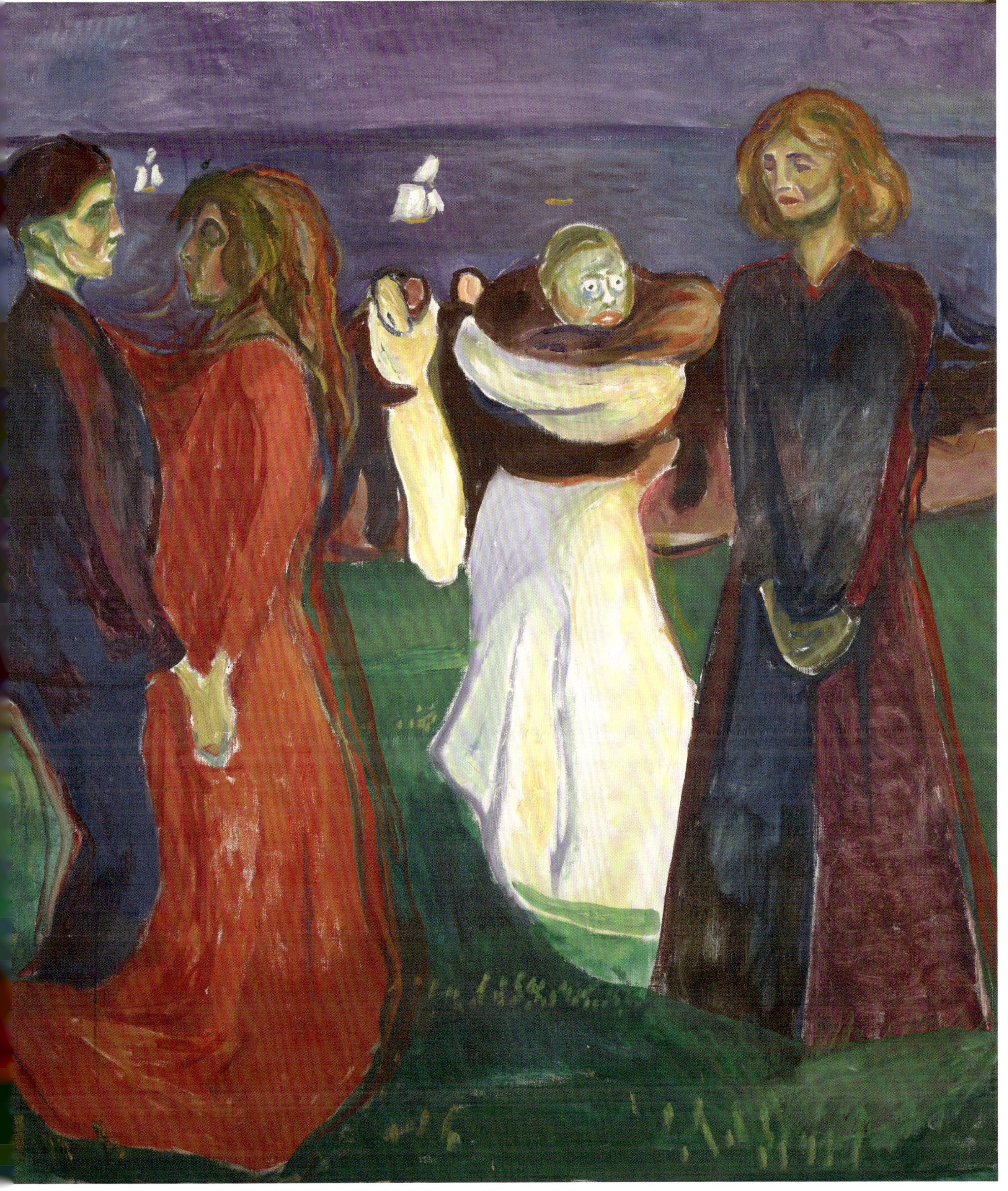

embracing death in an erotic *pas de deux*; the skeleton's bony leg thrust between the maiden's thighs suggests not just penetration but also dancelike movement.[102]

Munch's *Dance of Life* (fig. 66), painted in three versions, is one of the great examples of his use of dance to symbolize the stages of human existence. It was part of the *Frieze of Life*, and Munch saw it as encapsulating the cycle's principal themes: "the awakening of love, the dance of life, love at its peak, the fading of love, and finally death."[103] Against the backdrop of a glowing Nordic evening, an outdoor summer dance becomes the stage for an intense scene of mating rituals. The three women in the foreground represent types: the innocent, expectant virgin, reaching toward the flower; the dark-eyed temptress, locked in a swirling dance with her entranced partner; and the somber figure in black, her hands clasped in a gesture of resignation. The low-hanging moon casts a figural presence across the water—at once a phallus and crucifix—adding to the complex use of dance as a metaphor for life.

In the works that immediately followed *Dancers on a Plane*, Johns pushed crosshatching to the breaking point by inserting explicit symbols of sex and death, again inspired by the Tantric image of Samvara. The charcoal drawing *Tantric Detail* (fig. 67) and three closely related paintings (figs. 68, 69, and 70) all include a skull and testicles placed in the center.[104] They appear as if slipping behind panel divisions, prying apart the abstract surface to make shallow spaces for themselves. When the works were first exhibited in 1982, many viewers were dismayed by the intrusion of realistic images into the abstract pattern; as symbols they seemed "too loaded, too sudden, . . . horrifying in the context of what had become the more serene norm of his crosshatching."[105] Yet they reveal a tension that had been building in Johns's work since the introduction of crosshatching in 1972. In retrospect, their appearance confirmed a figural presence from the start of Johns's abstract phase and further belied the notion of crosshatching as neutral and nonrepresentational.

fig. 67 Johns, **Tantric Detail**, 1980, charcoal on paper, 58 x 41 in. (147.3 x 104.1 cm). Collection of the artist

fig. 68 Johns, **Tantric Detail I**, oil on canvas, 1980, 50 ⅛ x 34 ⅛ in. (127.3 x 86.7 cm). Donald L. Bryant Jr. and Marie-Josée and Henry R. Kravis, Promised gift to The Museum of Modern Art, New York

fig. 69 Johns, **Tantric Detail II**, oil on canvas, 1981, 50 x 34 in. (127 x 86.4 cm). Donald L. Bryant Jr. and Marie-Josée and Henry R. Kravis, Promised gift to The Museum of Modern Art, New York

fig. 70 **Tantric Detail III**, oil on canvas, 1981, 50 x 34 in. (127 x 86.4 cm). Donald L. Bryant Jr. and Marie-Josée and Henry R. Kravis, Promised gift to The Museum of Modern Art, New York

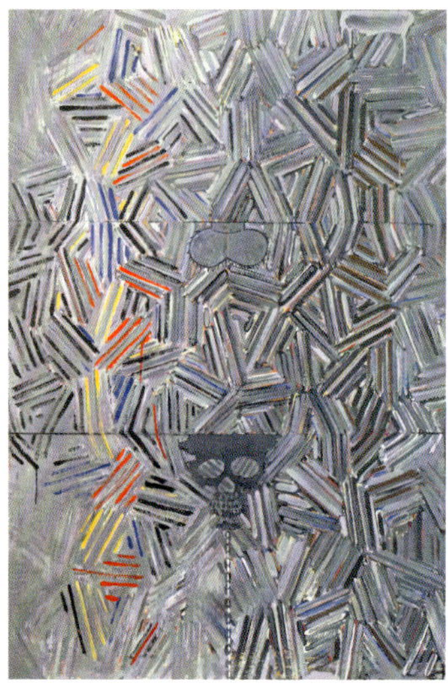
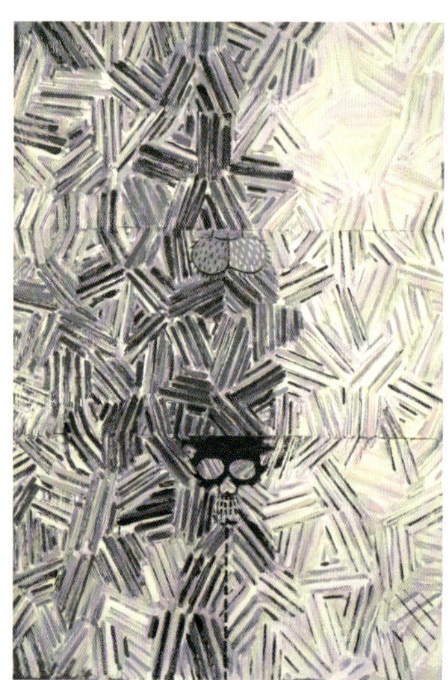
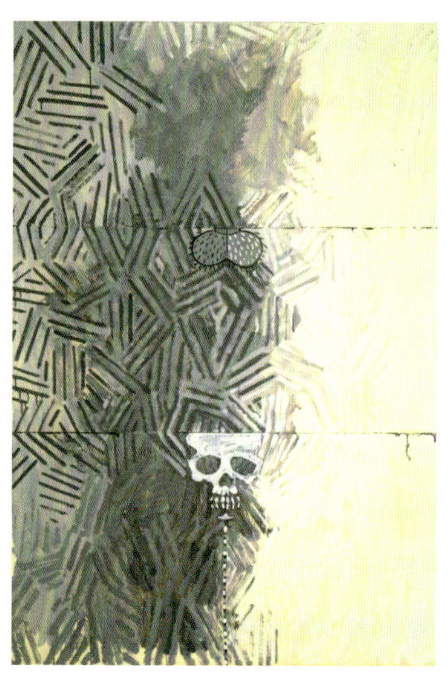

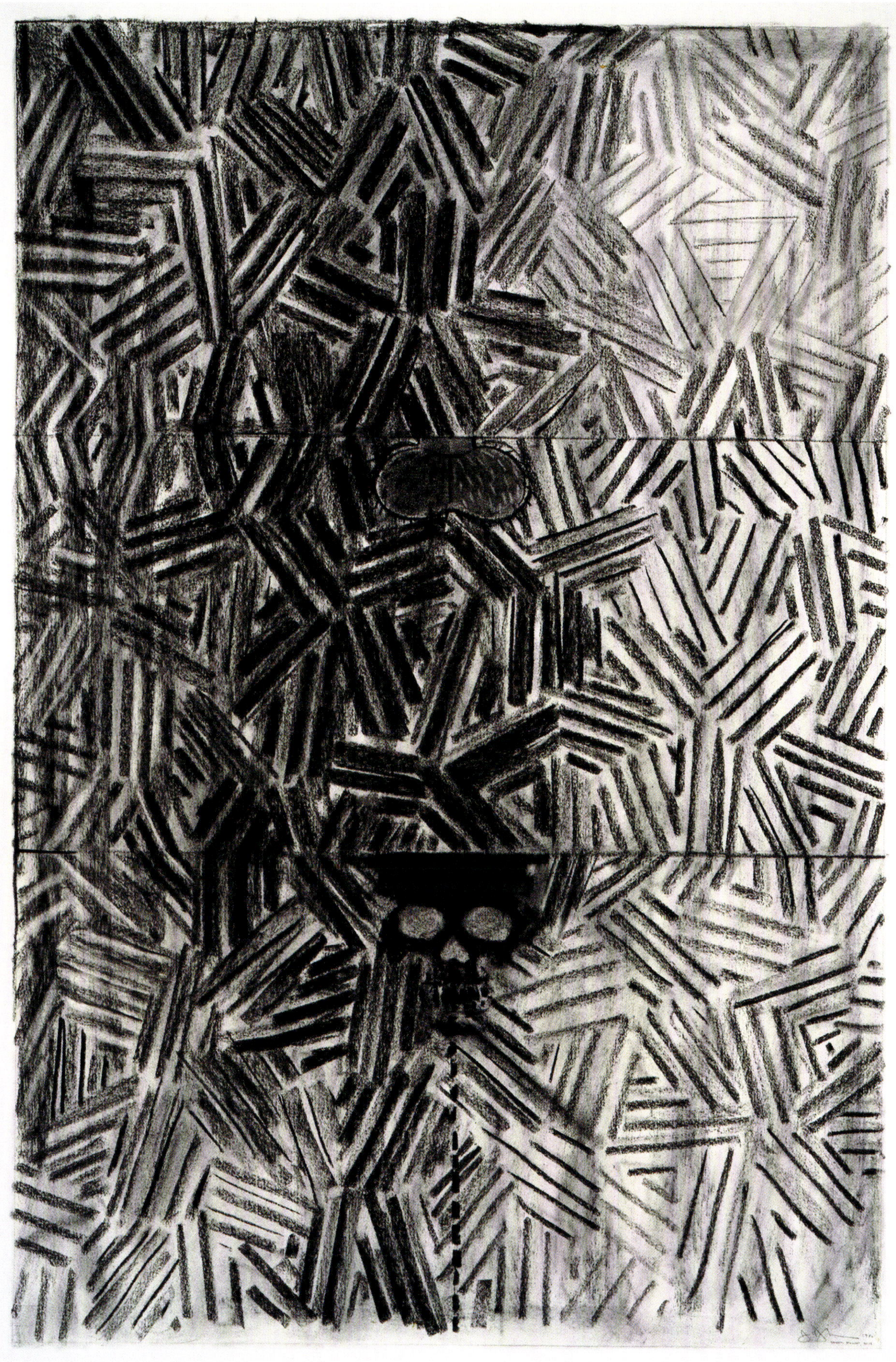

Between the Clock and the Bed

From 1981 to 1983, Johns completed the three monumental paintings that brought crosshatching to a grand conclusion. In titling each of them after Munch's late painting *Self-Portrait between the Clock and the Bed* (fig. 75), Johns offered his most overt confirmation of Munch's prominent role in his work. At the same time, he routed Munch's presence ever more deeply through his own creative process.

In keeping with the heightened complexity of late crosshatching, the three paintings are structured with multiple rules, partly apparent and partly hidden, that envisage them as both flat fields and volumes in space. Each of the works consists of three panels. In the first of the series, the two outer panels mirror each other (fig. 71).[106] In addition, if the painting could be rolled to form a cylinder, the hatch marks at the outer edges would connect with each other. At the inner edges of these

fig. 71 Johns, **Between the Clock and the Bed**, 1981, encaustic on canvas (three panels), 72 1/8 x 126 3/8 in. (183.2 x 321 cm). The Museum of Modern Art, New York, Gift of Agnes Gund

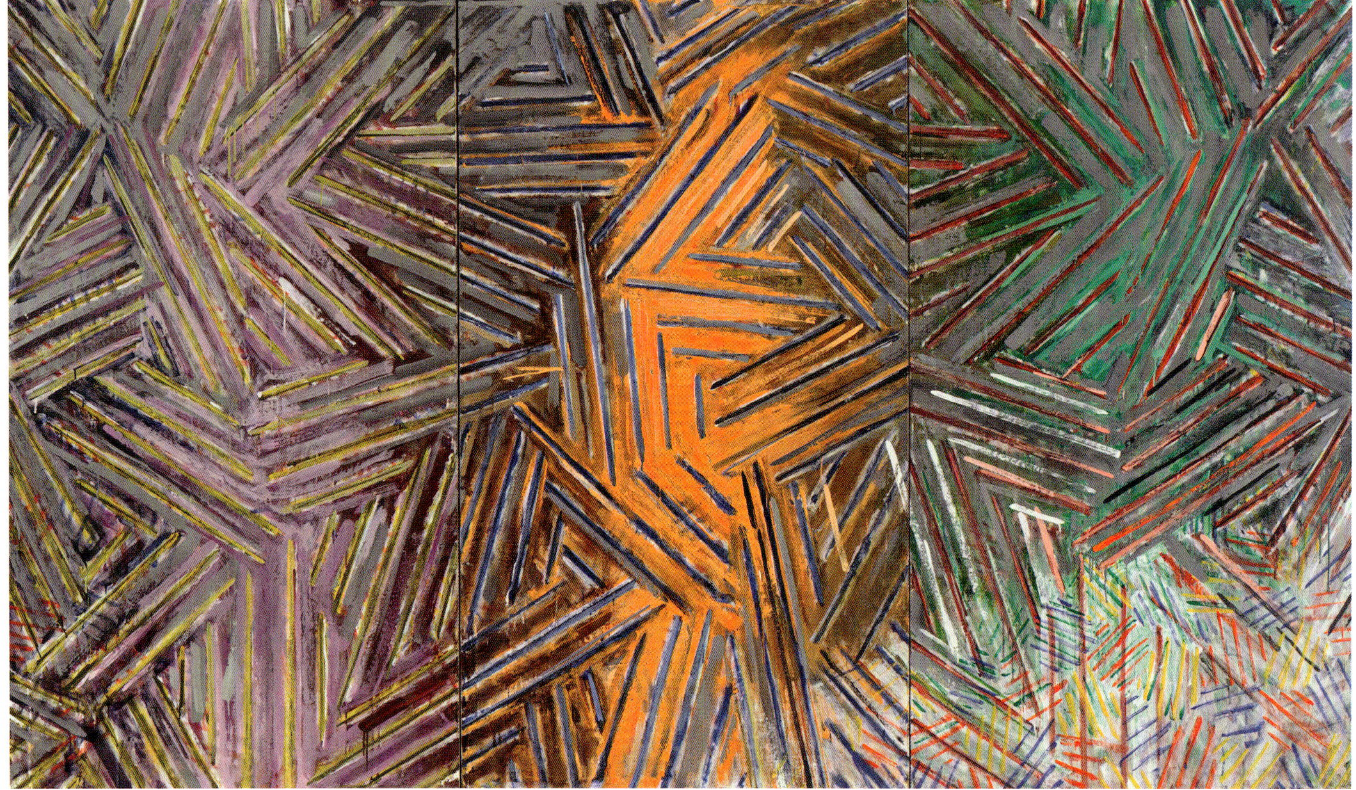

side panels, the lines connect across the seams to those of the central panel. The second painting, finished the same year (fig. 72), repeats this structure, though the position of the two side panels has been reversed—necessitating a new pattern for the center panel to maintain continuity of the hatches across the seams.

The third painting, started in 1982 and finished the following year, retains the pattern and position of the side panels from the second version, but the center panel is flipped (fig. 73). The hatches still connect across the seams, although they now make new configurations at the junctures. Aptly described by Mark Rosenthal as "a suite of rhapsodic elegies to the crosshatch,"[107] the three paintings together offer a complex exploration of the distinction between unique and repeating patterns.

Although the use of oil paint in the second painting lends a brighter tone than the encaustic of the first, both share a dominant palette of purples, oranges, and greens. Closer looking reveals that these secondary colors are the negative spaces

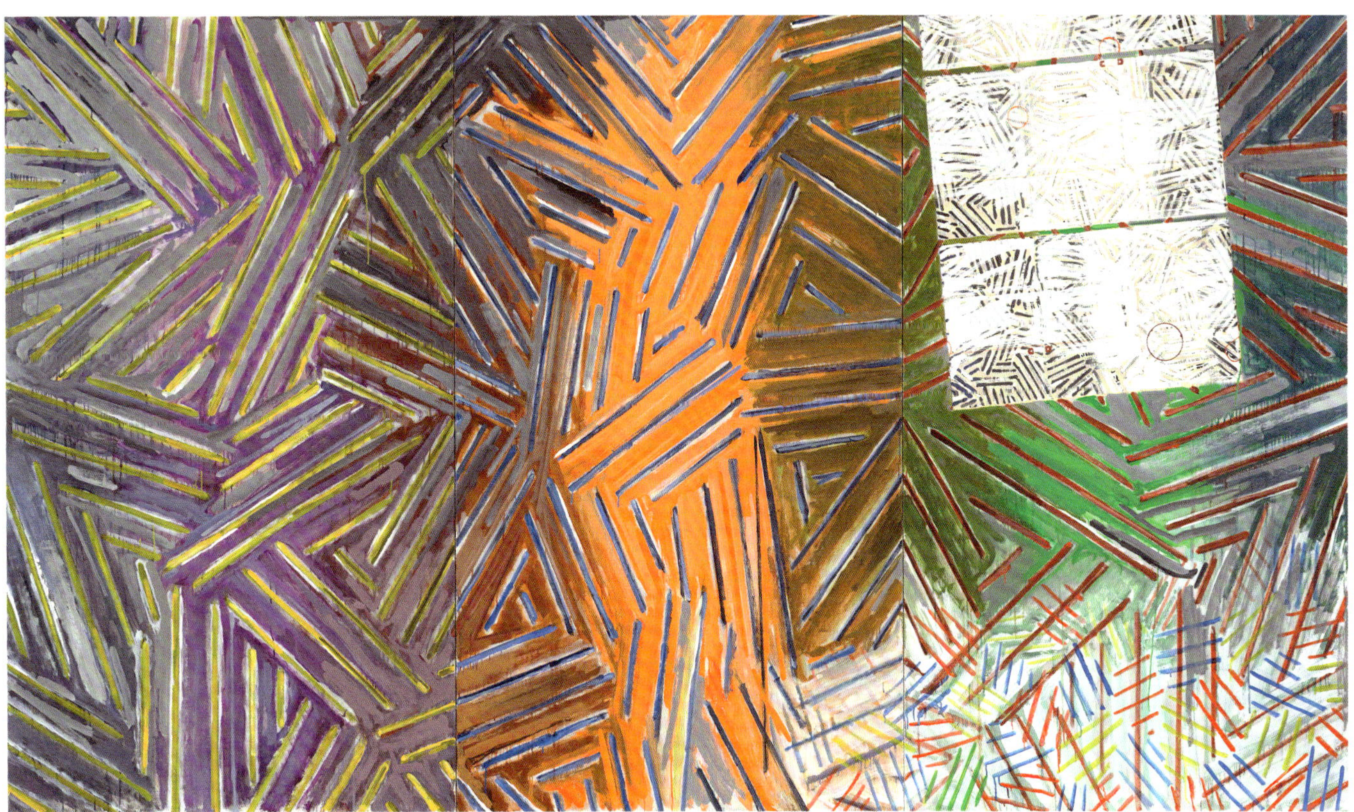

fig. 72 Johns, **Between the Clock and the Bed**, 1981, oil on canvas (three panels), 72 x 126 ¼ in. (182.9 x 320.7 cm). Collection of the artist

between hatches, which in each section are rendered in the complementary primary colors of yellow, blue, and red. Strokes of gray, white, and black further inflect each field. As a painting made primarily in shades of gray, the third work stands apart from the first two. The gray tones are in fact the negative spaces between the hatches, which are mostly black with parallel strokes of white. However, additional strokes in a full color spectrum punctuate the work, sometimes paralleling the black and white lines and sometimes as undertones to the gray.[108]

Also apparent in all three works is a light area at the lower right where smaller hatches cross larger ones—primary colors in the first two paintings and a range of colors dominated by secondary colors in the third work. These areas offer a rare example of true crosshatching in Johns's work and create the illusion of looking at an underlayer, as if the corner of the painting had been left unfinished. In the second painting, the image of another of Johns's works at the upper right further disrupts the field. It is a print version of the painting *Usuyuki* (fig. 74), rotated nearly ninety degrees and printed on the painting's surface with the original screens. Its presence

fig. 73 Johns, **Between the Clock and the Bed**, 1982–83, encaustic on canvas (three panels), 72 x 126¼ in. (182.9 x 320.7 cm). Virginia Museum of Fine Arts, Richmond, Gift of the Sydney and Frances Lewis Foundation

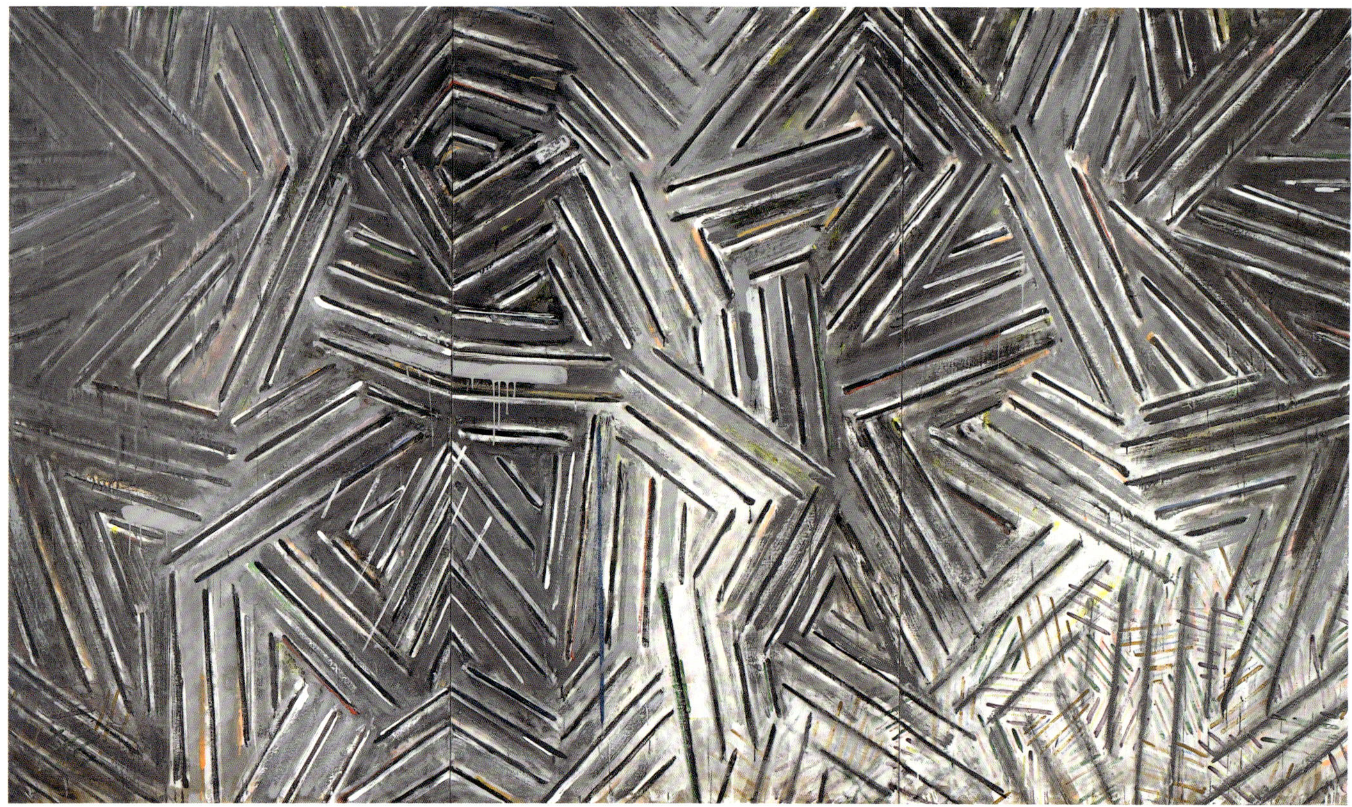

in *Between the Clock and the Bed* introduces a third, even smaller-scaled crosshatch pattern, governed by its own complex rules. In layering one work on another, it also joins printmaking and painting, as Johns had done earlier in the Savarin images.

When viewing these three resolutely abstract paintings, the question arises as to why Johns would title them after Munch's highly personal figurative painting from forty years before, deliberately linking his nonrepresentational work to an apparent opposite and implying the presence of similar content or, at least, importing that content by association. The use of encaustic in two of the three works provides one preliminary explanation. A mixture of pigment and melted beeswax, encaustic dries quickly and—unlike oil paint, where each subsequent stroke modifies the one beneath—creates a palimpsest of strokes, one atop another, preserving a history of accumulation over time. This frozen record of process suggests a parallel with the practice of embalming—a subtle metaphor that addresses mortality and offers a fitting analogy on a formal level with Munch's own encapsulation in his self-portrait of the quiet desperation of his final years.[109]

fig. 74 Johns, **Usuyuki**, 1981, screenprint, 29 ½ x 47 ¼ in. (74.9 x 120 cm). Ryobi Foundation

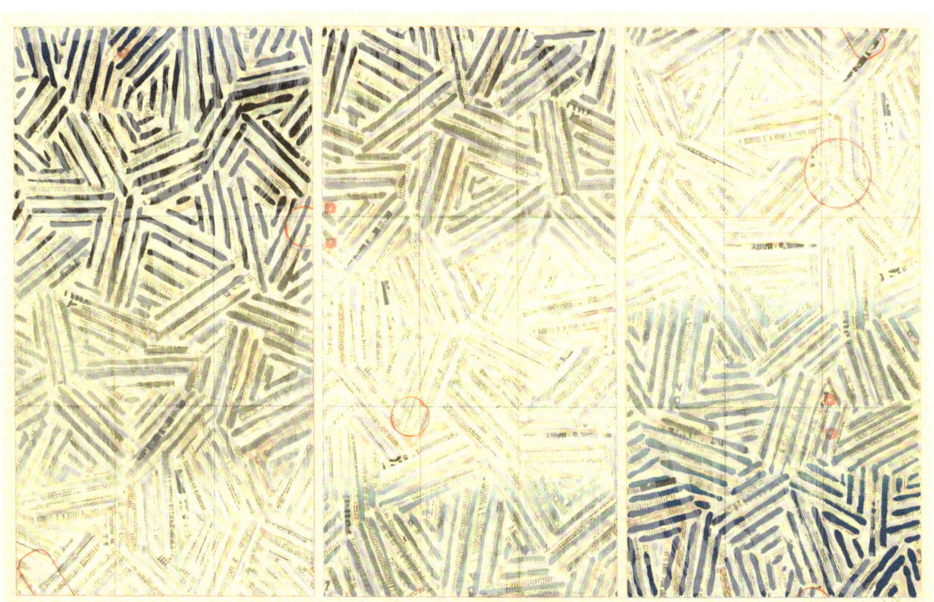

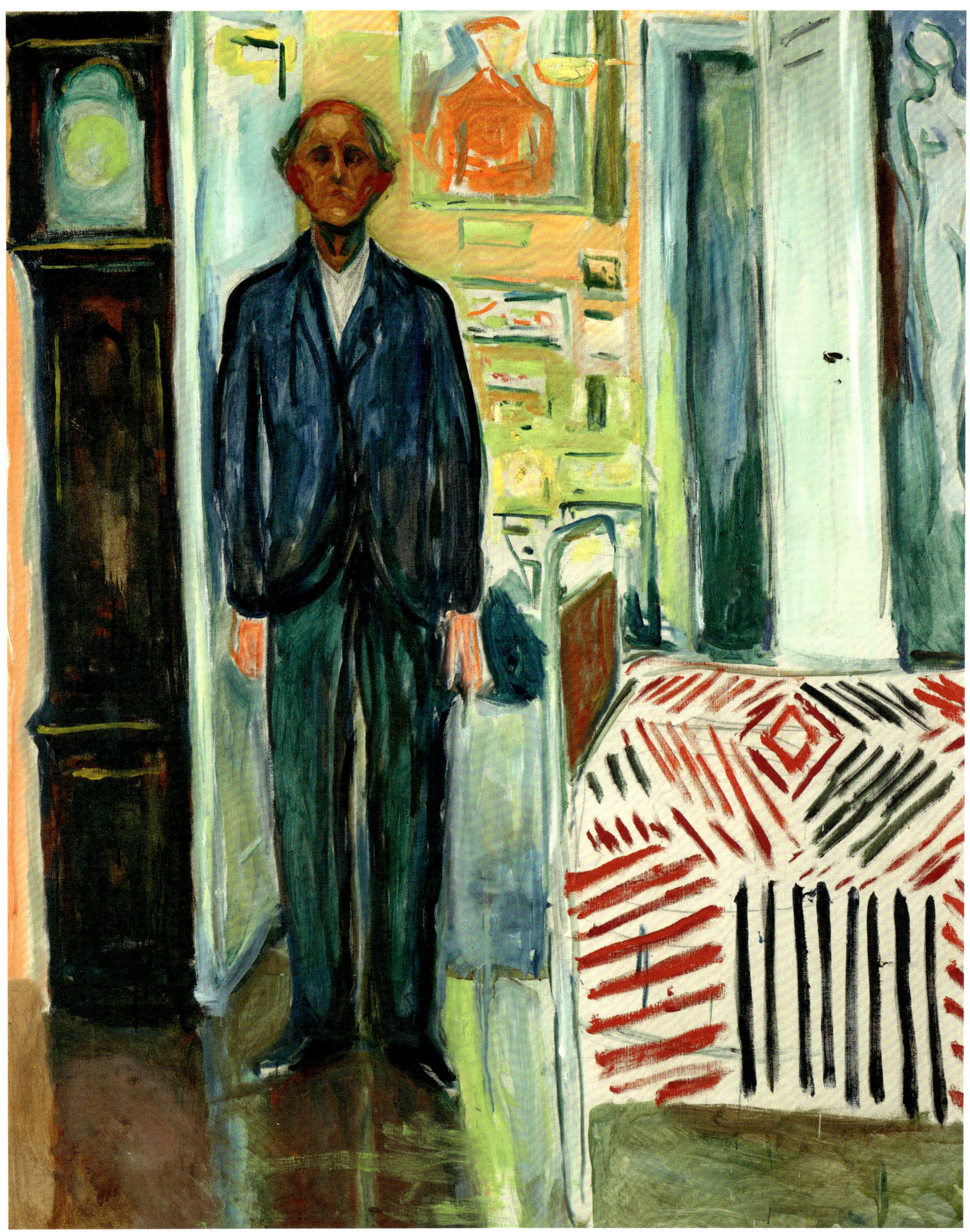

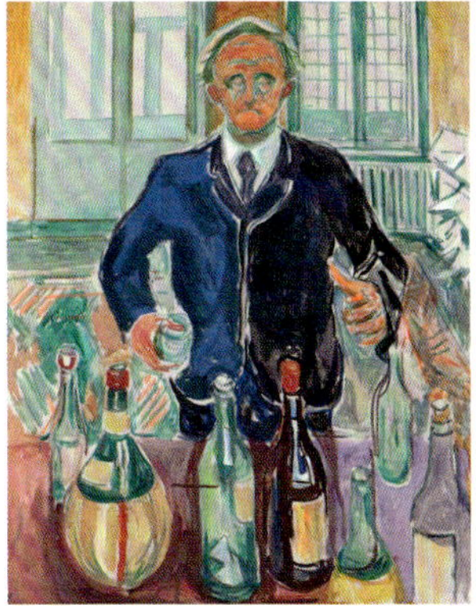

fig. 75 Munch, **Self-Portrait between the Clock and the Bed**, 1940–43, oil on canvas, 58 ⅞ x 47 ½ in. (149.5 x 120.5 cm). Munch Museum

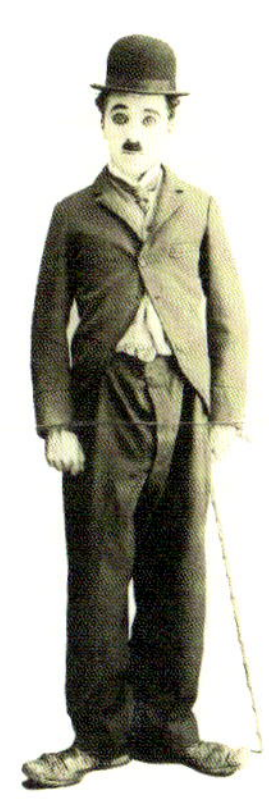

fig. 76 Munch, **Self-Portrait with Bottles**, 1938 (?), oil on canvas, 46 ½ x 36 ⅝ in. (118 x 93 cm). Munch Museum

fig. 77 Charlie Chaplin as **The Little Tramp**, ca. 1915, 4 ⁵⁄₁₆ x 9 ⁷⁄₁₆ in. (11 x 24 cm). Photograph from the archives of Roy Export Company Establishment

Munch painted *Self-Portrait between the Clock and the Bed* (fig. 75) when he was around age eighty. It shows him in his house at Ekely, just outside of Oslo, where he lived alone from 1916 until his death in 1944. The Ekely estate included a large main house, a winter studio with separate painting and print rooms, two summer studios, and an outdoor studio rimmed with a narrow roof and open to the sky in the center.[110] In his later years, Munch increasingly consolidated his studio space—his health began to fail and he wanted to lower his heating costs—so that by the end of his life he used just a few rooms of the main house for both living and painting. This is the setting for *Self-Portrait between the Clock and the Bed*.

Scholars have generally agreed on the symbolic nature of the self-portrait's clock and bed as portents of the inexorable passage of time and the finality of eternal rest.[111] Interpretations of the central figure, however, have varied. Frederick B. Deknatel described it in 1950 as a "caricatured old man, a little ridiculous in his posture . . . standing as if concentrating all of his attention on hearing the tick of the clock."[112] In a similar vein, Arne Eggum wrote in 1978 that in this work Munch "waxed ruthlessly ironic about his old age."[113] In the same publication, Ragna Stang perceived a more serious tone, writing that "the old Munch depicted himself standing at rigid attention while waiting for death, a death he no longer feared."[114] Iris Müller-Westermann's interpretation from 2010 aligns with Stang: "The artist stands on the threshold to death, upright and waiting. . . . His senses no longer perceive the outside world. Eyes and mouth are closed. Red spots top his ears like plugs."[115] Jon-Ove Steihaug recently emphasized the performative nature of Munch's self-portraits. He describes the figure as "a little bowed and shrunken, with his arms hanging limp by his sides and his gaze aimed directly at us. . . . Munch positions himself as though on a stage between the two objects in the room."[116]

In underscoring the artifice of Munch's self-presentation, Steihaug's reading resonates with those of Deknatel and Eggum, especially when he notes that Munch wears the same too-small blue jacket in a slightly earlier painting, *Self-Portrait with Bottles* (fig. 76), where he appears as "a Chaplin-like character, juggl[ing] with glasses and wine bottles, rings under his eyes and mouth pursed in a sad pout."[117] It could be argued that Munch appears even more Chaplin-like in *Self-Portrait between the Clock and the Bed*—with his hands pressed to his sides, feet turned out, and darkened eyes recalling the Little Tramp's characteristic stance and stage makeup (fig. 77). It may seem unlikely that Munch would undercut the solemnity of his existential contemplation with such a reference, but it is worth noting he was an ardent fan of both popular and art films, even announcing to the press in 1911 that he intended to open a cinema in Oslo.[118] It is conceivable that his pose is a conscious quotation, meant to inject a note of sardonic self-deprecation or gallows humor into an otherwise overwhelming awareness of death's approach.

Munch's self-presentation may also relate to a photograph taken on the occasion of his seventy-fifth birthday, a rarely allowed moment of public intrusion upon his privacy (fig. 78).[119] The image shows Munch in his winter studio. Although his hands are clasped rather than at his sides and he wears a dark suit and tie, the rest of his bearing is nearly identical to the painting.[120] He may have recognized the irony of transforming this commemorative image staged for the public into a private moment of self-reflection, knowing that it would soon enough become another public statement in a painting.

A sketch for *Self-Portrait between the Clock and the Bed* (fig. 79) shows the clock and bed not yet positioned as counterbalancing symbols. Instead, Munch's body overlaps the clock, allowing fuller visibility into the far room. A few lines on the bed indicate the coverlet's distinctive pattern. The sketch suggests that the clock and bed were actual elements in his living space, not imaginative insertions.[121] Munch seems to have recognized their full symbolic value only during the process of making the painting.[122]

Munch's paintings hang on the walls behind him; a dark green form beside his proper left hand may be a sculpture on a base, set slightly back into the second room. Its triangular shape recalls the sculpture *Workers in the Snow*, 1910/1932, in the 1938 birthday photograph and underscores Munch's interest in representing examples of his own art in his subsequent works, a practice shared by Johns.[123] The high polish of the floor in the painting also captures a detail of Munch's actual

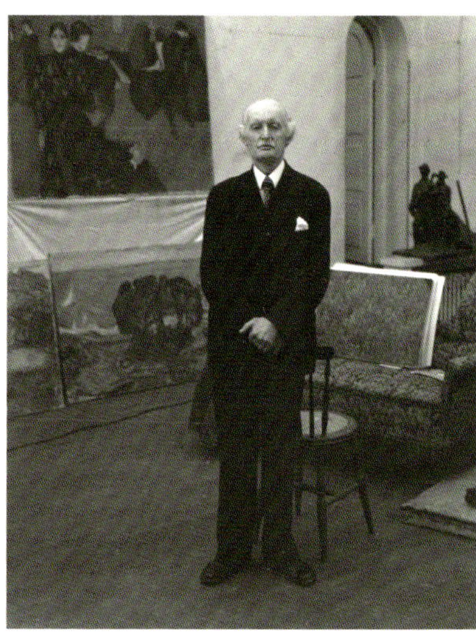

fig. 78 Munch in the Winter Studio at Ekely on the occasion of his seventy-fifth birthday, 1938, photographed by Ragnvald Vaering. Munch Museum Archives

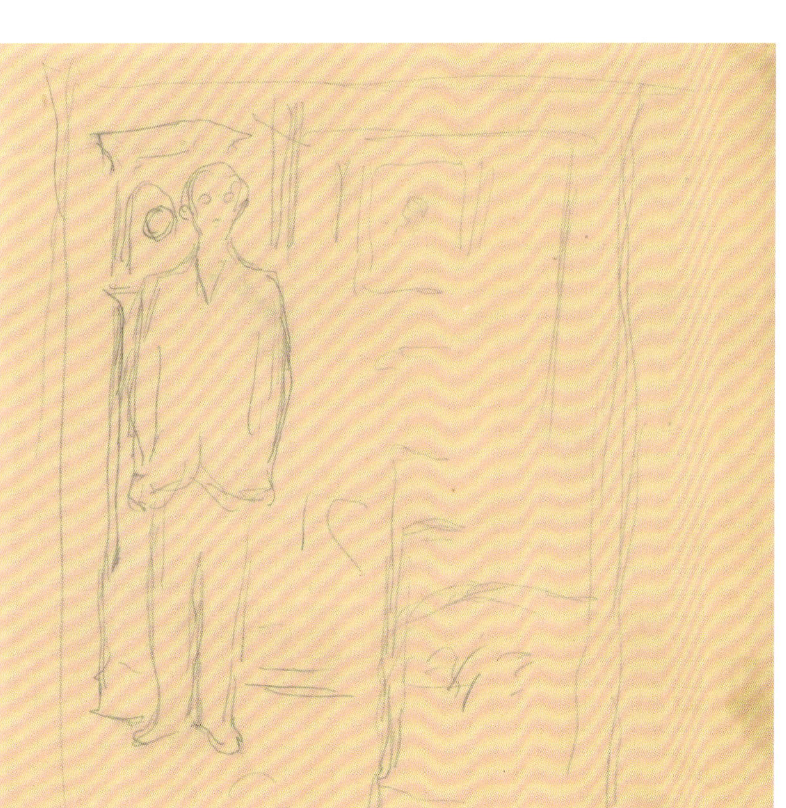

fig. 79 Munch, **Between the Clock and the Bed**, 1940–43, pencil on paper, 12⅝ x 19 in. (32.2 x 48.2 cm). Munch Museum

setting. In a photograph of the main house (fig. 80), likely one of the two rooms shown in the self-portrait, highlights bouncing off the two lowest paintings add gloss to the floorboards beside bolts of sunlight.

Müller-Westermann describes the floor in the painting as a metaphor, an "enigmatic, reflective surface" that "conveys no security" beneath the artist's feet as he confronts life's last great question.[124] Munch creates further spatial ambiguity with the various openings. He stands, literally, at a threshold, a few scant feet into the front room. The French doors beside him swing forward, partially obscuring the clock and a tall painting of a nude woman hovering over the bed. The painting is *Krotkaia*,[125] named after a Dostoyevsky character who committed suicide, though the cropping of its edges leaves unclear whether it is a mural, tapestry, or even a figment of the artist's imagination. Her nearly life-size presence confirms that Eros remained a powerful force to the end in the creative life of the artist. A tall narrow door infused with green and lavender mirrors the painting, making it difficult to determine where it belongs. The warmth of the rear wall and the yellow accents on the clock, floor, and door suggest a light-filled space, recalling the photograph of the house and contrasting with the grim figure clothed in cool blues and greens.

The placement of the single bed jutting halfway into the work is curious but supported by the sketch and suggestive of the crowded and haphazard nature of Munch's later years at Ekely. The bedspread's distinctive red-and-black geometric pattern is based on an actual textile (fig. 81)—a thin, summer-weight coverlet made of hand-cut cotton strips appliquéd to a linen backing.[126] Munch took liberties with the pattern, changing reds to blacks and diagonals to verticals. He also added a slight swell to his single bed, leading Eggum to equate it, in combination with the ceremonial bedspread pattern, to a sarcophagus.[127]

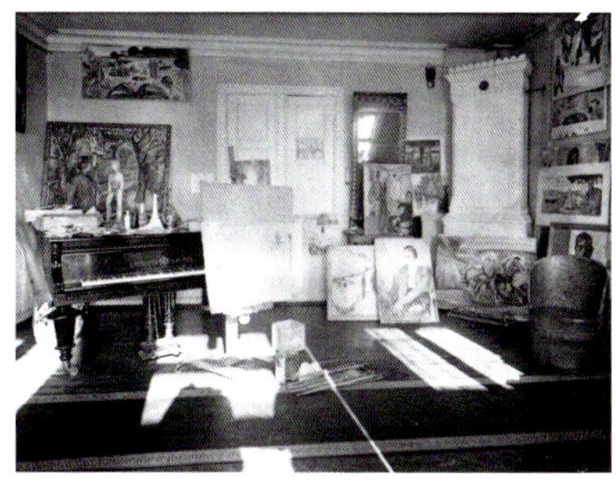

fig. 80 **Living room at Ekely**, 1937, photographed by Anders B. Wilse. Munch Museum Archives

fig. 81 **Edvard Munch's bedspread**, probably early 20th century, cotton applique on linen, 59 x 112½ in. (150 x 286 cm), irregular edge. Munch Museum, donated by The Friends of the Munch Museum, 1997

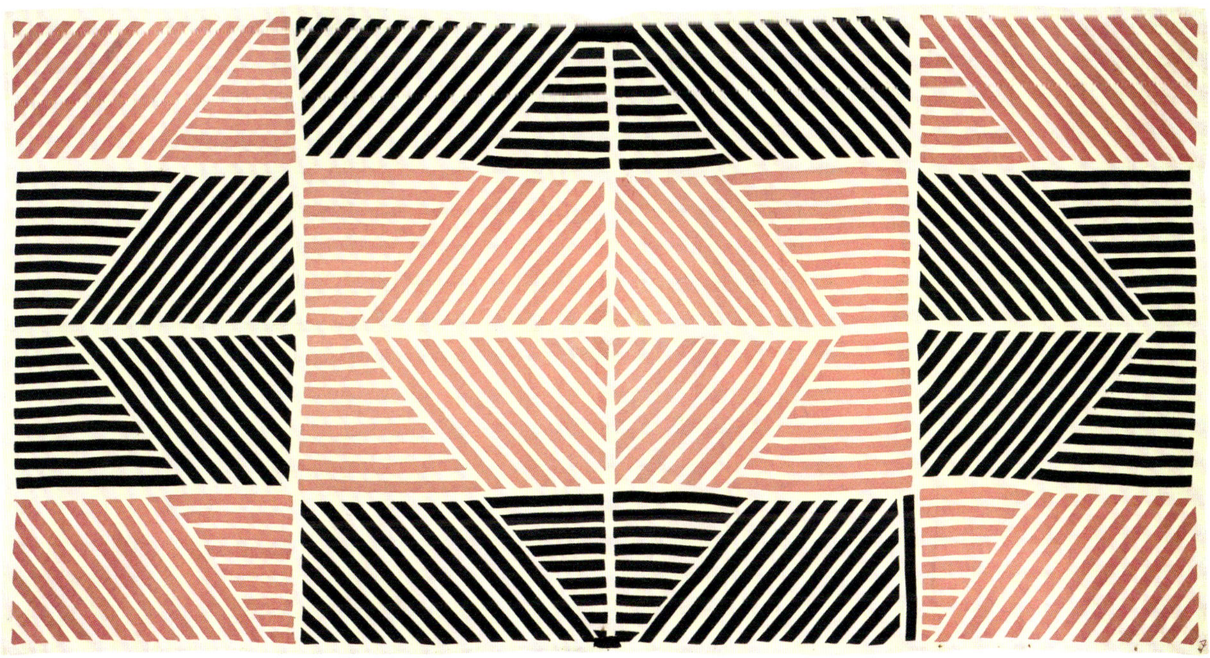

Munch, then, in weaving together elements of his everyday surroundings with only modest alteration, has shown the capacity of art to make a powerful statement about life. Surrounded by examples of his work, positioned between symbols of mortality, he offers an image of the artist on the cusp of a great transition. It is not surprising that Johns—already engaged with Munch's work for several years and on the cusp of his own great transition—found in this complex painting a way to signal the end of an entire phase of his work and cross a threshold into new territory. And yet, despite this rich parallel, the explanation for how Johns arrived at this culminating moment of reference to Munch has often come down to a simple anecdote. The account first appeared in 1992, in the revised version of Michael Crichton's monograph: "In 1981, a friend sent Johns a postcard of a self-portrait by Munch entitled *Between the Clock and the Bed*. The friend had noticed the bedspread, with its crosshatch motif so similar to Johns' own."[128] Following its publication, the story has appeared in a number of sources, sometimes with the date changed to 1980.[129] The easy embrace of this story may arise from its neat resemblance to the flag, flagstone, and crosshatch accounts and their shared sense of serendipity. Johns has confirmed receiving the postcard and for the first time revealed that it was sent by his friend Bill Katz.[130] But Katz believes he sent the card in 1974, not 1980 or 1981.[131] If true, Johns would have had the card in his possession for some six years before beginning the three paintings. (In addition, Johns would have seen the painting in the 1950 and 1978 Munch exhibitions and had access to its reproduction among the books in his library.[132])

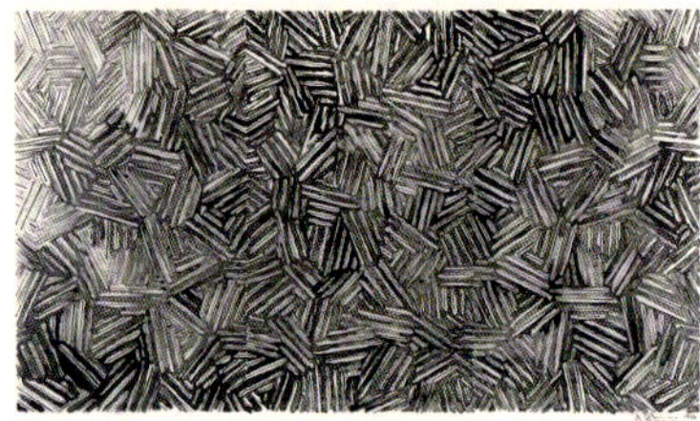

fig. 82 Johns, **Untitled**, 1980, ink on plastic, 17 x 24 ⅞ in. (43.2 x 63.2 cm). Collection of Barbaralee Diamonstein and Carl Speilvogel, New York

fig. 83 Johns, **Between the Clock and the Bed**, 1980/1988, ink and watercolor on plastic, 13 ¼ x 22 ½ in. (33.7 x 57.2 cm). Private collection

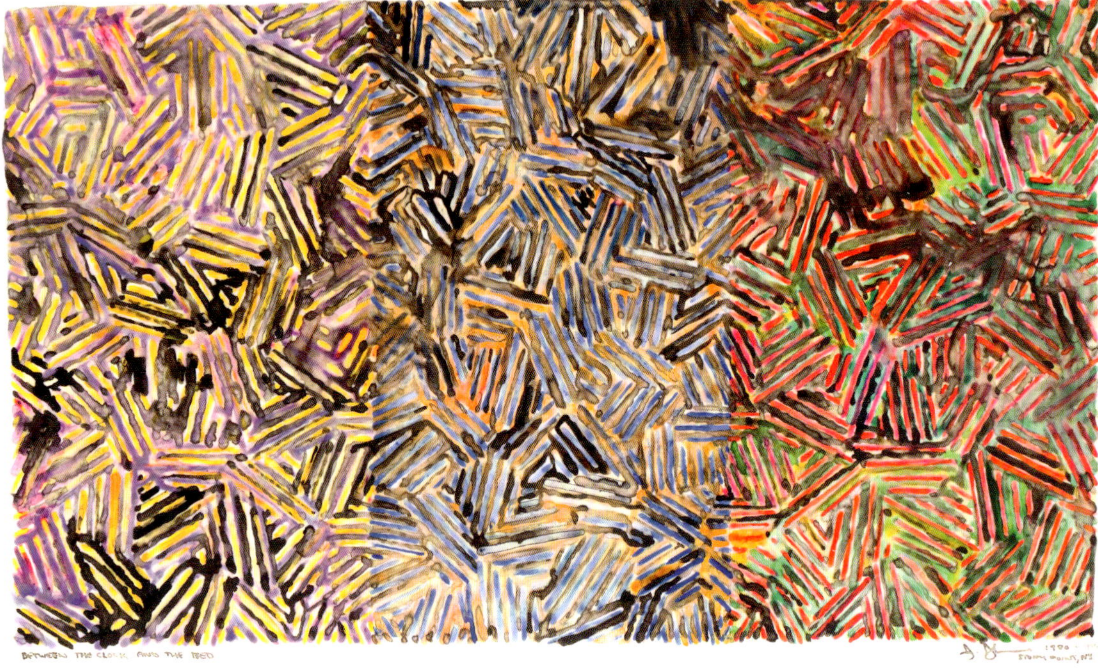

Johns seems to have first considered the *Between the Clock and the Bed* composition in an untitled ink-on-plastic drawing from 1980 (fig. 82), which, like the paintings, is divided into three parts and pairs each hatch mark with its opposite— here black and white instead of color. The drawing also includes the mirroring of left and right panels and the joining of lines into the center panel. A lighter section in the upper left corner of the drawing appears in the lower right in the paintings.

Two drawings from 1980—a luminous ink and watercolor on plastic (fig. 83)[133] and a two-tiered pastel on paper (fig. 84)—are the first to be titled *Between the Clock and the Bed*. Both display the three-part structure, mirroring side sections, and continuity of hatches into the center, along with the complex play of complementary colors.

None of these drawings, however, contains the additional visual references to Munch's self-portrait that appear in Johns's three large paintings: the distinctly brighter areas in the center of the left and middle panels and the lower right of

fig. 84 Johns, **Between the Clock and the Bed**, 1980, pastel on paper, 27 ¹³⁄₁₆ x 23 ⁷⁄₁₆ in. (71.1 x 59.7 cm). Collection of Marsha and Jeffrey Perelman

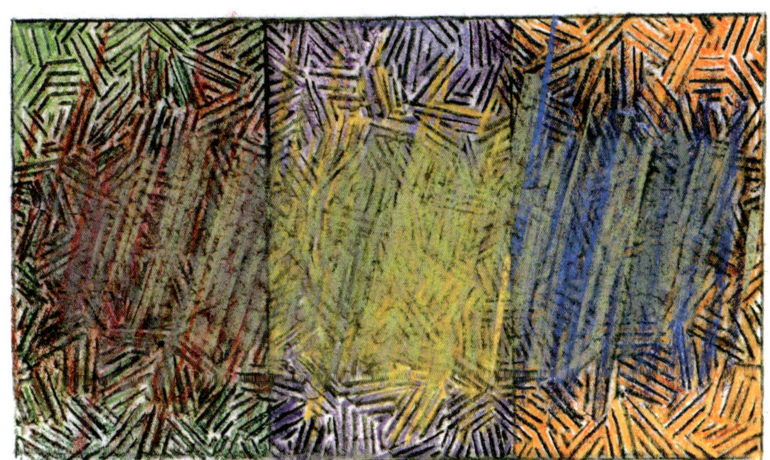

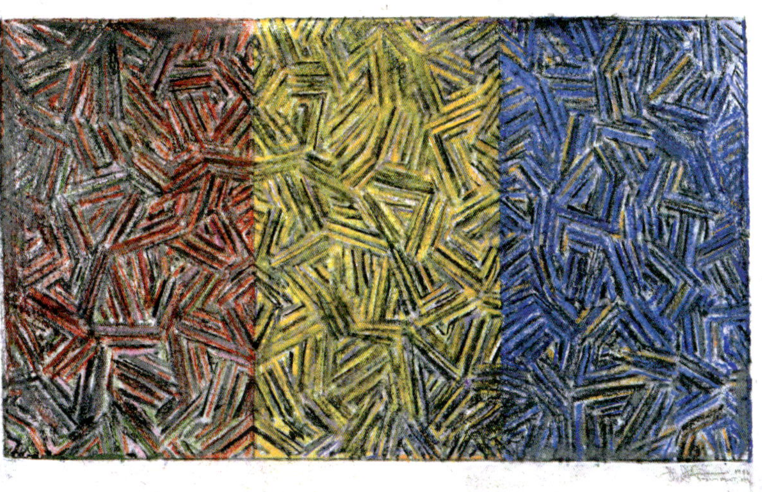

the third panel. Together, these areas have inspired scholars to identify them as the clock, full-length figure, and bed. Richard Francis saw Johns's paintings as an "abstracted version of Munch's image" and read the lower right corner as the bed.[134] Mark Rosenthal, too, described Johns's paintings as "abstract analogues" for Munch's self-portrait. Addressing the light tone in the center of each of the three paintings, he wrote: "Once lifted visually from their surroundings, the white-tinged focal configurations of the 1983 painting and the orange patterns in the first two works might even be read as abstract, energetically gesticulating figures."[135] Crichton, also, in conversation with Johns, pointed to a figure in the center:

> The friend [who sent the card] had noticed the bedspread, with its crosshatching motif so similar to Johns' own. But it is likely that Johns was more interested in the possibility of suggesting a figure. He was struck by the title: "The Munch painting is tantalizing, but I don't think the title is even his [said Johns]. You would think it would be called *The Artist Between the Clock and the Bed*." [Johns] notes further that "Between the clock and the bed implies three things, not two." That third thing, unstated in the title, is the image of the artist himself.[136]

The imprint of *Usuyuki* onto the second version of *Between the Clock and the Bed*, which Johns beautifully re-created in a watercolor from 1984 (fig. 85), can be seen as making a further reference to Munch's painting. While its shape, angle,

fig. 85 Johns, **Between the Clock and the Bed**, 1984, watercolor and graphite pencil on paper, 24 ⅜ x 36 ⅛ in. (61.9 x 91.8 cm). Robert and Jane Meyerhoff Collection

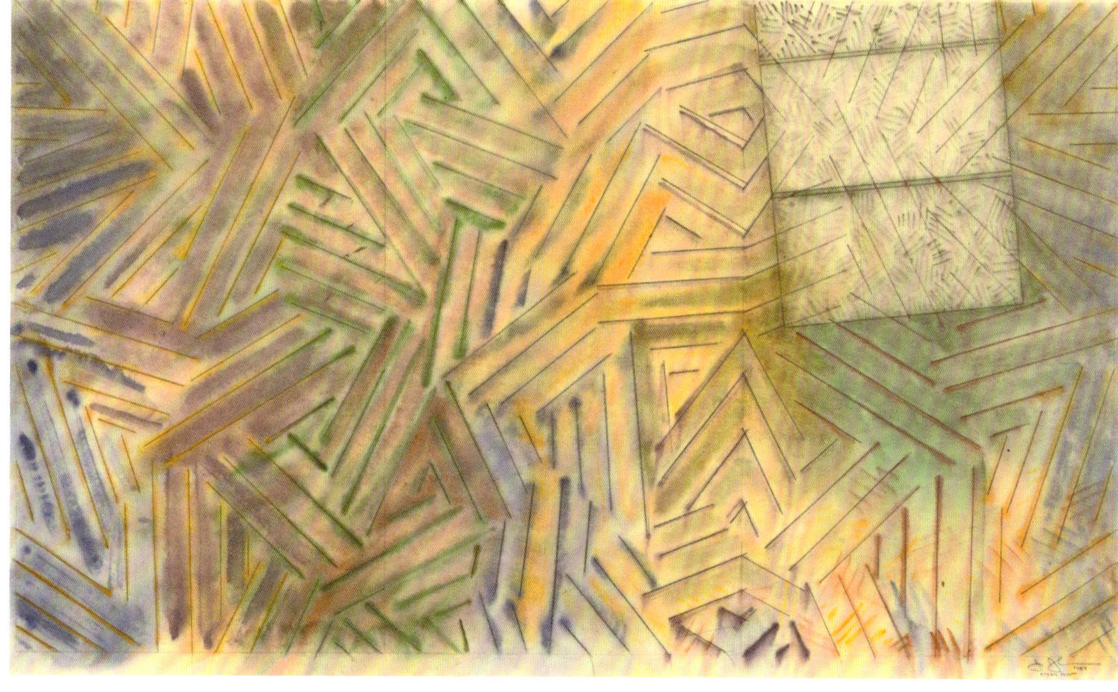

and placement derive from the superimposed window in his earlier painting *Harlem Light* (fig. 86)[137]—implying both an inserted work of art and an opening onto a space beyond the surface—the imprint of *Usuyuki* creates an opening that parallels the painting of Kotkaia, the French doors, and the rear door in Munch's self-portrait. Johns has further remarked that the superimposed image of *Usuyuki* can be read as a bed, which makes sense given the connection of the title *Usuyuki* with love and longing, and he drew a parallel with Munch's placement of the female nude over his single bed.[138]

> Author: Is it accurate to see the light-colored lower right corner of *Between the Clock and the Bed* as related to Munch's bedspread?
> JJ: It probably relates in some way, just as the inclusion of *Usuyuki* relates to the idea of a bed. It's a romantic conception of beauty.
> Author: The inclusion of *Usuyuki* recalls both window and doorway, as in *Harlem Light*. In Munch's *Self-Portrait* there's passage through a door into a back room, and also the representation of his own art, which all pertain to *Usuyuki*.
> JJ: You also have this nude.
> Author: And the clock with no hands and the bed on which he'll lie down and die.
> JJ: In which he was also born.
> Author: Yes.
> JJ: In which he had sex . . .
> Author: Yes.
> JJ: With that lady above it.

The questions that remain are why Johns turned his attention at this particular moment in 1980–81 to Munch's late self-portrait and what exactly led him to use the title *Between the Clock and the Bed* for some but not all of the preliminary studies.[139] Johns told curators Ruth Fine and Nan Rosenthal that he may have assigned the titles in 1981 to the two 1980 studies, after they were finished and once the first of the three paintings with this title was underway.[140] And there is passing mention that Johns may have received a second postcard of Munch's self-portrait at around this time, but this has not been confirmed and may never be as Johns does not recall receiving it (nor the date on which he received the one from Katz).[141] In themselves, a card or cards are not sufficient explanations for Johns's engagement with Munch. Whether sent in 1974 or later, they remain a detail in a far more complex, substantial, and consequential narrative—one that continues to the present, as shown by Johns's acknowledgment of the connection between his *Regrets* series (2012–14) and Munch's *Self-Portrait between the Clock and the Bed*.[142]

fig. 86 Johns, **Harlem Light**, 1967, oil and collage on canvas (four panels), 78 x 172 in. (198.1 x 436.9 cm). Seattle Art Museum, partial and promised gift of John and Mary Shirley, in honor of the 75th Anniversary of the Seattle Art Museum

Savarin Monotypes

In early 1982, shortly after finishing the first two *Between the Clock and the Bed* paintings, Johns created a group of monotypes that are his last to date with the Savarin can motif. Taken together, they show his sustained engagement with Munch as he worked through a number of variations on the Savarin can, armprint, wood grain, and crosshatching.

The series began with leftovers from the 1981 *Savarin* lithograph (fig. 47). The large dimensions of that earlier print had exceeded the limits of sheet paper available at the time and required paper rolls, which were cut to size and flattened. The ULAE staff used up one roll for part of the edition, then purchased a second roll to complete it. After printing, the new paper was discovered to be brighter and the later, mismatched prints were set aside.[143] When Johns returned to ULAE in January 1982, he decided these prints could serve as the basis for a monotype.

Painting on a plastic surface, Johns created seventeen new images, some printed on blank paper and some on the leftover 1977–81 lithographs.[144] For the

fig. 87 Johns, **Savarin**, 1982, monotype over lithograph, 50 ¼ x 38 ⅛ in. (127.6 x 96.8 cm). Whitney Museum of American Art, New York; Gift of The American Contemporary Art Foundation, Inc., Leonard A. Lauder, President

fig. 88 Johns, **Savarin**, 1982, monotype, 50 x 38 in. (127 x 96.5 cm). Whitney Museum of American Art, New York; Gift of The American Contemporary Art Foundation, Inc., Leonard A. Lauder, President

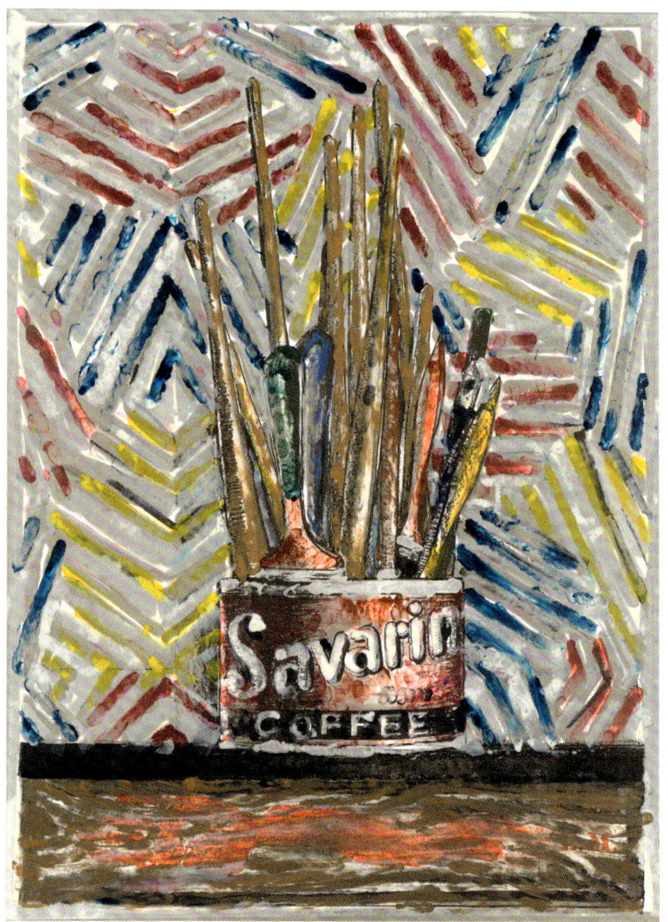

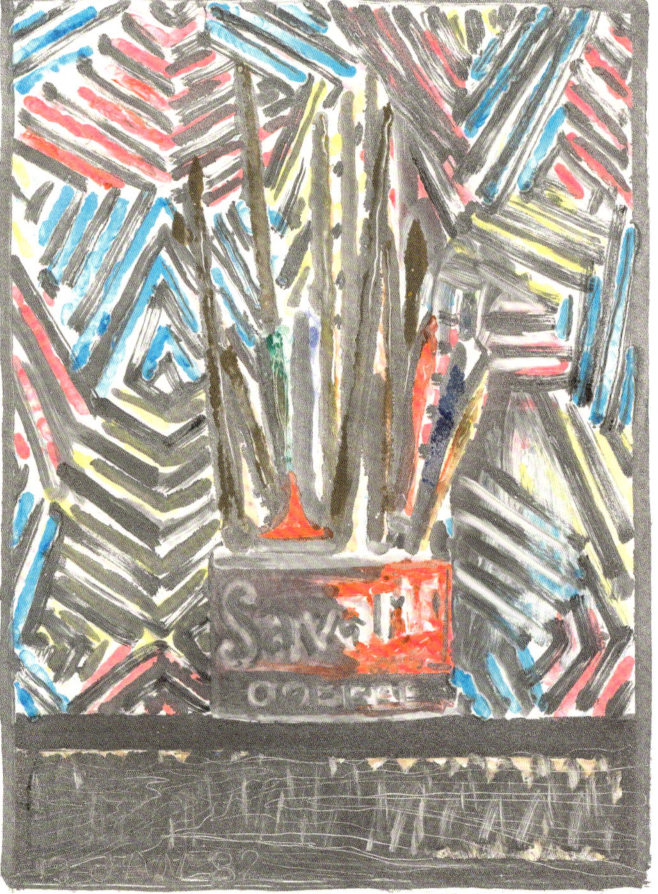

first of the group (fig. 87), Johns added primary colors to the can, brushes, and hatching, and he overlaid the armprint with thick brown wood grain. Number three (fig. 88) presents a completely new painting of the can and brushes set against crosshatching. Printed on blank paper, the image includes a lower section with a thin wood-grain pattern that is scratched into dark paint and suggests a landscape—recalling Munch's dual reference to wood grain and landscape in *The Scream*, *Angst*, and *Kiss in the Field*.

In number five (fig. 89), Johns superimposed handprints in secondary colors on the lithograph's gray hatching. His fingers align for the most part with the pattern beneath, underscoring the connection between the two and echoing related works from 1977 and 1978. Number six in the series (fig. 90) makes use of the same painting as number five but is printed on blank paper, resembling even more closely the 1977 drawing on plastic (fig. 91). The wood-grain pattern beneath the bright yellow ledge again suggests landscape, as in number three, but here recalls Japanese woodcuts and the stylized landscapes and seascapes of dry-rock Zen gardens.

Several of the 1982 prints have an oval frame, which Johns also used for one of the 1978 Savarin lithographs (fig. 40), and here again he makes a connection to

fig. 89 Johns, **Savarin**, 1982, monotype over lithograph, 50 ¼ x 38 ⅛ in. (127.6 x 96.8 cm). Whitney Museum of American Art, New York; Gift of The American Contemporary Art Foundation, Inc., Leonard A. Lauder, President

fig. 90 Johns, **Savarin**, 1982, monotype, 50 x 38 in. (127 x 96.5 cm). Whitney Museum of American Art, New York; Gift of The American Contemporary Art Foundation, Inc., Leonard A. Lauder, President

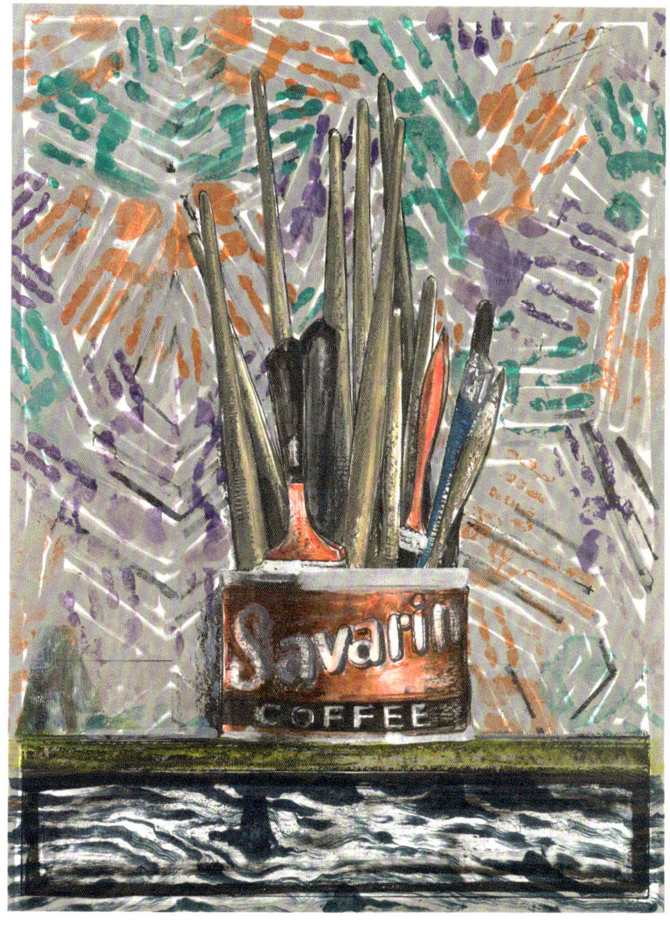

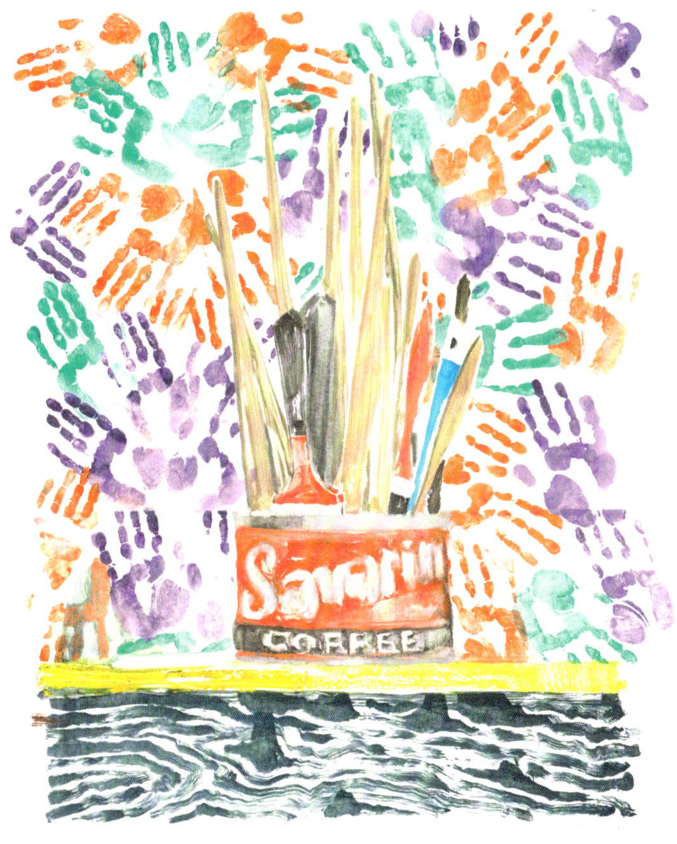

portraiture.[145] In number seven (fig. 91), a red handprint directly beneath the can and atop the red armprint fits within the curve of this frame. Number nine (fig. 92) adds illusionistic pushpins to the upper corners, suggesting an image tacked to a wall and creating a representation of a representation. Two light squiggles beneath the pins are reflections and also evoke sperm—an association developed further in number eleven (fig. 93), where a single large sperm floats in darkness beneath the can. Behind it the faint wood-grain pattern doubles as water ripples. Splatters surrounding the can reinforce the sense of an environment at once close and damp yet also infinitely expansive—a cosmic moment of creation linking human conception with the origins of the universe. The presence of the sperm also confirms Johns's earlier interest in the sperm surrounding Munch's *Madonna* (fig. 53), which may have inspired Johns's decision the year before to surround

fig. 91 Johns, **Savarin**, 1982, monotype with hand additions over lithograph, 50 ¼ x 38 ⅛ in. (127.6 x 96.8 cm). Whitney Museum of American Art, New York; Gift of The American Contemporary Art Foundation, Inc., Leonard A. Lauder, President

fig. 92 Johns, **Savarin**, 1982, monotype over lithograph, 50 x 38 ⅛ in. (127 x 96.8 cm). Whitney Museum of American Art, New York; Gift of The American Contemporary Art Foundation, Inc., Leonard A. Lauder, President

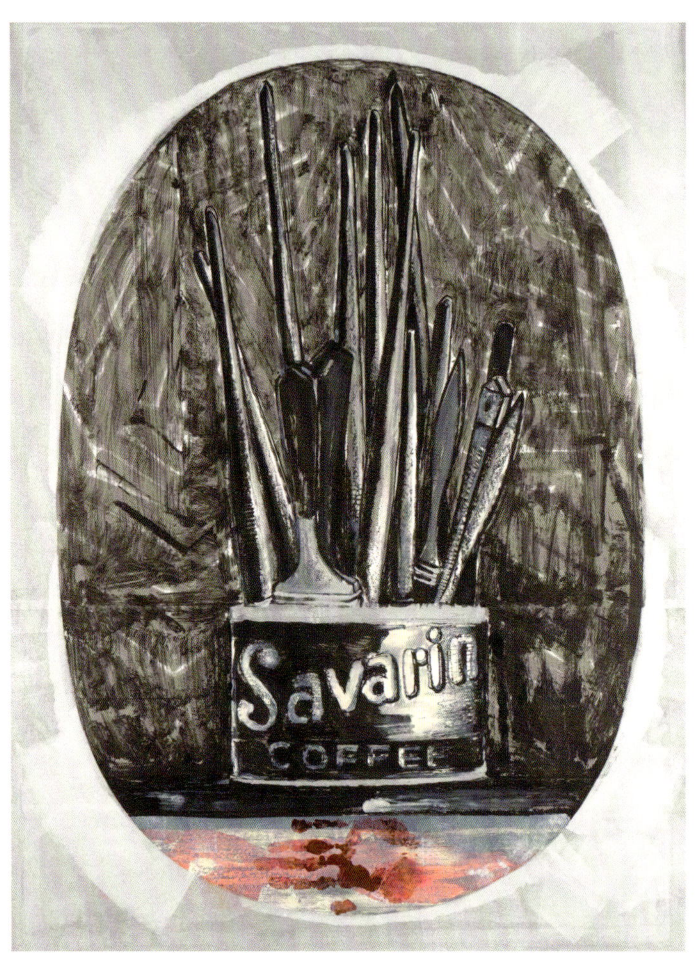

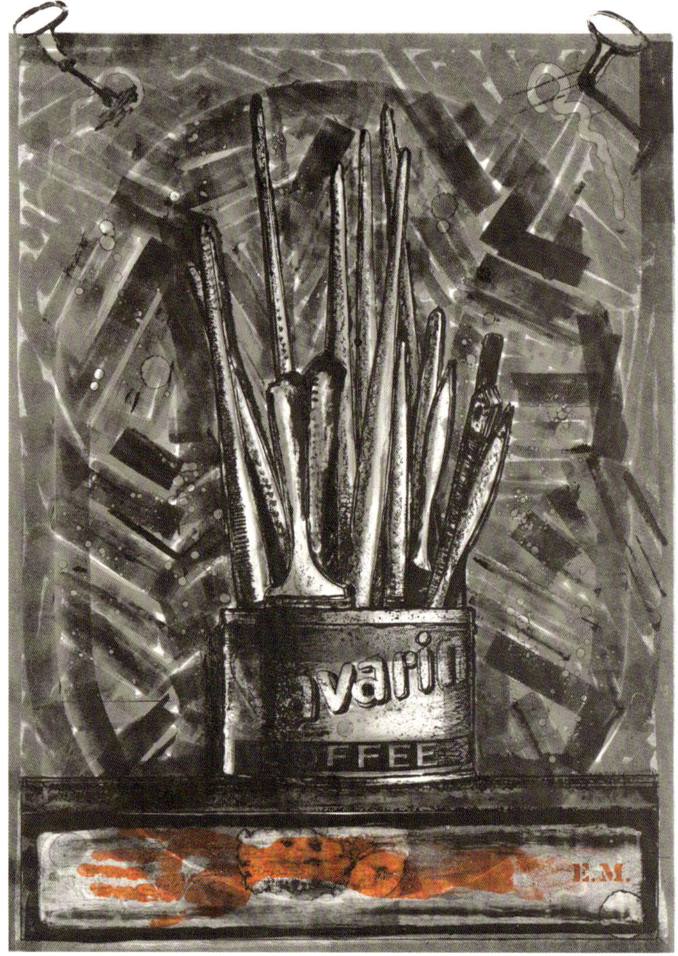

Dancers on a Plane with forks, knives, and spoons. The sperm also reappears in a major painting two years later, discussed below.

The twelfth print in the series (fig. 94) saturates the lithograph with a field of blood-red marks, unaligned with the pattern beneath. An arrow on the arm recalls a motif from the 1960s that Johns revisited in prints in the early 1980s; the arrow also developed into a marker of time in *The Seasons* paintings in the mid-1980s. Nine more prints exploring further variations complete the series. By the end, the course of the seventeen images finally exhausted Johns's twenty-two-year engagement with the Savarin can motif, as there have been no more prints to date and just one more appearance in a painting. Both wood grain and armprint, however, are present in the works of the early to middle 1980s, extending the references to Munch into new contexts.[146]

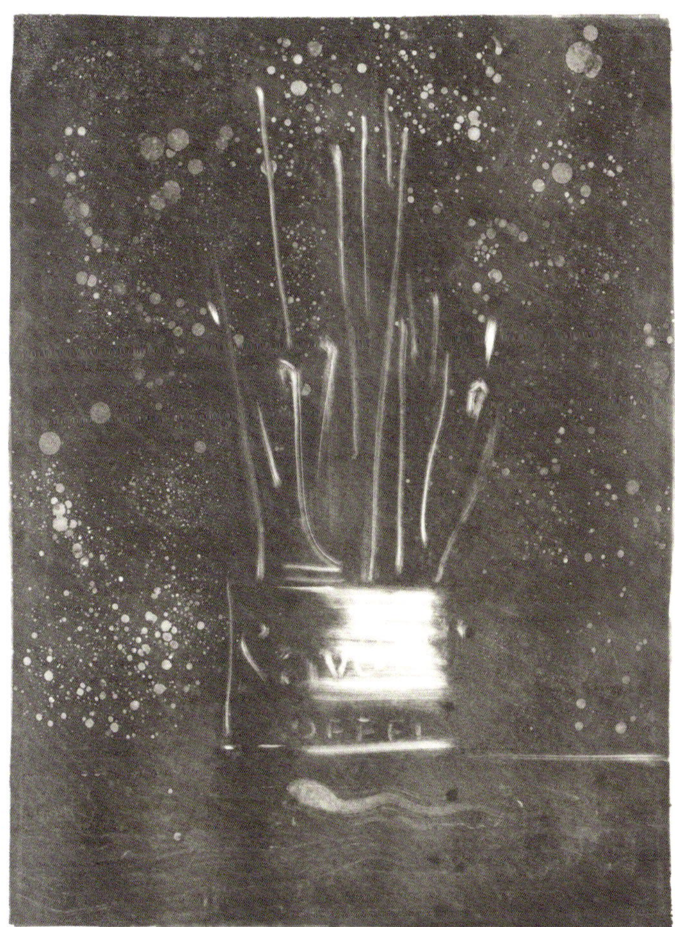

fig. 93 Johns, **Savarin**, 1982, monotype, 50 x 38 ⅛ in. (127 x 96.8 cm). Whitney Museum of American Art, New York; Gift of The American Contemporary Art Foundation, Inc., Leonard A. Lauder, President

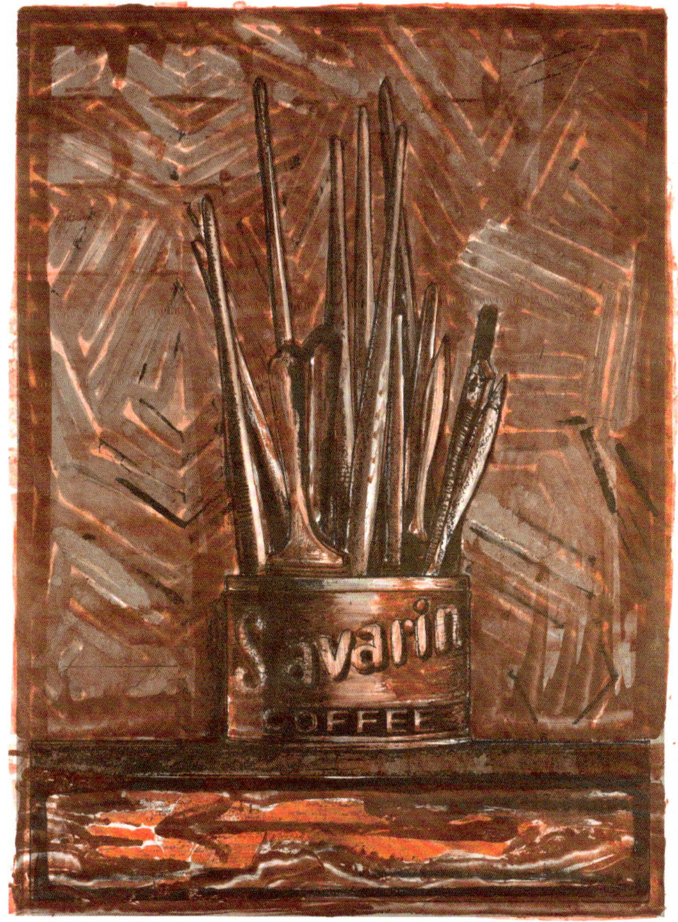

fig. 94 Johns, **Savarin**, 1982, monotype over lithograph, 49 ¾ x 38 in. (126.4 x 96.5 cm). Whitney Museum of American Art, New York; Gift of The American Contemporary Art Foundation, Inc., Leonard A. Lauder, President

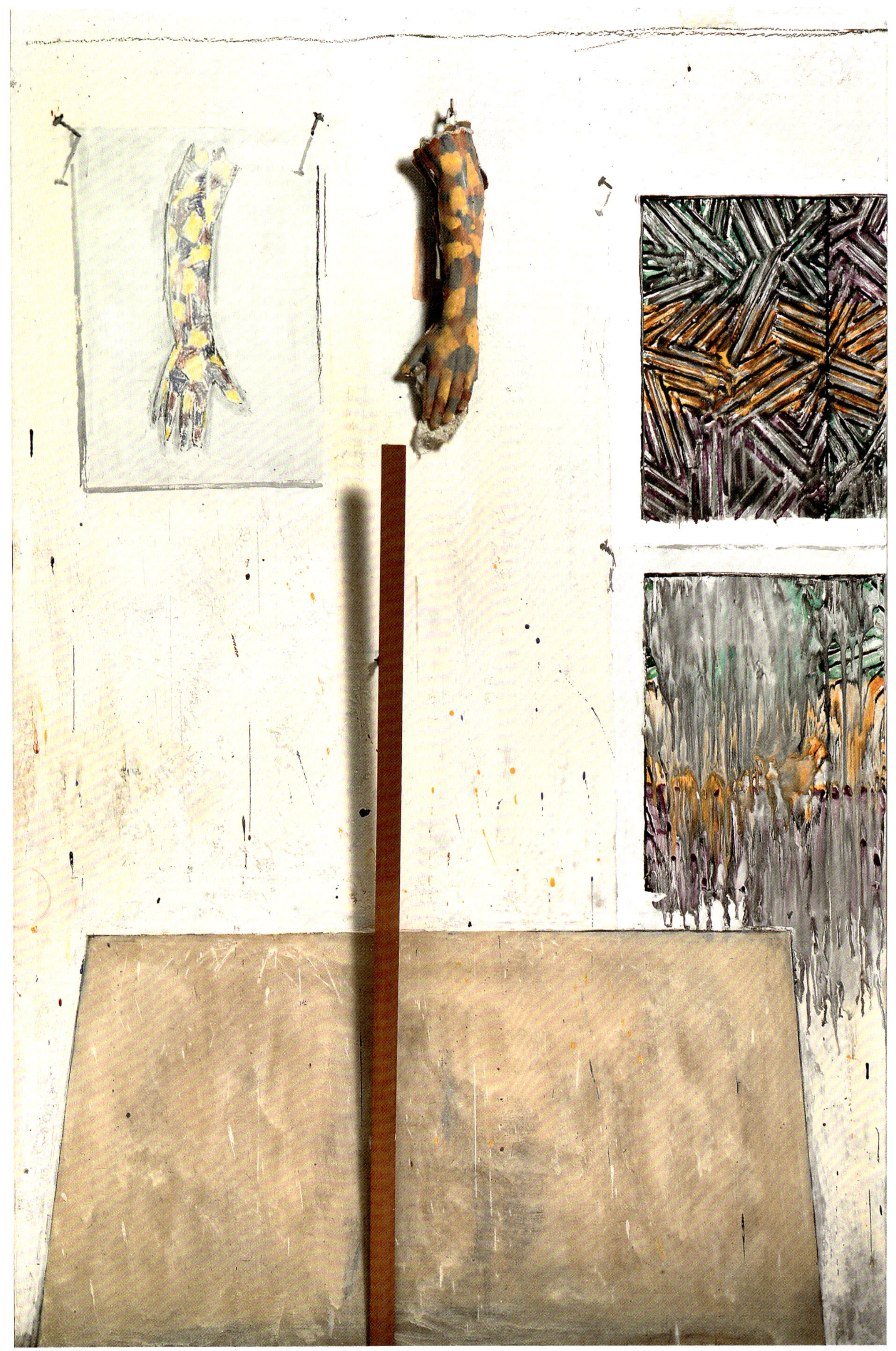

Sea Change: Illness and Mortality

In 1982, the year Johns completed the Savarin monotypes, his painting underwent a sea change. With the exception of the last version of *Between the Clock and the Bed*, which was already in progress, Johns ended his decadelong focus on crosshatching and returned to recognizable imagery. The representational motifs that had infiltrated the paintings two years earlier—at the margins of *Dancers on a Plane* and between the seams in the *Tantric Detail* paintings—now moved front and center. Johns announced the change with *In the Studio* (fig. 95), where several elements previously absent from his work—such as a specific location (his studio)—make a first appearance and others reappear in new ways. A cast-wax arm hanging against the paint-splattered surface recalls the arms of the Savarin prints and the two- and three-dimensional arms of the 1950s and 1960s. Beside it hangs a trompe l'oeil drawing with trompe l'oeil pins. The "drawing" mirrors the arm but with fingers spread. (Two independent drawings relate to the one in the painting, while differing in important ways. One of them [fig. 96] shares the curve of the forearm but not the spread of the fingers, thus more closely resembling the cast. The other [fig. 97] presents a stiff forearm while the spread fingers are closer to the illusionistic drawing.)[147] The pairing of the cast and the drawing reinforces the studio setting and once again allows Johns to unite drawing, painting, and sculpture in a single work.

A beige trapezoid at the bottom of the canvas represents a painting turned away from the viewer and leaning against the wall. Its slight tilt introduces the notion of shallow space, an illusion countered by a strip of wood held by a hook that leans out several inches from the surface. Johns would surely have noticed the plunging depth in Munch's paintings and prints, especially in iconic early works such as *The Scream* and *Despair* (fig. 98), where roads, bridges, and railings accelerate movement

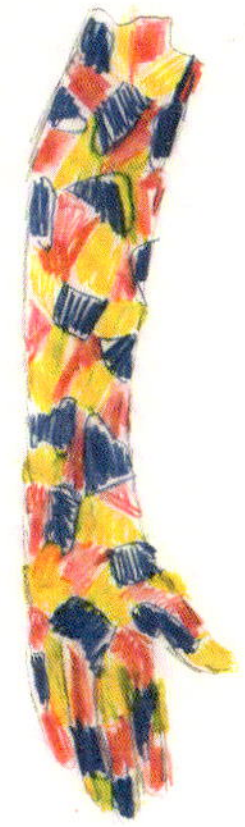

fig. 95 Johns, **In the Studio**, 1982, encaustic and collage on canvas with objects, 75 x 50 x 5 in. (190.5 x 127 x 12.7 cm). Collection of the artist

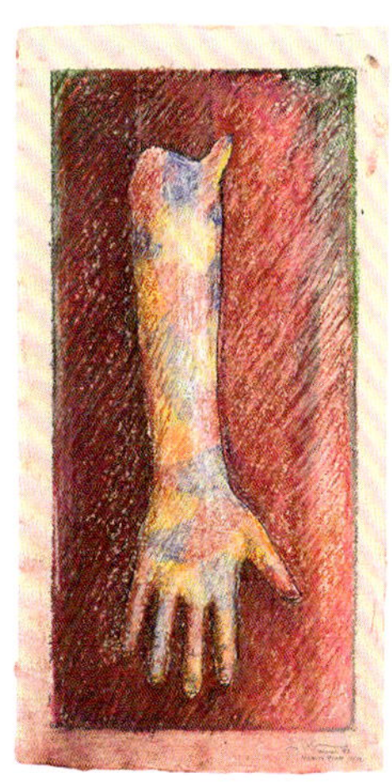

fig. 96 Johns, **Untitled**, 1982, oil, crayon, and graphite pencil on plastic, 18 ⅞ x 12 in. (47.9 x 30.5 cm). Collection of the artist

fig. 97 Johns, **Untitled**, 1982, pastel and graphite pencil on paper, 17 ⅛ x 8 ⅜ in. (43.5 x 21.3 cm), sight. Collection of the artist

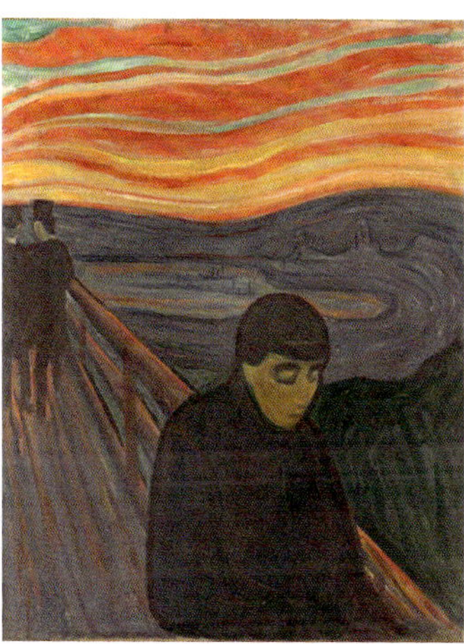

fig. 98 Munch, **Despair**, 1894, oil on canvas, 36 1/4 x 28 ½ in. (92 x 72.5 cm). Munch Museum

into space. The gentle lean of his reversed canvas has no such drama but may be an understated nod to Munch's deep spaces. It is worth remembering that the only previous appearance of illusionistic space in Johns's work is in the images of Savarin cans with crosshatch backgrounds, which initiated Johns's references to Munch. In addition, the new theme of the artist's studio resonates deeply with Munch's image of himself surrounded by his art in *Self-Portrait between the Clock and the Bed*, and *In the Studio* is conceivably an additional outgrowth of Johns's engagement with this painting during the years 1981 to 1983, when he was working on the three large crosshatch works.[148]

Although *In the Studio* marks the end of crosshatching as the sole subject of Johns's paintings, the pattern still appears as a motif within the new work—in the harlequin pattern on the arm and, more directly, in two trompe l'oeil crosshatch works on paper tacked to the wall.[149] The images suggest before and after versions, the lower one dripping onto the canvas below in a vivid reminder of the properties of encaustic: applied as a liquid, quickly hardening to a solid, and easily converted back to liquid with heat. At the same time, melting suggests the demise of cross-hatching as Johns's primary subject, the downward slide reflecting its loss of purchase on his imagination.

Johns may not have known Munch's painting of Stanisław Przybyszewski (fig. 99), as it was not included in the 1950 or 1978 exhibitions, but it offers a telling example of a much-discussed feature of Munch's work. A portrait of the Polish writer and art critic who was part of Munch's Bohemian circle in Berlin in the late 1890s, it also prominently represents Munch's "kill-or-cure" treatment.[150] As Munch described,

> Just wait till the painting has been exposed to a couple of showers, been gashed a little by some sharp nails and so forth, and then has been carted around the world in all sorts of miserable, leaking boxes. . . . Oh yes, in due course I think this could be good! It only needs a few flaws in order to become really good.[151]

Eyewitness accounts describe how Munch "manhandled his pictures. He might fly at them in a rage, kick them, tear them apart."[152] In other accounts, he actually encouraged visitors to damage his works: "Go ahead and trample all over them. It will only make them better."[153]

Munch's harsh treatment of his work appeared as early as the mid-1880s, where scraping, scratching, and gouging served simultaneously to call attention to the materiality of paint and canvas and to add another expressive layer to the representation of the subject. Around 1894, while in Berlin, Munch began another phase of this treatment in which he exposed his works to the elements. The Przybyszewski portrait belongs to a group of works that he allowed wind, sun, and rain to disfigure. By this time, he had already begun painting thinly and leaving large areas of the canvas blank. Deliberate weathering of his works took this dematerialization to another level. By incorporating the chance actions of nature, he downplayed his subjective will while suggesting that his creative

fig. 99 Munch, **Stanisław Przybyszewski**, 1894, casein and distemper on canvas, 29 ½ x 23 ⅝ in. (75 x 60 cm). Munch Museum

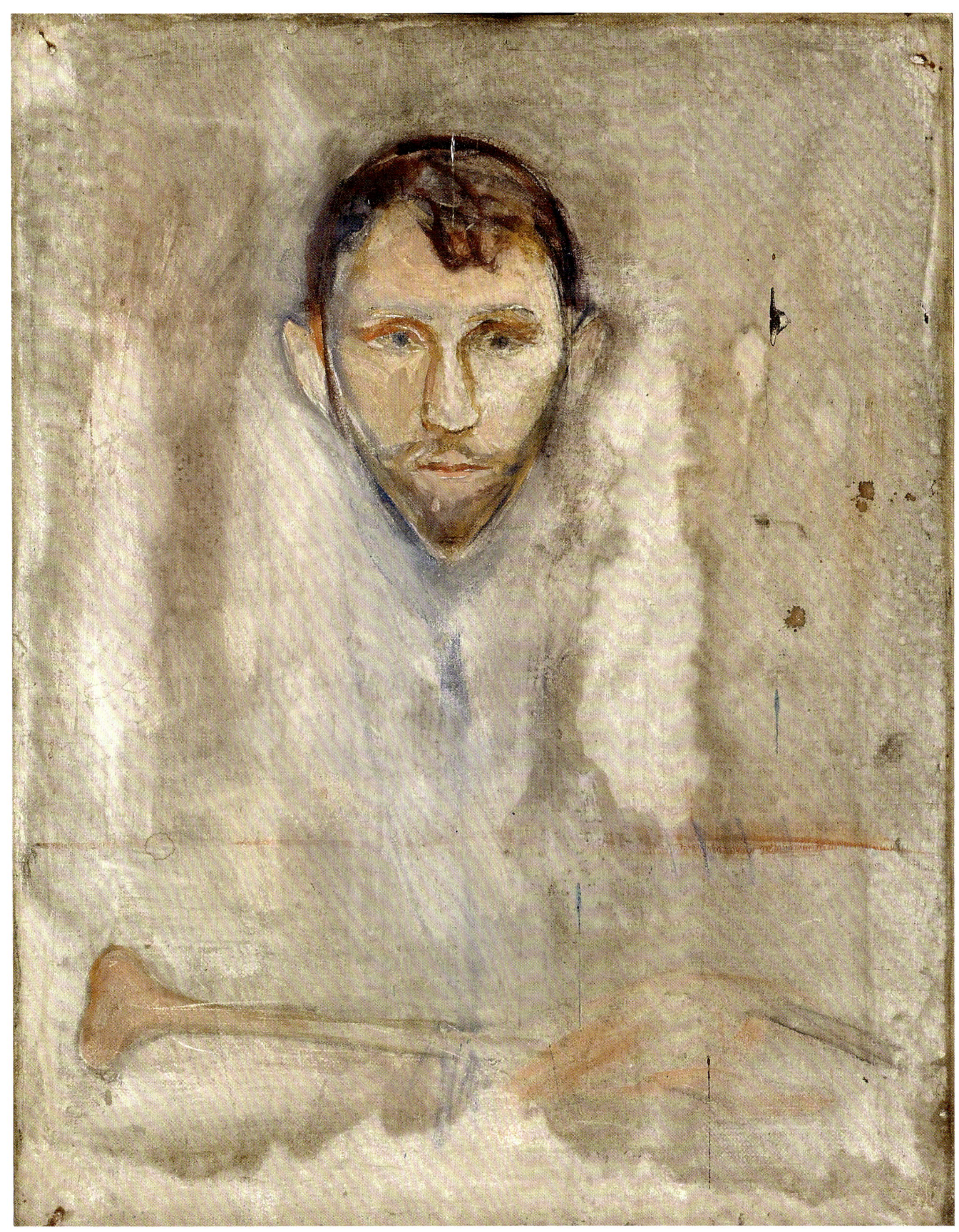

process harnessed the force of nature itself. The resulting degradation embodied a dialectic of creation and destruction, materiality and temporality.

Munch continued variations of the kill-or-cure practice throughout his career, including painting in an outdoor studio at Ekely through the winter with only minimal protection from snow, ice, and rain (fig. 100). Given that his idiosyncratic process was well known among contemporary artists, including Joseph Beuys, Dieter Roth, and Anselm Kiefer,[154] it is conceivable that Johns is subjecting his trompe l'oeil crosshatch painting to his own version of a kill-or-cure treatment at the moment of its end as his principal subject. The melting of actual encaustic calls attention to its distinct properties while also creating the illusion of a watercolor left in the rain.

Coincidentally, the Przybyszewski portrait is the first of Munch's works to feature the detached, skeleton arm, which a year later became a prominent element in the 1895 self-portrait lithograph (fig. 46). The isolated arm also appears in a version of *Dance of Death,* where Munch has cut off the bottom portion of the image and inserted the limb, not skeletal but severed and holding what appears to be a communion wafer (fig. 101).

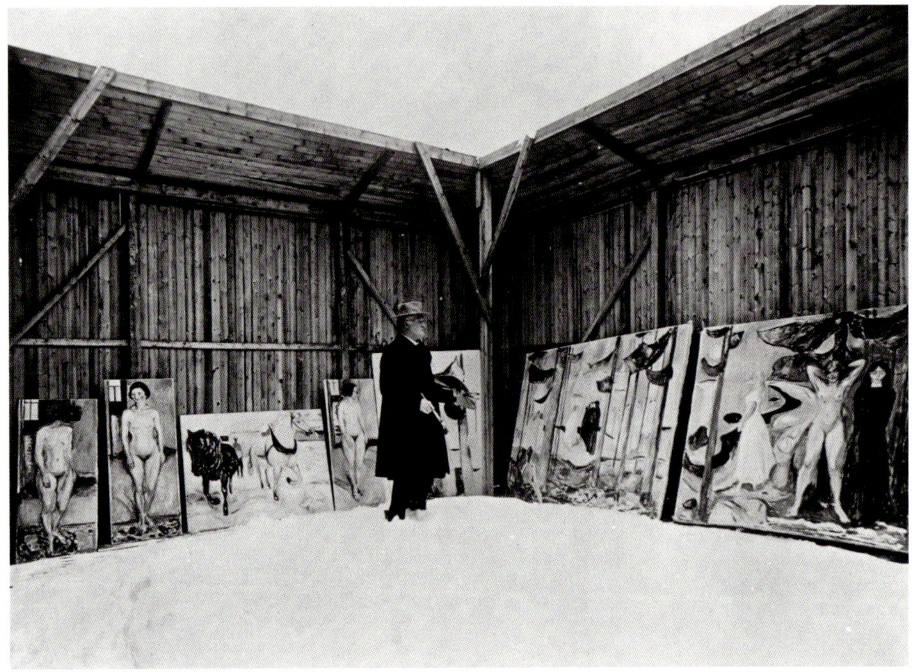

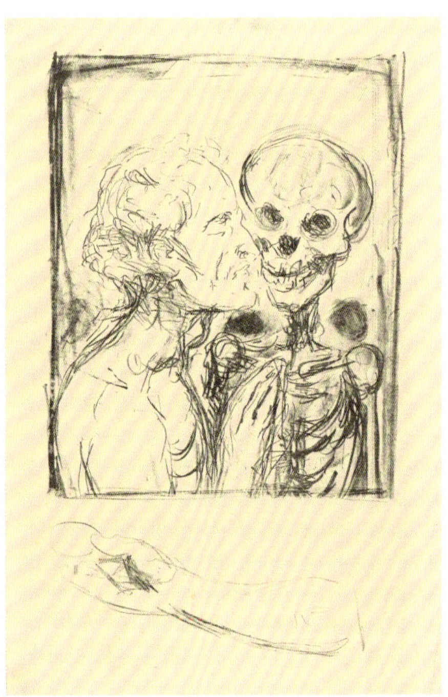

fig. 100 **Munch in his outdoor studio at Ekely**, 1933, photographed by Ragnvald Vaering. Munch Museum Archives

fig. 101 Munch, **Dance of Death (III)**, 1915, lithograph, 21 ⅞ x 14 ⅜ in. (55.6 x 36.6 cm). Munch Museum

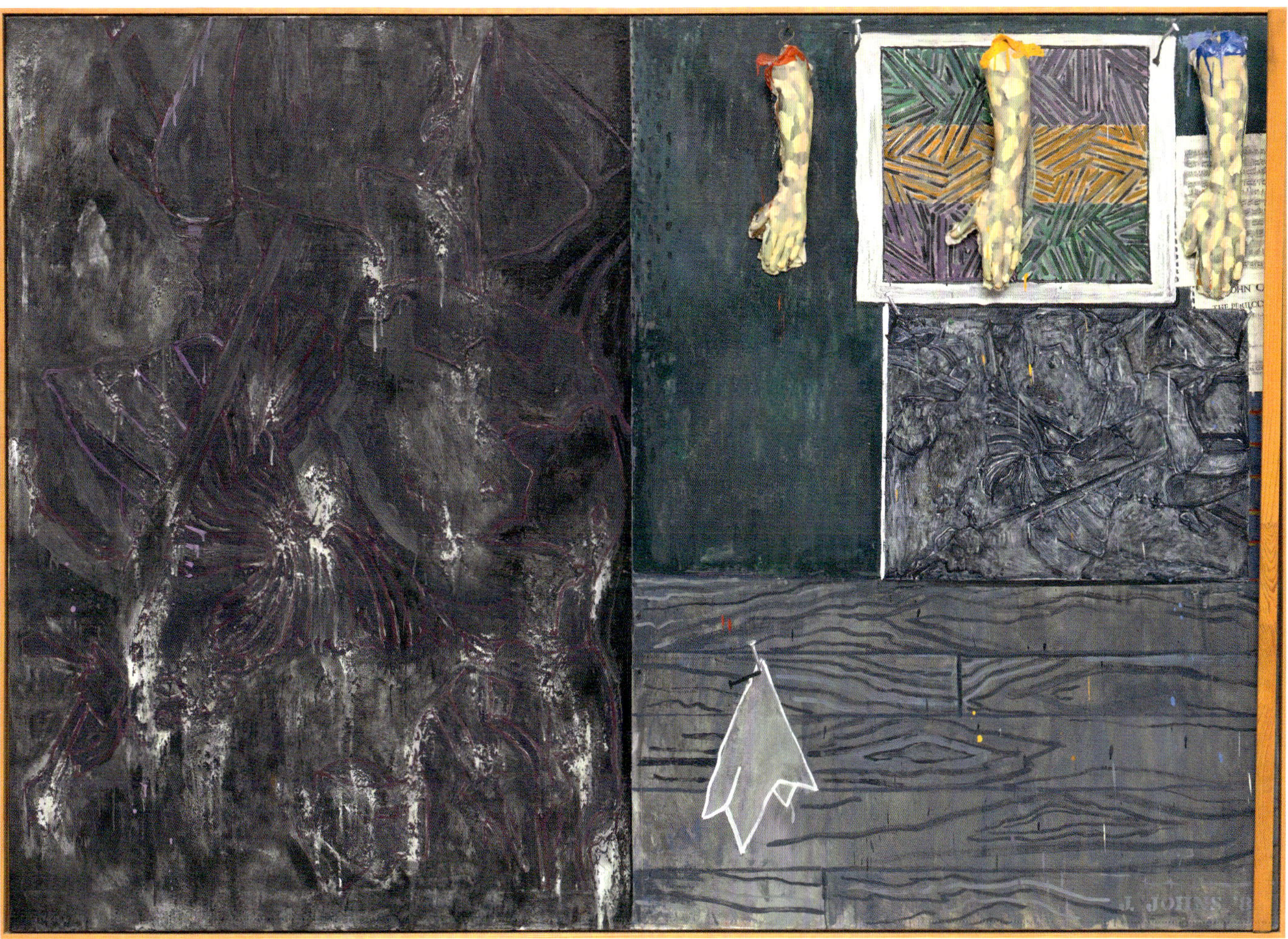

fig. 102 Johns, **Perilous Night**, 1982,
encaustic on canvas with objects,
67 ⅛ x 96 ⅛ x 6 ¼ in. (170.5 x 244.2 x 15.9 cm).
National Gallery of Art, Washington, DC,
Collection of Robert and Jane Meyerhoff

Johns's next painting, *Perilous Night* (fig. 102), builds on several elements from
In the Studio, including the detached arms. Here three limbs of graduated sizes
punctuate the upper right of the work. These examples were cast at three-year
intervals from the arm of a friend's son and together indicate change over time.[155]
The harlequin pattern is less distinct now, its mottled flesh-and-gray patches
resembling bruises. Bright primary colors splashed onto the truncated tops and
dripping below create an effect at once cheerful and disturbing. Behind the center
arm, the crosshatch drawing from *In the Studio* reappears whole. The far-right arm
extends over *The Perilous Night*, a 1943–44 score by Johns's friend and mentor John
Cage that lends the painting its title.

Wood grain reappears on an expanded scale in *Perilous Night*. A cartoonish
handkerchief pinned to the wood with an illusionistic nail implies a vertical plane,
but the wood also suggests a floor meeting a wall, where a small, slightly trapezoidal

illusionistic painting seems to lean (as in *In the Studio*). Johns contradicts the hint of recession, however, by "nailing" this painting to the wall, making it hang as much as sit. Similarly, an actual strip of wood at the right leans away from the surface, in contrast to the shallow space suggested by the small painting within the painting.[156]

The left half of *Perilous Night* introduces a new motif of darkness and anxiety. It is derived from the Isenheim Altarpiece by German Renaissance painter Matthias Grünewald. Johns focused on the foreground of the *Resurrection* panel, a night scene where two stunned soldiers fall over at the sight of the risen Christ (fig. 103). Reduced by Johns to their contours, flipped, and then rotated counterclockwise by ninety degrees, the soldiers can still be recognized by select details, such as the sword and pleated tunic of the foreground figure. One soon understands the subject of the painting on the right side of *Perilous Night*, just above the wood planks, as a smaller, un-flipped and un-rotated version of the left side.

The role of this and other Isenheim motifs in Johns's work has been much discussed.[157] Pertinent in relation to Munch is the iconography of physical and emotional distress they introduce into Johns's growing repertoire of motifs concerning sex, death, and the cycle of life. Johns saw the Isenheim Altarpiece in 1976 and again in 1979 when visiting a close friend who was dying in a hospital in nearby Basel.[158] In 1980, a German dealer sent Johns a large book of reproductions of the altarpiece, inspiring him to begin making tracings from several of the images.[159] The experience of the visits, the gift of the portfolio, and the appearance of the imagery in his work overlap precisely with the creation of the Savarin prints and first two *Between the Clock and the Bed* paintings.

The Isenheim Altarpiece was painted for the Monastery of St. Anthony in northwestern France.[160] The monks specialized in hospital work and were known for taking care of plague sufferers. They also treated skin diseases, especially a mysterious affliction named St. Anthony's fire after their monastery and the burning pain it caused. (Some 150 years after the altarpiece was commissioned it was discovered that this disease stemmed from a fungus on rye.) Grünewald's paintings were part of the overall program of care for the stricken, intended to help them meditate on their salvation.

Just a year after introducing the ghostly hint of a full figure in *Between the Clock and the Bed,* Johns found in the Isenheim images the opportunity to include full figures in his work once again, also in a highly abstracted manner. Johns's description of his motivation is at once straightforward and complex.

> I thought how moving it would be to extract the abstract quality of the work, its patterning, from the figurative meaning. So I started making these tracings. Some became illegible in terms of the figuration, while in others I could not get rid of the figures. But in all of them I was trying to uncover something else in the work, some other kind of meaning.[161]

From embedding body parts into the abstract paintings of the late 1970s to embedding abstracted figures into representational paintings in the early 1980s, Johns continued to mine the ambiguities of the terms abstraction and representation.

A related drawing, also called *Perilous Night* and made at the same time (fig. 104),[162] highlights the painting's expression of mourning and foreboding. A single imprint

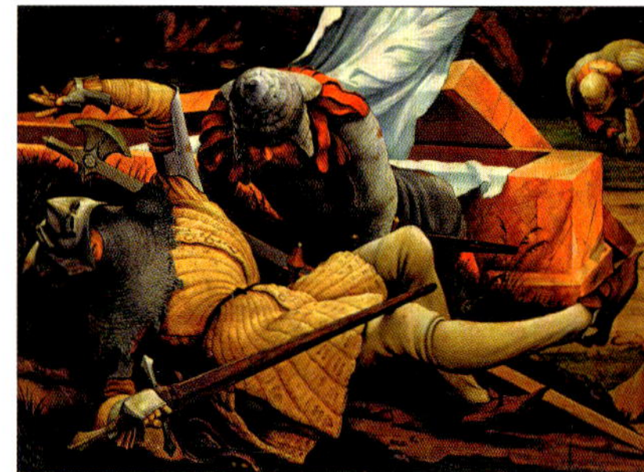

fig. 103 Matthias Grünewald (German, ca. 1480–1528), **Soldiers Guarding Christ's Tomb at the Resurrection**, detail from the Isenheim Altarpiece, ca. 1512–16, oil on panel, 105 7/8 x 56 5/16 in. (269 x 143 cm). Musée Unterlinden, Colmar, France

of the artist's arm and hand replaces the child's arm casts. It recalls the red arm of the Savarin print, but now in black, the funereal replacing the visceral. The hand extends downward into a cloud of black and blue ink whose ominous quality recurs on the left, where the soldiers are present in the same configuration and orientation as in the painting. In contrast to the painting, however, the score at the right of the drawing is entirely visible, its two pages aligned. The long rectangular shape, along with the slight angle and increased scale, link it to the imprint of *Usuyuki* in *Between the Clock and the Bed* (fig. 72), adding yet another layer to the already existing association with a bed: Cage said that his composition was inspired by an Arthurian legend, related by Joseph Campbell, about a "perilous" bed that severely tests Sir Gawain in his efforts to seduce a maiden.[163] Cage was thinking of this bed, its relation to the breakup of his marriage, and the "loneliness and terror that come to one when love becomes unhappy"[164] as

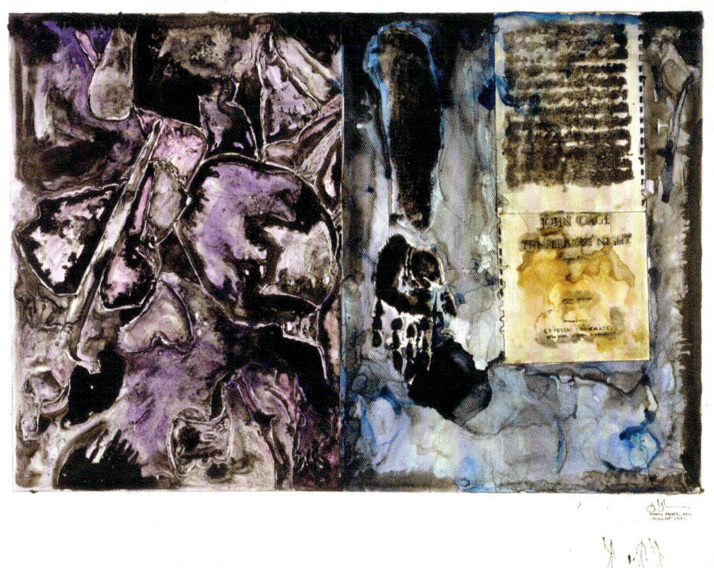

fig. 104 Johns, **Perilous Night**, 1982, ink on plastic, 39 ½ x 94 ½ in. (100.4 x 240 cm). Through prior gift of Mary and Leigh Block; Harold L. Stuart Endowment. The Art Institute of Chicago

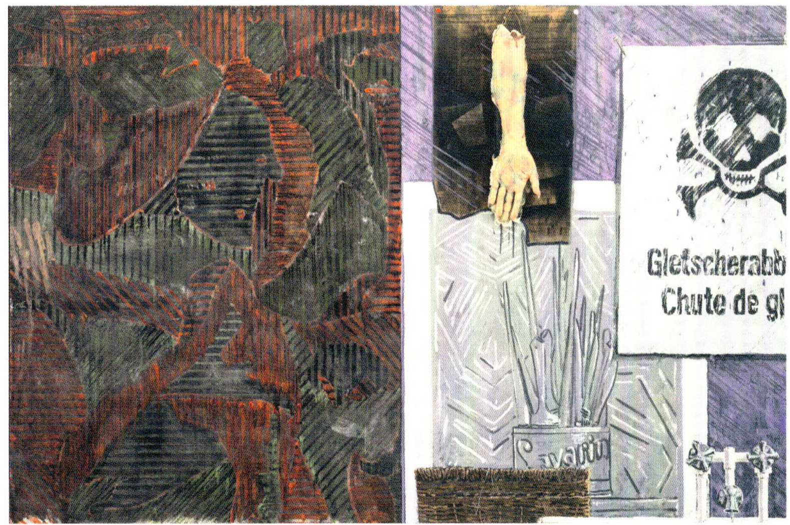

fig. 105 Johns, **Untitled**, 1983, encaustic and collage on canvas with objects, 48 ⅛ x 75 ⅛ in. (122 x 191 cm). Kravis Collection

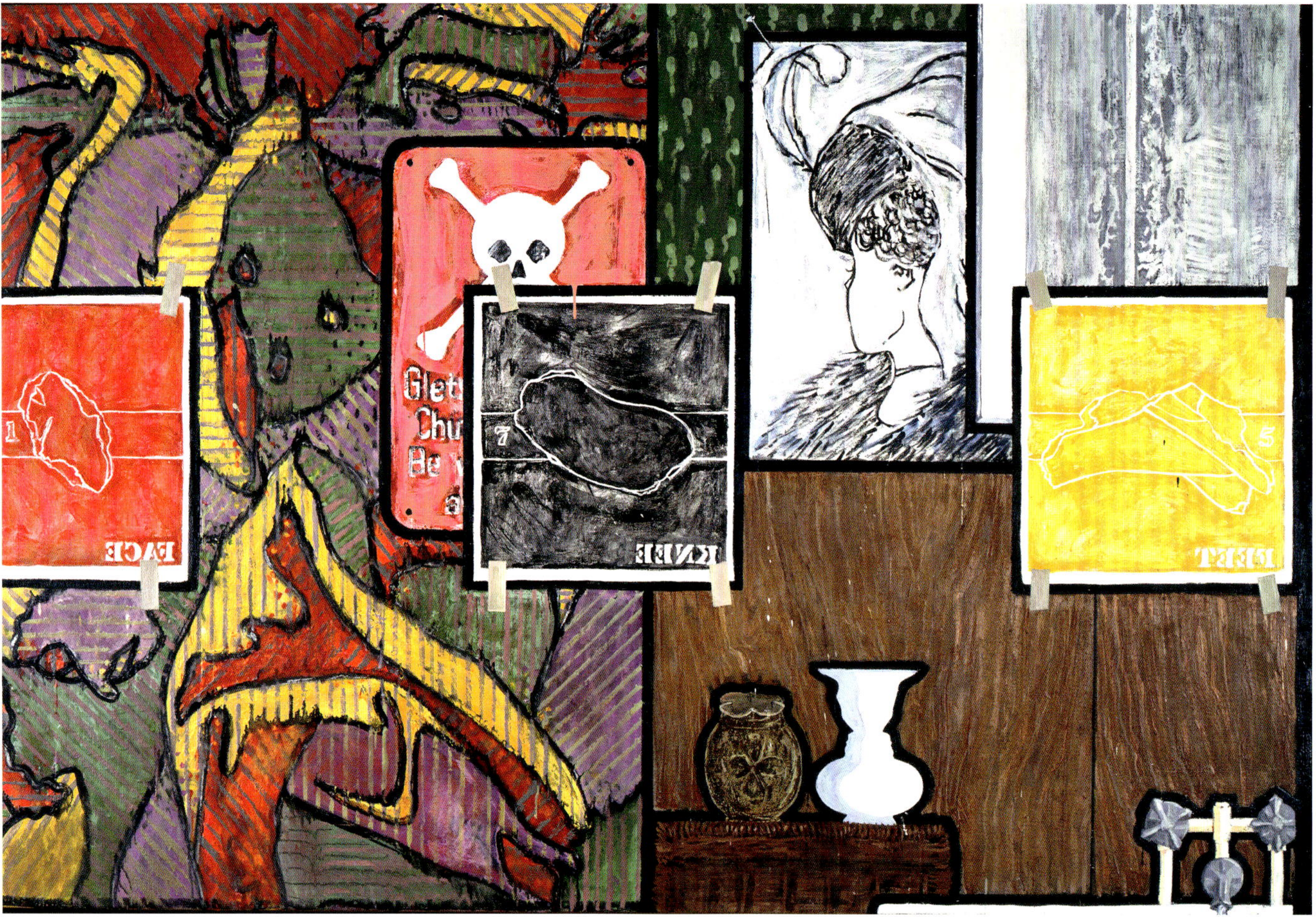

fig. 106 Johns, **Untitled**, 1984, encaustic on canvas, 50 x 75 in. (127 x 190.5 cm). Collection of the artist

he changed "Bed" to "Night" in the title of his work. Johns retains the darkness of night and Cage's emotional tone, and reinserts the allusion to the bed, weaving an ever tighter connection among *Usuyuki, Between the Clock and the Bed,* and Munch's self-portrait of the same title.

Themes of illness and anxiety continued to define Johns's work over the next two years, in particular a group of works known as the "bathtub's-eye view" paintings. An untitled painting from 1983 (fig. 105) offers the Savarin can's last appearance in Johns's work to date. The right side of the canvas shows a wall in Johns's bathroom, seen from within the tub (the rim and fixtures are at the lower right). The image behind the clothes hamper is sometimes identified as the Whitney poster but is better understood as the 1981 *Savarin* lithograph with the red arm. Cut off by the bottom of the painting, the arm is displaced to the three-dimensional cast above, where it seems to reach for the artist's tools. The futile gesture, set beside the image of a skull taken from a Swiss avalanche warning sign,[165] restates the analogy

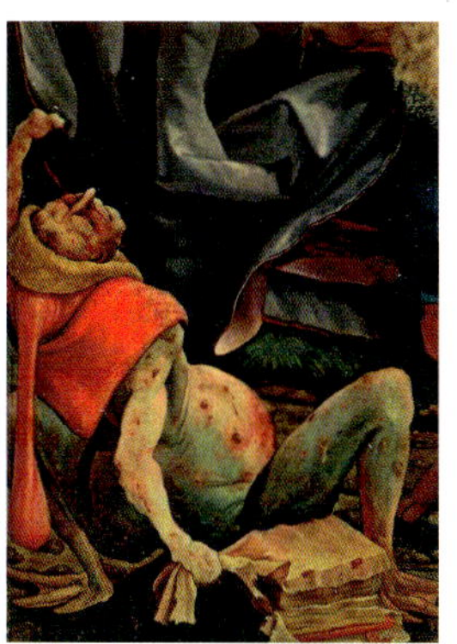

fig. 107 Matthias Grünewald (German, ca. 1480–1528), **Suffering Man**, detail from the reverse of the Isenheim Altarpiece, ca. 1510–15, oil on panel, 104 ¹¹⁄₁₆ x 54 ¹¹⁄₁₆ in. (265 x 139 cm). Musée Unterlinden, Colmar, France

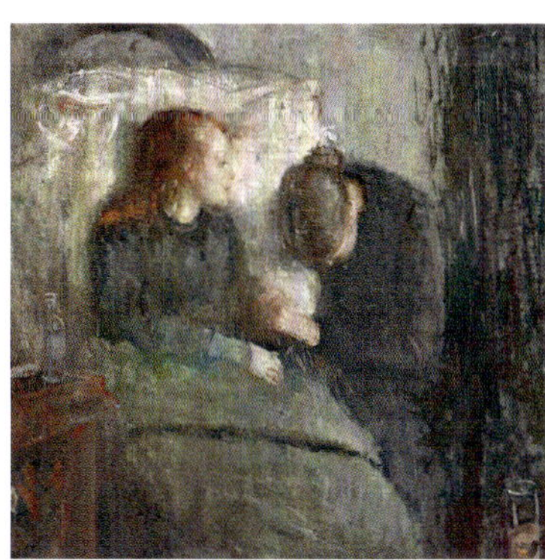

fig. 108 Munch, **The Sick Child**, 1885-86, oil on canvas, 47 ¼ x 46 ⅝ in. (120 x 118.5 cm). National Museum of Art, Architecture and Design, Oslo

between fingers, brushes, and crosshatching, along with the tension between creativity and mortality.

The left side presents a new figure from the Isenheim Altarpiece that furthers the themes of sickness and vulnerability. It derives from the panel *Saint Anthony Tormented by Demons Sent by Satan* and shows a barely human personification of St. Anthony's fire, with webbed feet, bloated belly, and skin covered with boils and lesions (fig. 107). Johns turned the figure upside down and fragmented it into interlocking puzzle pieces filled with hatch marks.

The suffering figure reappears in another untitled bathtub painting from the following year (fig. 106), again filling the left side but now in sickly green and purple intermingled with yellow and red. Other borrowed images include a Barnett Newman print at the upper right, the avalanche warning sign, two ceramic vessels, and an optical illusion that oscillates between a young maiden and an old crone as one stares at it.[166] Notable in connection to Munch, a pattern of light-green sperm swimming against a darker green ground appears above panels of wood grain and behind the ambiguous female.

Across the front of the image, Johns "taped" three prints from a 1974 series based on the cast body parts in the far right panel of the painting *Untitled*, 1972 (fig. 3), adding further reference to the fragmented, vulnerable body. The reversed lettering is original to the prints but here adds to the dizzying complexity of the composition. Surfaces and images pile on top of and slide beneath each other, creating a space that shifts back and forth like the young woman/old woman image. The density of the whole is matched by the layering of images of illness, anxiety, and death onto those of conception and creation.[167]

Although recent scholarship places Munch in the context of his surrounding environment—not only literature and the arts but science, technology, and popular culture[168]—Johns would initially have encountered a view of Munch that emphasized his isolation and Nordic melancholy. Munch's own statements and writings encouraged this view: "I arrived in the world on the point of death. . . . Sickness and insanity and death were the black angels that hovered over my cradle and have since followed me throughout my life."[169] In addition to being part of Munch's personal experience, these themes were familiar subjects in late nineteenth-century Scandinavian art. Munch's *The Sick Child* (fig. 108) recalled a painting from five years before by his teacher, Christian Krohg, but its differences established it as his breakthrough work. When he first exhibited it, the controversy generated by its aggressive brushwork and unfinished appearance garnered him recognition as the most progressive of the new generation of Nordic painters. The image is based on Munch's memories of his older sister, Sophie, who suffered from tuberculosis and died at age fifteen. Munch restaged her sickbed for the painting, using his aunt and housekeeper as models. Overpainting and scoring with a palette knife (even more evident in later versions)—suggesting the view through a veil of tear-laden lashes— push a familiar genre scene to a heightened level of expression.[170]

The Sick Child became one of Munch's most repeated images in paintings and prints. *The Sick Child I* (fig. 109) belongs to a series of variously colored lithographs that focus on the girl's head against the pillow. Strong crosshatching captures the knife work of the painting and enmeshes her in a force field of agitated lines. Splotches of yellow and red set off the pale face and imply illness. Munch's many repetitions of this image have been seen as obsessive—a psychological need to revisit and exorcise painful memories. At the same time, recent scholarship has explored other motivations, including market pressures and the desire to retain important images for his own collection. Most significant in connection to Johns, Munch viewed repetition as a way to deepen his engagement with a motif; with

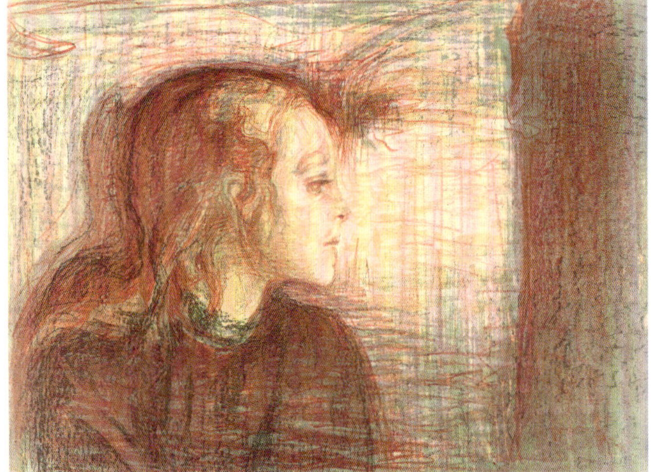

fig. 109 Munch, **The Sick Child I**, 1896, lithograph, 16⅜ x 26⅛ in. (41.3 x 66.3 cm). Munch Museum

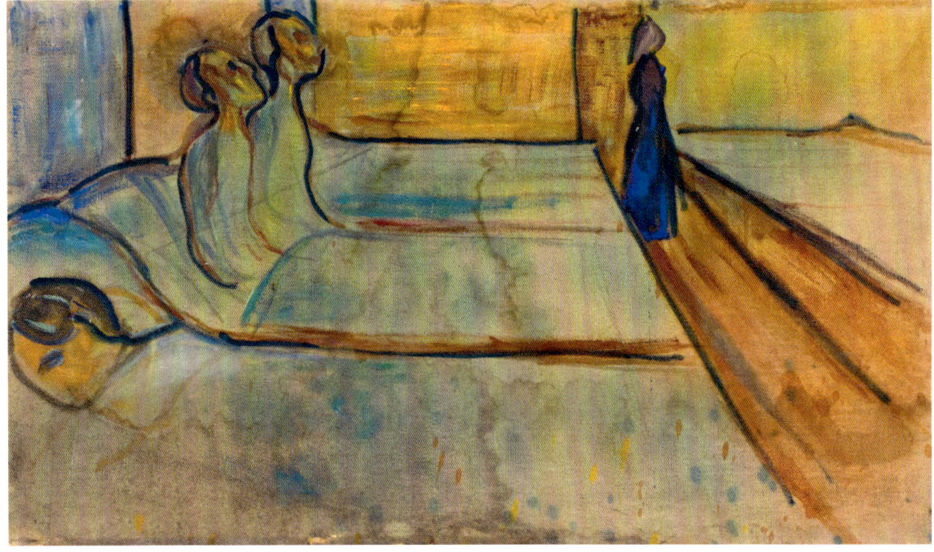

fig. 110 Munch, **Hospital Ward**, 1897–99, oil on unprimed canvas, 31½ x 55⅛ in. (80 x 140 cm). Munch Museum

each new iteration he opened the image to new meanings based on shifts in color, scale, perspective, and medium. The repetition inherent to printmaking became central to Munch's thinking over time and influenced his painting, in ways very similar to Johns.[171]

Munch's paintings from the 1890s continued his preoccupation with illness. In *Hospital Ward* (fig. 110), he presents stricken, ghostlike men in their beds attended by a lone figure that seems as much reaper as nurse, anchoring the end of a steeply receding path characteristic of his work during this period. The loose application of diluted paint to an unprimed canvas creates an anemic quality that underscores the evanescent nature of the suffering souls. Water staining enhances the effect, a result either of the painting process or deliberate exposure to the elements, which Munch had begun by this time. Green and yellow splatters in the foreground add to the sickly mood and bring to mind the diseased skin of the Isenheim creature in Johns's paintings.

Inheritance (fig. 111) also foregrounds the ill body. The inheritance is syphilis, on full display in the deformed proportions and pale, spotted skin of the infant, presented like a corpse in a shroud or a fetus in a womb and recalling the framing

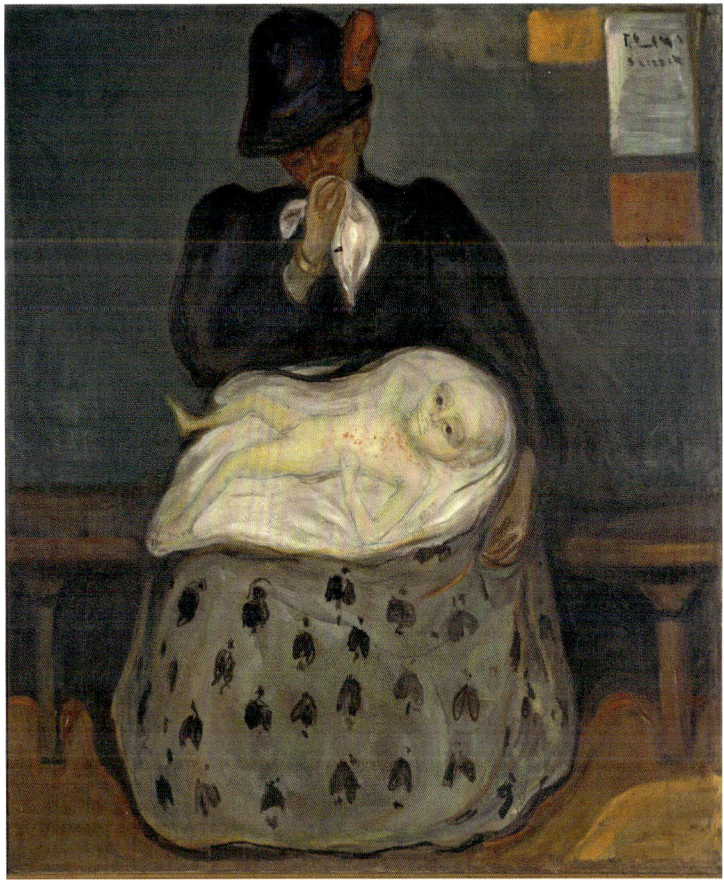

fig. 111 Munch, **Inheritance**, 1897–99, oil on canvas, 55 ½ x 47 ¼ in. (141 x 120 cm). Munch Museum

figures in the Madonna images. Munch's interest in the subject was not just in drawing attention to a prevalent social scourge; it also addressed his worries about the physical and mental illness in his own family. Despite having recovered from a childhood bout with tuberculosis, he lost not only his sister but his mother and paternal grandfather to the disease—although there was some suspicion that his grandfather had died of syphilis. (This circumstance led Munch to identify with Oswald, the character in Ibsen's *Ghosts* whose deceased father, Captain Alving, left him a legacy of insanity from syphilis.) Whether or not syphilis plagued the family, Munch never married, concerned about passing on what he saw as his father's mental instability, and he sometimes said that his own "weak nerves" were his unfortunate inheritance.[172]

Munch's ill health, heavy drinking, and emotional stress led to a collapse, and he admitted himself to a clinic for eight months in 1908–9. Yet even after he recovered, he continued to probe the anxiety he felt about his health in numerous images, including a series from ten years later showing him with Spanish flu (fig. 112).

This pandemic is thought to have killed some 25 to 50 million people in 1918–19, though there is some debate over whether Munch actually had the illness.[173]

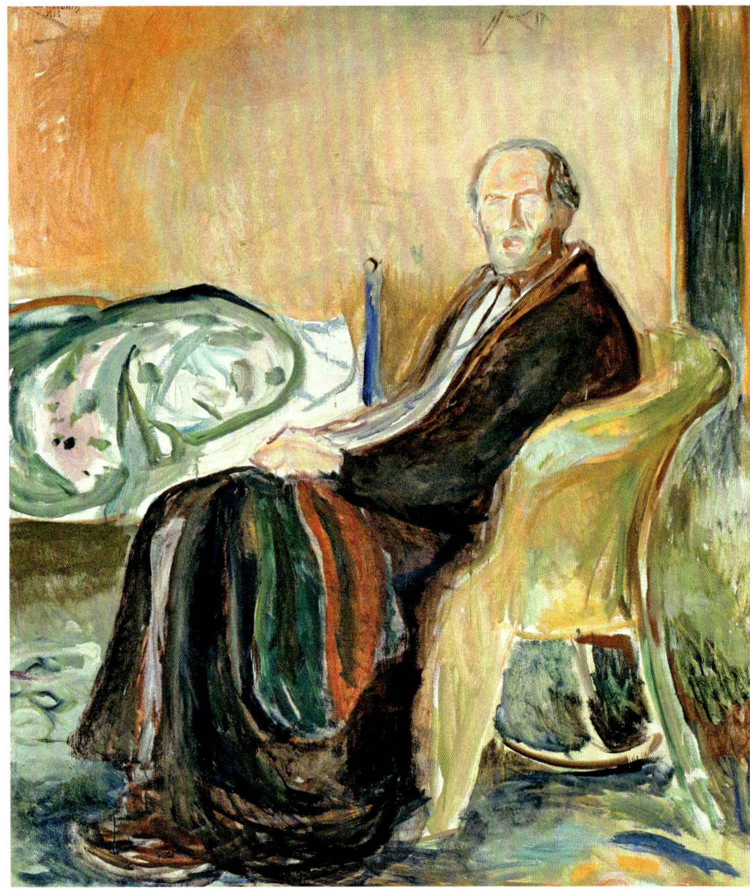

fig. 112 Munch, **Self-Portrait with the Spanish Flu**, 1919, oil on canvas, 59 x 51⅝ in. (150 x 131 cm). National Museum of Art, Architecture and Design, Oslo

In any case, he used its ravages to dramatize his own fears, showing himself slack-jawed and listless. In a conversation about this work, Munch asked a young art collector, "Does it seem repellent? . . . Can you smell it? . . . Yes, can't you see that I'm in a state of decay?"[174] A related drawing seems to present him even closer to the moment of death (fig. 113).

While Johns would have seen Munch's images of illness and mortality in exhibitions and publications, the precise extent of their impact is uncertain. But what we do know is that after Johns chose to conclude his decadelong focus on crosshatching with a public declaration of his interest in Munch, he then moved on to several bodies of work concerning illness, anxiety, isolation, and death—the themes that preoccupied Munch throughout his life and form the core of his art. Addressing this monumental shift in his work, Johns answered in general terms.

> In my early work, I tried to hide my personality, my psychological state, my emotions. That was partly due to my feelings about myself and about painting at the time. I sort of stuck to my guns for awhile but eventually it seemed like a losing battle. Finally one must simply drop the reserve. I think some of the changes in my work relate to that.[175]

Munch, too, should be seen as one of the catalysts for this change—not just as the inspiration for the Savarin images with armprints and the *Between the Clock and the Bed* paintings, but also as a gateway to an entire realm of human experience that was previously all but exiled from Johns's work.

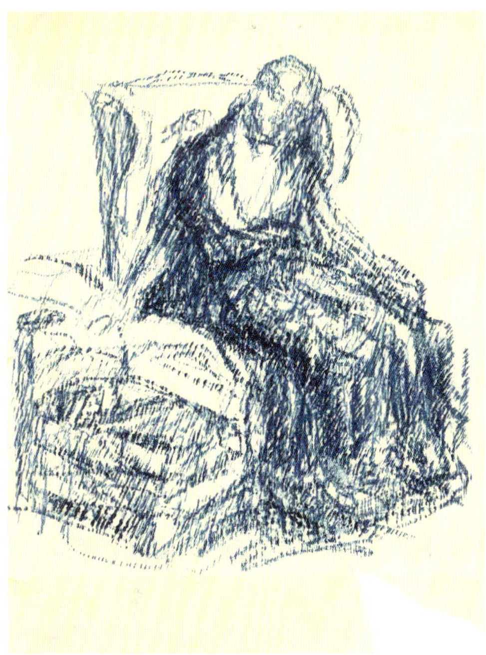

fig. 113. Munch, **Self-Portrait in Wicker Chair (Spanish Flu)**, 1919, crayon on paper, 11 ⅜ x 8 ¾ in. (29 x 22.3 cm). Munch Museum

Shadows and Ghosts: The Passage of Time and the Transience of Life

Even if Johns had finally "dropped the reserve" and opened his work to more autobiographical and emotionally expressive imagery, *The Seasons* paintings of 1985–86 still marked a surprising new level of self-reference and self-reflection. In four closely related paintings, a dark figure based on a tracing of Johns's own shadow stands within environments of the changing seasons.[176] Directly behind the figure, four varied surfaces are usually understood as references to the flooring of Johns's residences and studios at the time: terra-cotta tile from St. Martin in *Spring* (fig. 115); brick from Stony Point, New York, in *Summer* (fig. 116); wooden planks from the Provident Loan Society building on Houston and Essex Streets in downtown New York in *Fall* (fig. 117); and stone from the courtyard of his Upper East Side Manhattan townhouse in *Winter* (fig. 118).[177]

In each work, the figure stands beside piles of his belongings, some in states of collapse, including Johns's own work and that of other artists. Each painting also features a large black semicircle with an armprint that recalls the Savarin prints of the 1970s and 1980s. The placement of the arm in the circle and its boardlike forearm also recall prints of the 1960s (see fig. 36), but unlike their suggestion of endless, futile circling, the movement of the arm here is meant to show a sequence of stages from top to bottom, marking time's steady passage through the seasons of life.

Along with this traditional allegorical content, *The Seasons* have generally been seen as referring to the transitions that preoccupied Johns during the mid-1980s. He painted *Summer* first, in 1984–85, during the time he was establishing a new studio on St. Martin, in the Caribbean. He worked on the subsequent paintings in 1985–86 as he was moving back into Manhattan from Stony Point and relocating another studio from downtown to uptown.[178] Around this time, he saw a reproduction in a book by David Duncan of Picasso's 1936 painting *Minotaur Moving His House* (fig. 114), which Picasso had painted in response to his own time of transition after separating from his first wife, Olga, following the birth of a child to his mistress Marie-Thérèse Walter.[179] Johns was apparently struck by the imagery in this small work as it related to his own situation, and he borrowed many of its elements for his paintings—including the large stars in the sky; the wheel of the cart, half black and half white, which was transformed into Johns's semicircle; and the rope bundling a ladder, painting, and other objects. Picasso's pregnant horse, so tired it rides in the cart, became the seahorse in *Summer,* while the Minotaur, Picasso's alter ego, became Johns's self-portrait shadow. Another Picasso painting, which Johns may have glimpsed in the same book and also recalls seeing in a Paris exhibition, provided an additional source for the shadow as self-portrait. In *The Shadow* (fig. 119), Picasso presents himself as a silhouette darkening the doorway to his studio, contrasting with the pale painted representation of his mistress, Françoise Gilot, who had recently taken the two children and left him alone in Southern France. Johns seems to have been interested

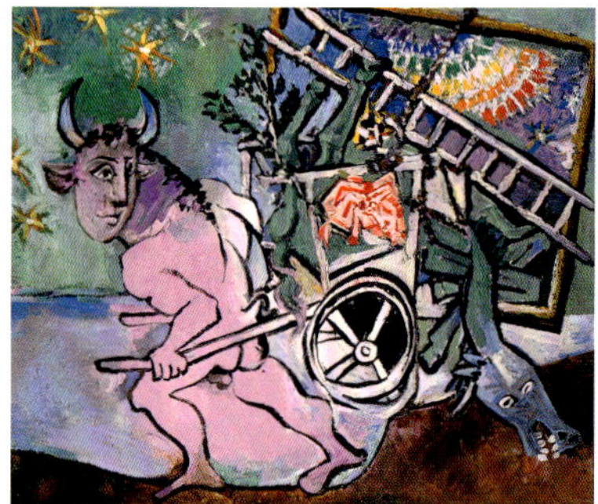

fig. 114 Pablo Picasso, **Minotaur Moving His House**, 1936, oil on canvas, 18 ⅛ x 21 ⅝ in. (46 x 54.9 cm). Private collection

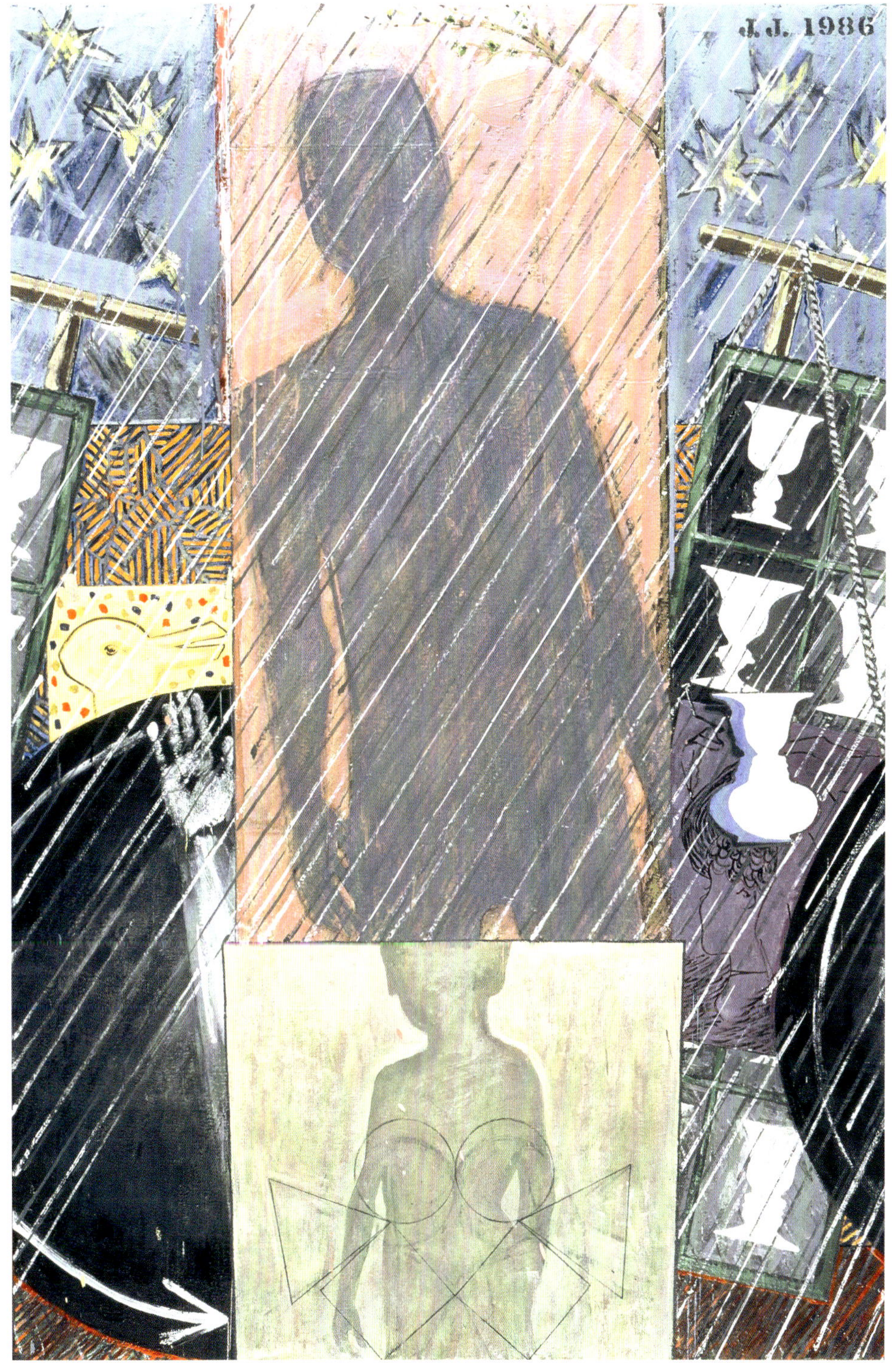

fig. 115 Johns, **Spring**, 1986, encaustic on canvas, 75 x 50 in. (190.5 x 127 cm). Robert and Jane Meyerhoff Collection

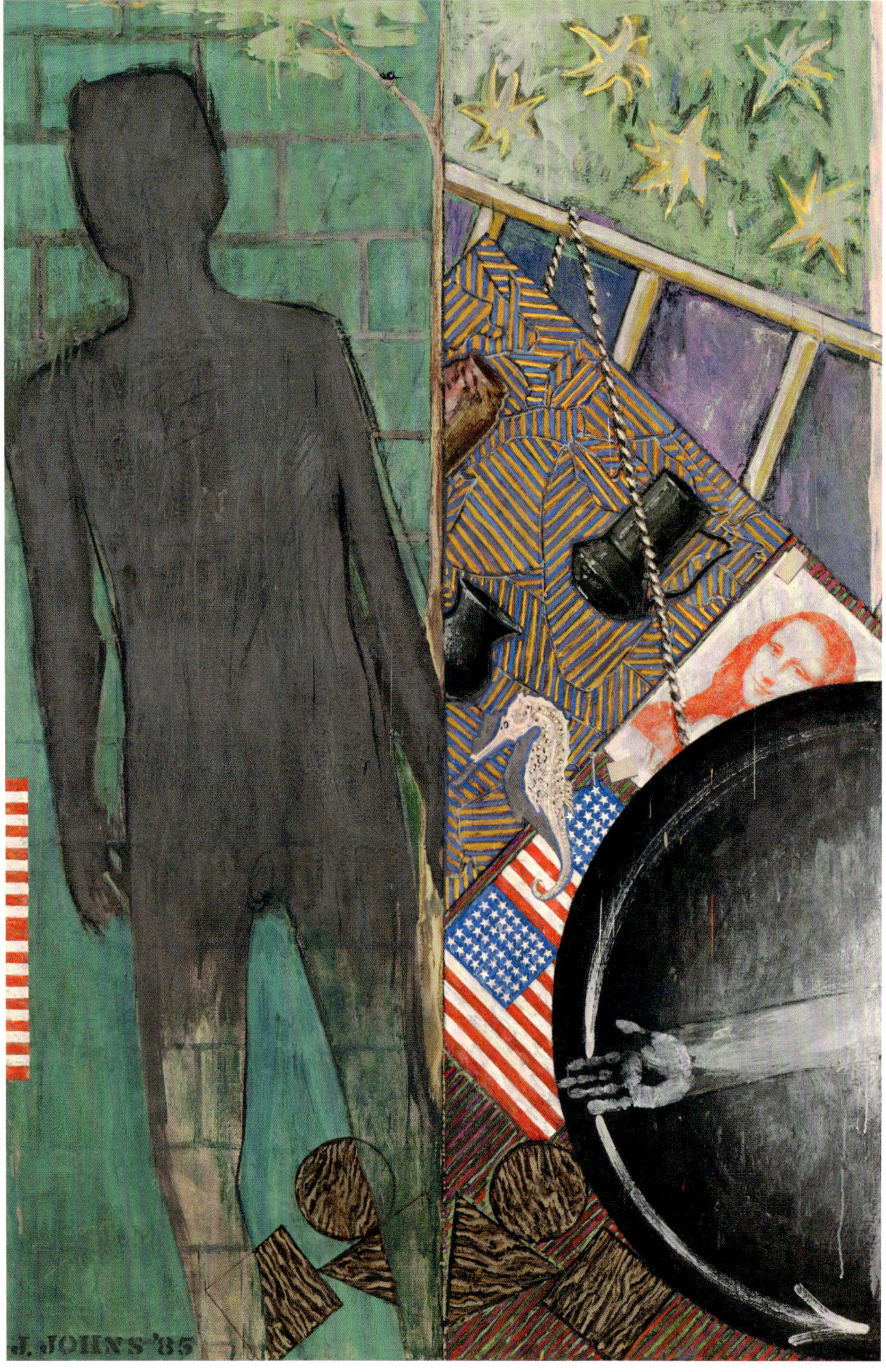

fig. 116 Johns, **Summer**, 1985, encaustic on canvas, 75 x 50 in. (190.5 x 127 cm). The Museum of Modern Art, New York, Gift of Phillip Johnson

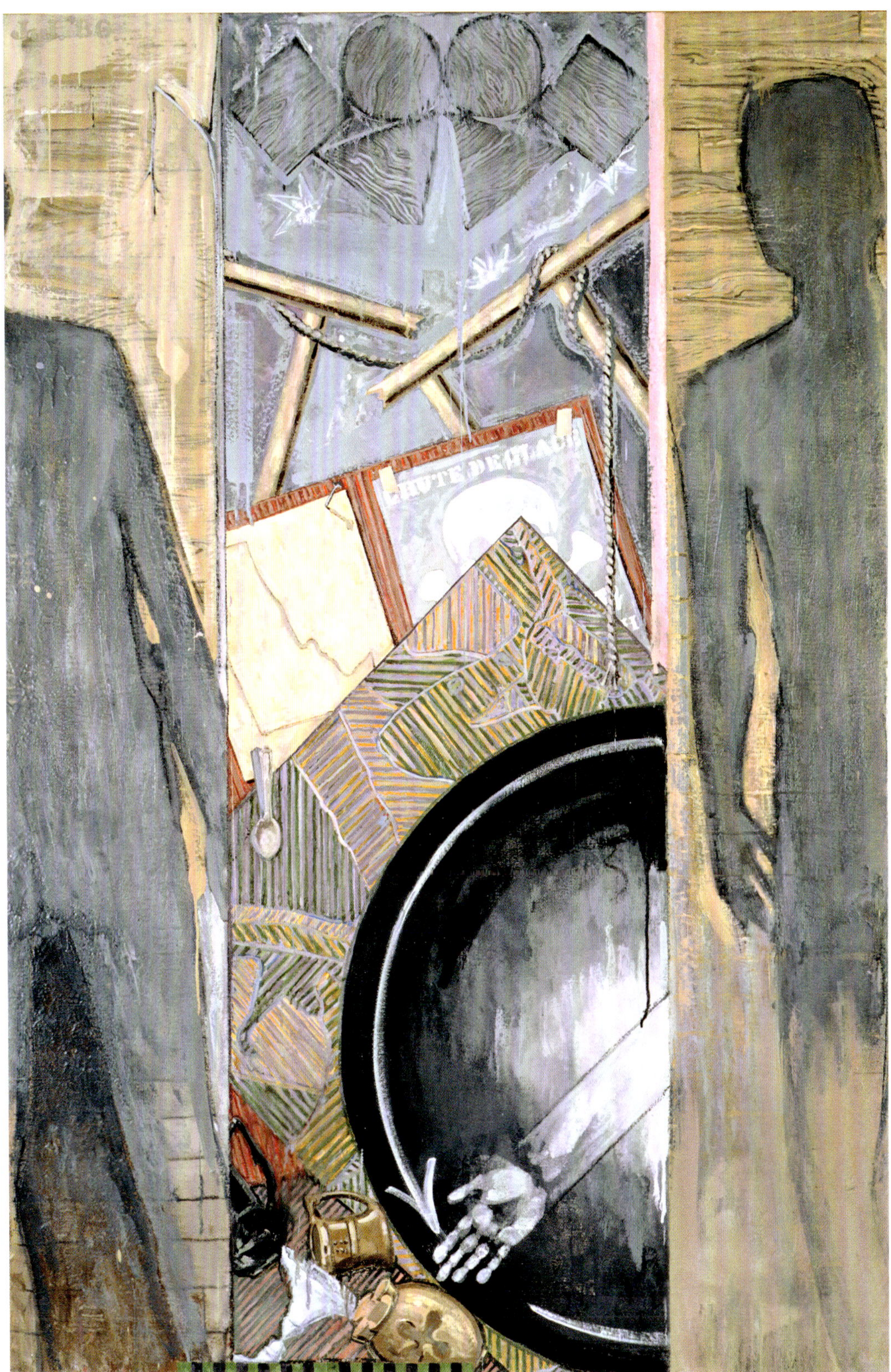

fig. 117 Johns, **Fall**, 1986, encaustic on canvas, 75 x 50 in. (190.5 x 127 cm). Collection of the artist

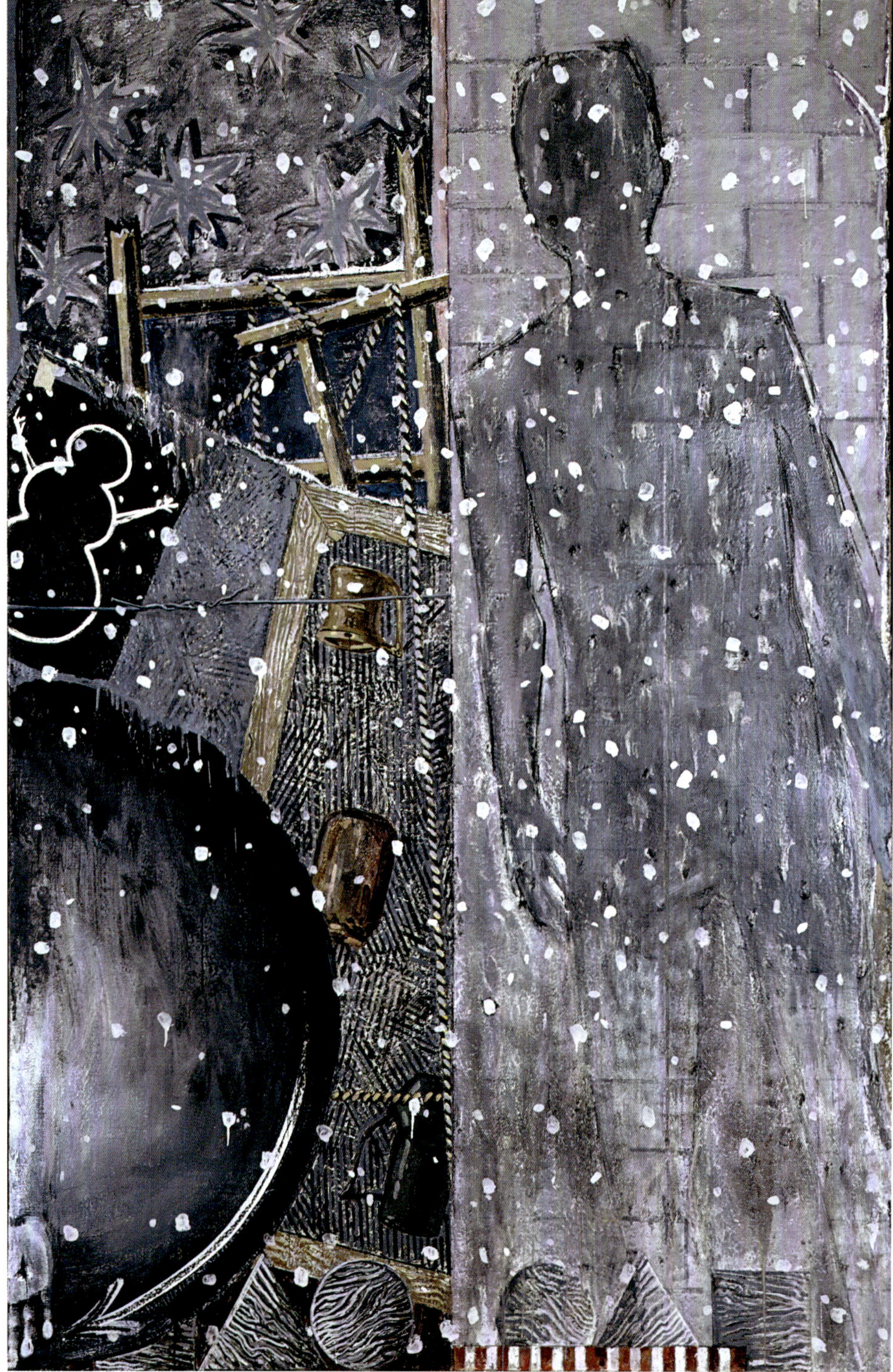

fig. 118 Johns, **Winter**, 1986, encaustic on canvas, 75 x 50 in. (190.5 x 127 cm). Private collection

not only in the artist-as-shadow, but also in an environment defined by the artist's work and possessions, and in the sense of a chapter of life coming to a close, with the attendant play of memory and feelings.

The shadows in *The Seasons* are often described as the first whole figures in Johns's work.[180] It is true the figure is now easily seen, but this assertion ignores the figurative presence at the center of the *Between the Clock and the Bed* paintings and also the soldiers and suffering creature from the Isenheim Altarpiece in the paintings that followed. In *The Seasons*, however, the full figure finally shed its abstract camouflage and in doing so emerged in the guise of a self-portrait. This can be seen as a joining of two formerly parallel tracks, both Munch-inflected: the surrogate self-portrait of the Savarin can and the bodies erupting from within crosshatching. Without negating the importance of Johns's encounter with the Picasso paintings that he saw at the moment of starting *The Seasons,* the account of these paintings is enriched by including in their arc his long engagement with Munch.

In addition, any connection between *The Seasons* and Munch should include discussion of the central role of shadows in Munch's art, especially in his many self-portraits. While these works, many of which were on view in the New York and Washington exhibitions, do not appear to be explicit sources as the Picasso paintings

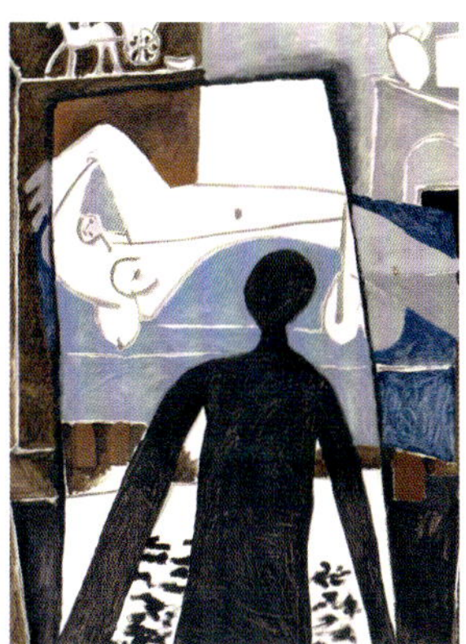

fig. 119 Pablo Picasso, **The Shadow**, 1953, oil and charcoal on canvas, 49 ½ x 38 in. (125.7 x 96.5 cm). Musée Picasso, Paris

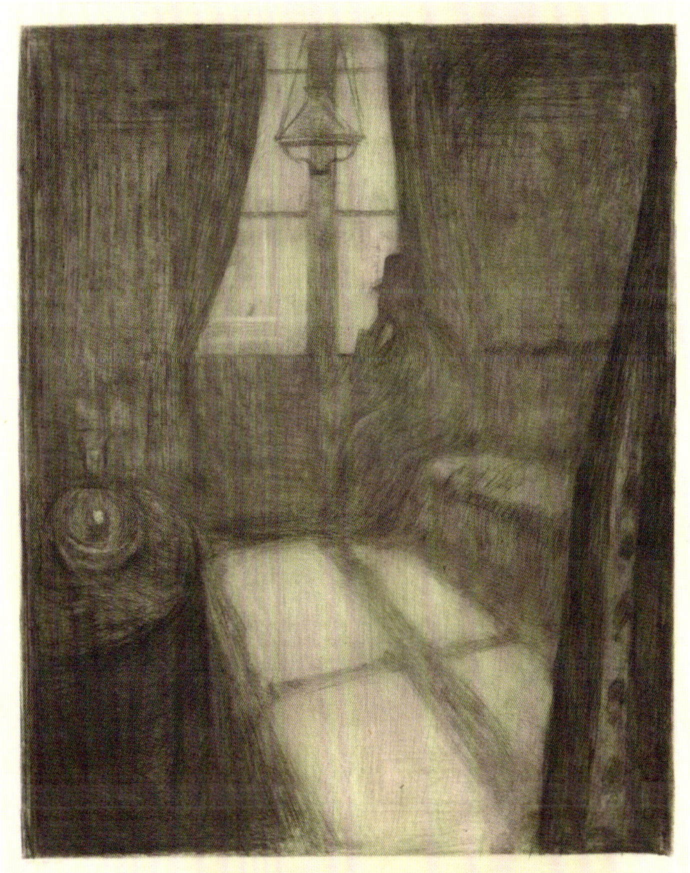

fig. 120 Munch, **Moonlight: Night in Saint-Cloud**, 1895, drypoint, 24 ⅝ x 17 ⅝ in. (62.6 x 44.7 cm). Munch Museum

were, they do offer another layer of association between Johns and Munch—one that involves not only formal affinities but related themes of the passage of time and the transience of life. One of Munch's earliest prints, *Moonlight: Night in Saint-Cloud* (fig. 120) presents a shadowy figure lost in thought seated beside a window. The image refers to a painting from 1890, when Munch was in Paris on a Norwegian state grant. The model was Danish poet Emanuel Goldstein, but the melancholic figure perched at the foot of a large crucifix-shaped shadow is often interpreted as a surrogate self-portrait—a reflection of the spiritual and artistic crisis Munch experienced in the year after his father's death, when he decisively rejected Scandinavian naturalism and French Impressionism in favor of a symbolist art of memory and feeling.

Munch continued to embed himself in shadow for some of his most famous self-portraits. In *Self-Portrait with Cigarette* (fig. 121), he is dramatically lit from below as if on stage, his elegant, spectral persona merging with the surrounding darkness. *Self-Portrait in Hell* (fig. 122) shares the use of theatrical footlighting and the shadowy backdrop. But here he is nude and set within warm and hot colors that dramatically convey his feelings as a tormented artist existing in a living hell.[181] A woodcut begun the following year (fig. 123) places him outdoors at night, where a dark looming form both shelters and threatens the wary figure below.

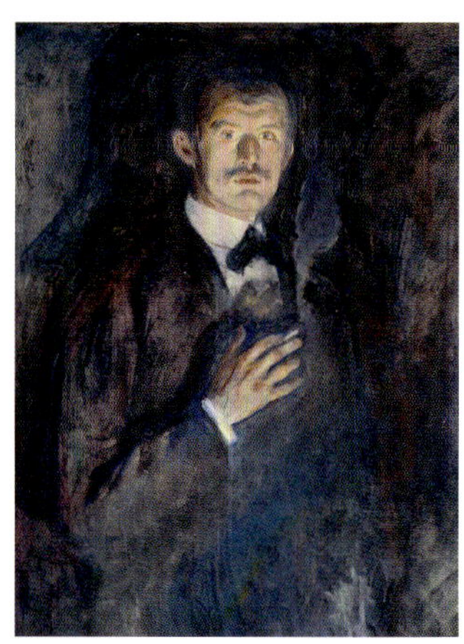

fig. 121 Munch, **Self-Portrait with Cigarette**, 1895, oil on canvas, 43 ½ x 33 ⅝ in. (110.5 x 85.5 cm). National Museum of Art, Architecture and Design, Oslo

fig. 122 Munch, **Self-Portrait in Hell**, 1903, oil on canvas, 32 ¼ x 26 in. (82 x 66 cm). Munch Museum

fig. 123 Munch, **Self-Portrait in Moonlight**, 1904–6, woodcut, 25 ⅞ x 19 ½ in. (65.9 x 49.5 cm). Munch Museum

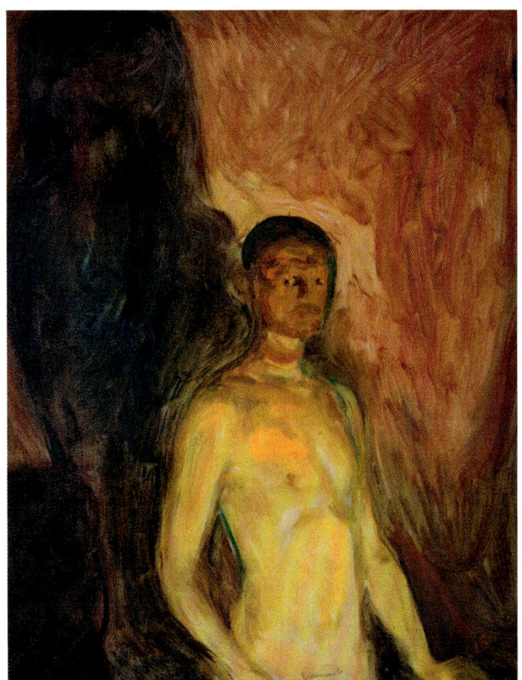

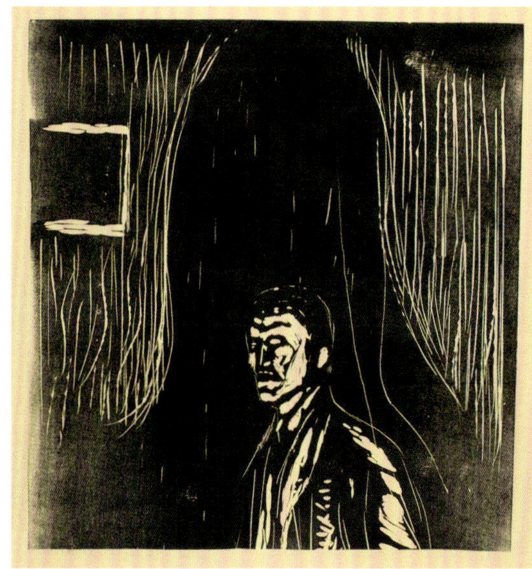

In addition to using shadow as a dramatic setting, Munch also employed it as a mask. A notebook sketch (fig. 124) offers his distinctive profile, defined by the strong jaw and prominent nose, partially veiled in a patch of darkness. Two years later he rendered his entire head as a shadow, the use of woodcut increasing the contrast of light and dark (fig. 125). Thin lines pick out details from within the black mass, while irregular cuts along the front edge describing blocked light show that Munch has used the dynamic of backlighting to transform himself into a ghoulish, menacing figure. More than a decade later, he re-created this effect in lithography (fig. 126), blacking out his features to assume the appearance of an ominous death's head.

The projection of the figure's silhouette onto the surrounding environment is the third principal way that shadow appears in Munch's work, and it resonates most

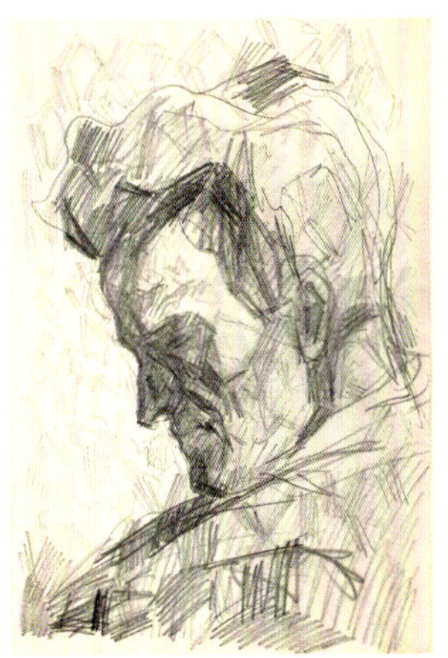

fig. 124 Munch, **Self-Portrait in Profile**, ca. 1910, pencil in sketchbook, 16¾ x 10⅝ in. (42.5 x 27.1 cm). Munch Museum

fig. 125 Munch, **Self-Portrait Facing Right**, 1912–13, woodcut, 20⅜ x 16¼ in. (51.8 x 41.1 cm). Munch Museum

fig. 126 Munch, **Self-Portrait in Backlight**, 1930, lithograph, 19⅝ x 14¾ in. (50 x 37.7 cm). Munch Museum

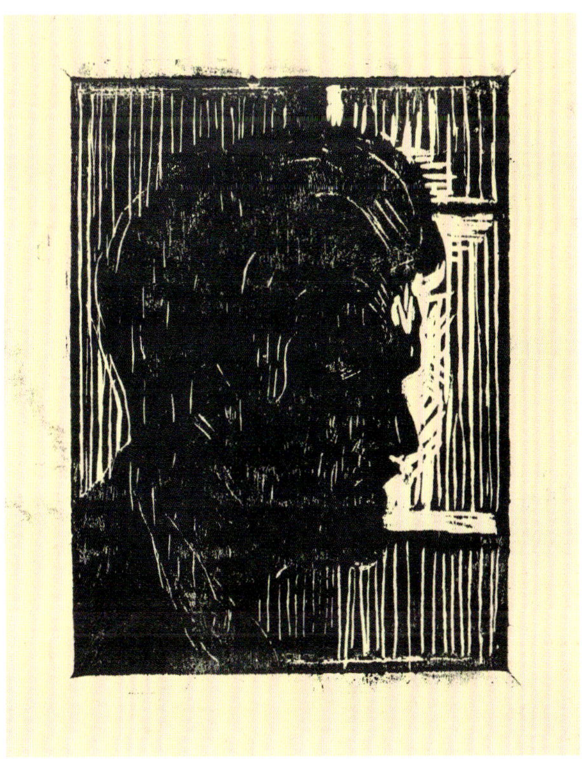

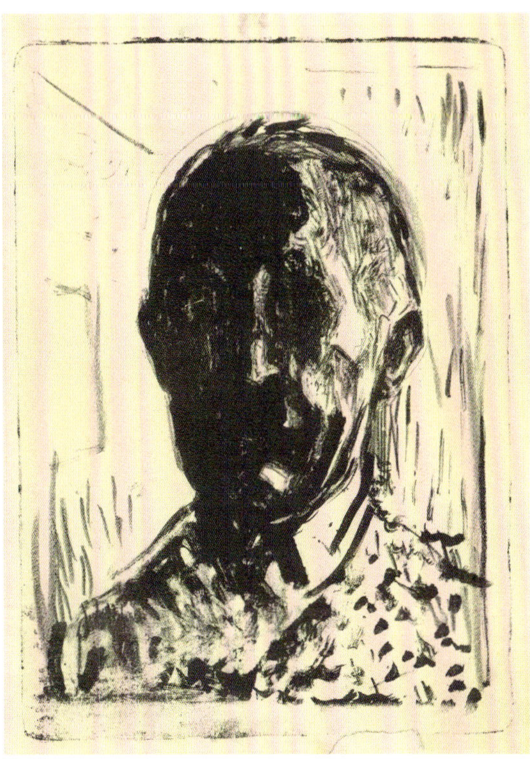

closely with John's self-portrait shadow in *The Seasons*. An early print of lovers
(fig. 127), inspired by Munch's romance with an older, married woman and set in
the coastal town of Åsgårdstrand where he spent many summers, casts the couple's
shadows across a garden onto a white fence and grove of trees. Echoed by two low
stars reflecting on the water, the shadows join them to the landscape and move
them closer to each other.[182]

Munch had explored the setting for this print, devoid of figures, in his first
Starry Night painting (fig. 128). It is one of his early psychological landscapes,
where the artist's mood and memory expressively distort nature's appearance.[183]
Munch returned to this motif three decades later for some of his most intensely
felt landscapes, which he described as addressing "the great force of Eternity."[184]
Starry Night II (fig. 129) from the early twenties, now a winter scene, depicts
a radiant nocturnal setting at Ekely.[185] The portrayal of nature's glory in the
early painting is now infused with a new sense of loneliness and anxiety. In

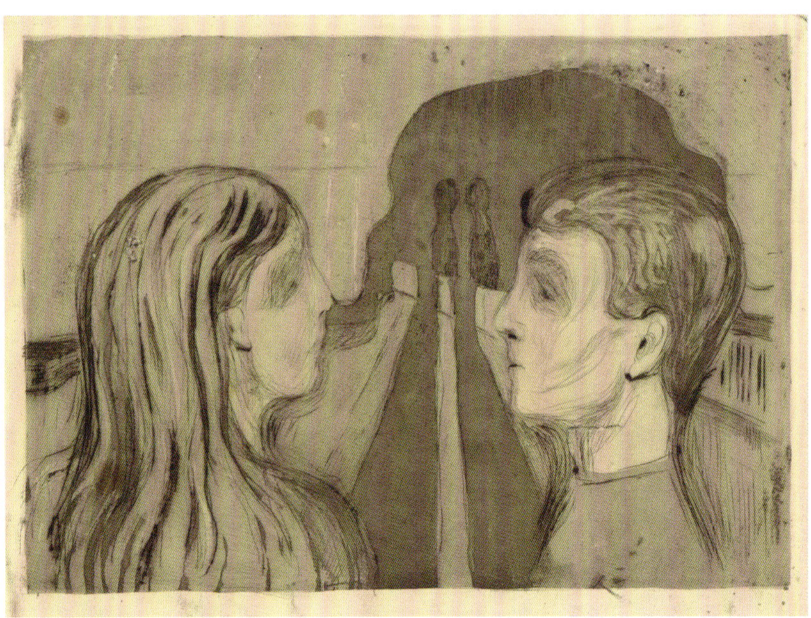

fig. 127 Munch, **Attraction II**, 1895,
etching and drypoint, 14 ¼ X 18 ¾ in.
(36 X 47.7 cm). Munch Museum

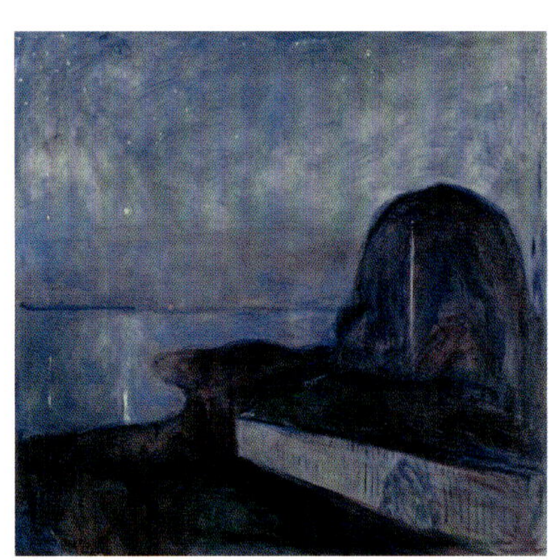

fig. 128 Munch, **Starry Night**,
1893, oil on canvas, 53 ⅜ x 55 ⅛ in.
(135.5 x 140 cm). The J. Paul Getty
Museum, Los Angeles

fig. 129 Munch, **Starry Night II**, 1922–24,
oil on canvas, 47 ½ x 39 ⅓ in. (120.5 x
100 cm). Munch Museum

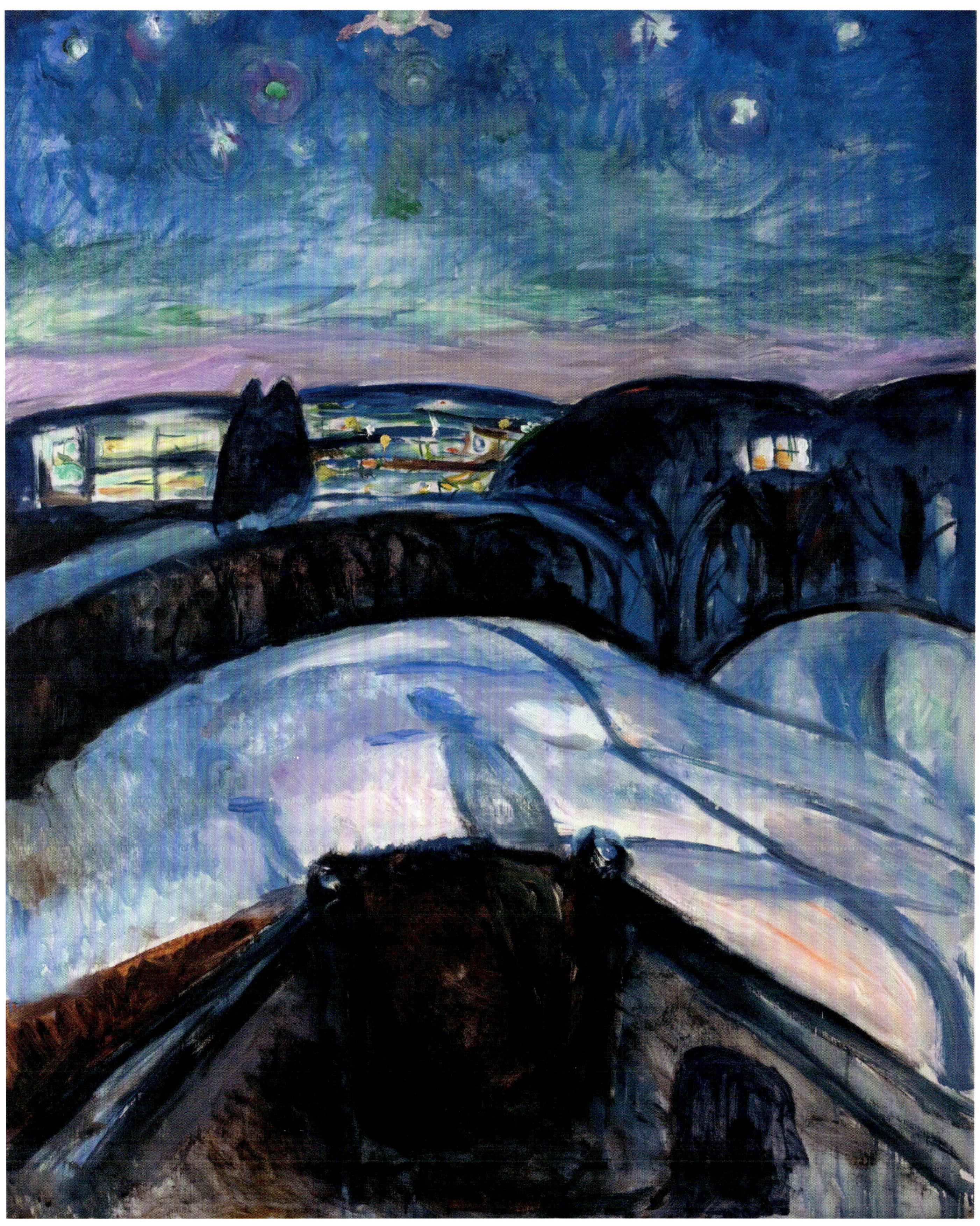

the foreground the steps and railing from Munch's porch lead down to the front yard, beyond which glow the lights of Oslo and the star-filled sky.[186] A prominent shadow at the center of the image is generally seen as Munch's own, a ghostly self-portrait cast outward onto the snowy ground. This identification is supported by related paintings, drawings, and prints discussed below, but it is important first to recognize it as the shadow of the distinctive newel post adorned with a large ball that anchored the bottom of the railing (fig. 130), and whose companion appears to the left in the painting. Munch is playing with the ambiguity of shadows, transforming the inanimate into the animate in a moment of slippage that enhances the uncanny quality of the overall scene. In a sketch from one of his notebooks, made around the same time as *Starry Night*, Munch underscores the headlike quality of the post ball, making it look like the back of a woman's head underneath a narrow-brimmed hat (fig.131). Next to the post Munch placed a postlike woman with her own brimmed hat, creating a standoff between the two "figures."[187]

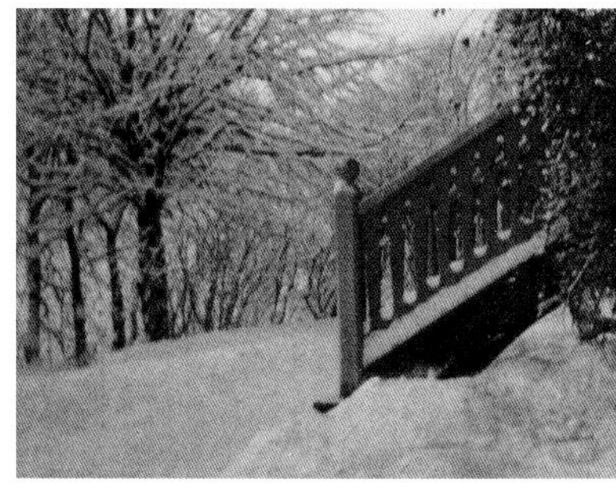

fig. 130 Munch, **Steps from veranda, Ekely** (detail), ca. 1927, gelatin silver print, 3⅛ x 4⅛ in. (7.8 x 10.5 cm). Munch Museum

Munch developed these echoes and ambiguities further in the many works related to *Starry Night* while also signaling the close connection to Ibsen's *John Gabriel Borkman*. Written in 1896, the play concerns a former bank president who was jailed for illegal speculation. Now released from prison, Borkman has exiled himself to the top floor of a house belonging to his wife's twin sister, Ella, his first love. His wife lives on the floor below, but the three do not speak to each other until a heartrending argument over the son whom Borkman and his wife had together. Borkman finally flees the house, only to suffer a fatal heart attack within view of the distant lights of the city; he dies convinced its inhabitants will one day vindicate him. Munch considered the play to be "the most powerful winter landscape in Scandinavian art."[188] At the same time, he understood Borkman as Ibsen's self-portrait—an embattled response to conservative countrymen who ignored or misunderstood him upon his return to Norway after twenty-seven years away and great international acclaim. Munch in turn identified closely with Ibsen's plight, especially in light of the chilly reception he, too, received after returning to Norway in 1909 following years abroad and his own international success. Munch invested his bitterness in the self-affirming precedent of Borkman, reading Ibsen's play entirely from the point of view of the title character, whom he considered a long-suffering victim of lesser minds.

A charcoal drawing from the same time as the *Starry Night II* painting (fig. 132) shows how Munch, in reengaging with this psychologically loaded landscape theme after some thirty years, infused the setting with "an entirely new constellation of symbols."[189] The view is the same as in the paintings, with the distant lights of Oslo seen from the porch of Ekely, but here the focus is on three long shadows stretching across the snow. Unattached to any architectural feature, they read solely as figures, related directly to the final scene of the play when Borkman leaves in a rage, followed by Ella and his wife. The rounded shadow on the right represents Borkman, who will soon die in the snow, while the two on the left are the shrouded sisters who will watch his demise.[190]

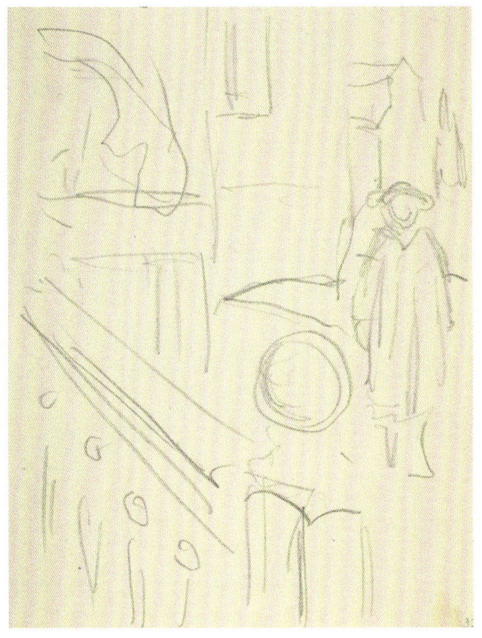

fig. 131 Munch, **Woman between the Veranda and Studio at Ekely**, 1922, crayon in sketchbook, 10⅜ x 8⅛ in. (26.5 x 20.6 cm). Munch Museum

fig. 132 Munch, **Starry Night**, 1922–24, charcoal on paper, 27⅝ x 24⅝ in. (70 x 62.5 cm). Munch Museum

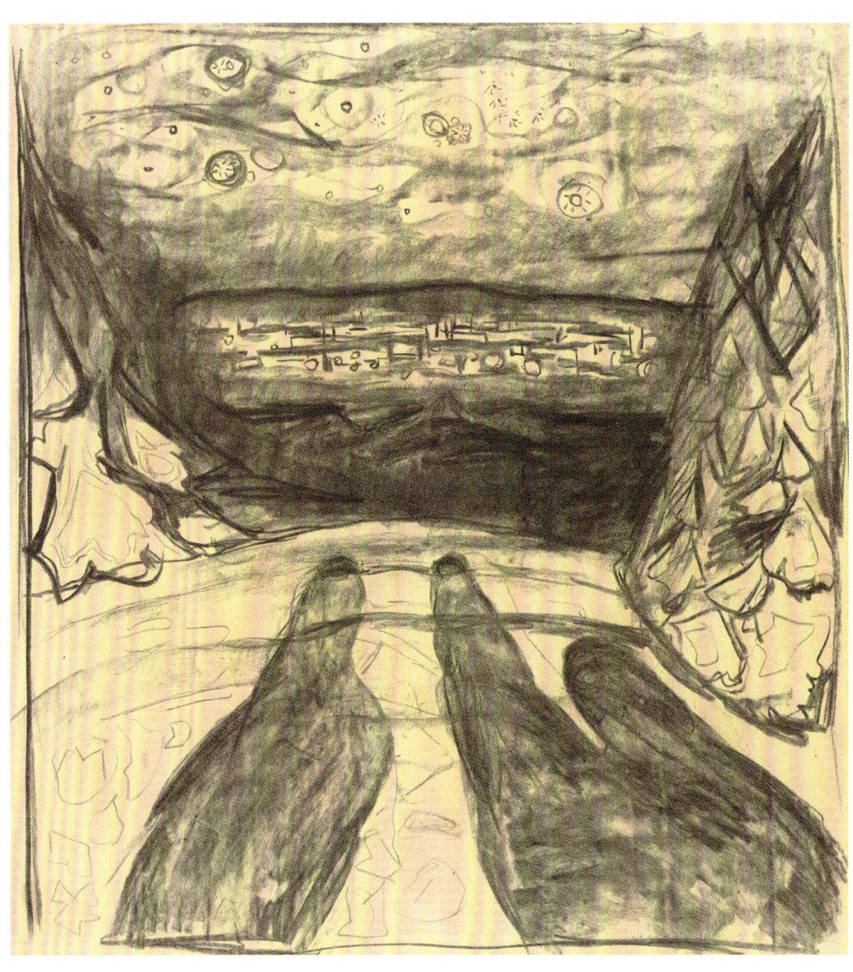

Munch illustrated Borkman's tragic denouement in a lithograph (fig. 133) that shows the sisters casting their forms across the snow toward the body slumped on the bench, in Ella's words "A dead man and two shadows." An arched top suggests both a church window and a tombstone. A woodcut from the same year (fig. 134) distills the scene to a solitary shadow darkening an abstracted landscape, alone and cut off from the longed-for redemption represented by the distant city lights. In adapting Borkman as his fictional precursor, the aging Munch found a vehicle to envisage his own death, thereby infusing the beauty of his beloved Ekely landscape with a sense of the deep pessimism that he carried throughout his life.

Munch made some eighty variations from 1909 into the 1930s on the theme of Borkman, almost all concerning the final scene. One of them (fig. 135) shows Borkman in the flesh rather than as a shadow, about to descend Munch's own stairs, identified by the Swiss-style detail of the railing. The shadow of the newel post below echoes Borkman's own. Ella stands on the porch, ghostly beside the yellow electric light. Borkman's face in profile resonates with another shadow that appears in the immediate foreground of the *Starry Night II* painting, a

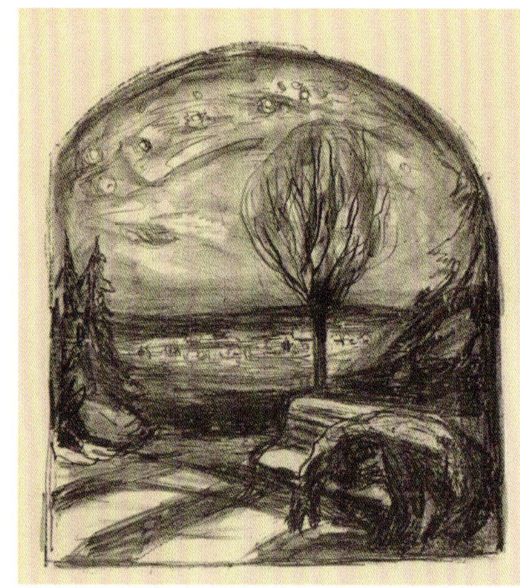

fig. 133 Munch, **Starry Night: John Gabriel Borkman**, 1930, lithograph, 29¾ x 22 in. (75.8 x 56.1 cm). Munch Museum

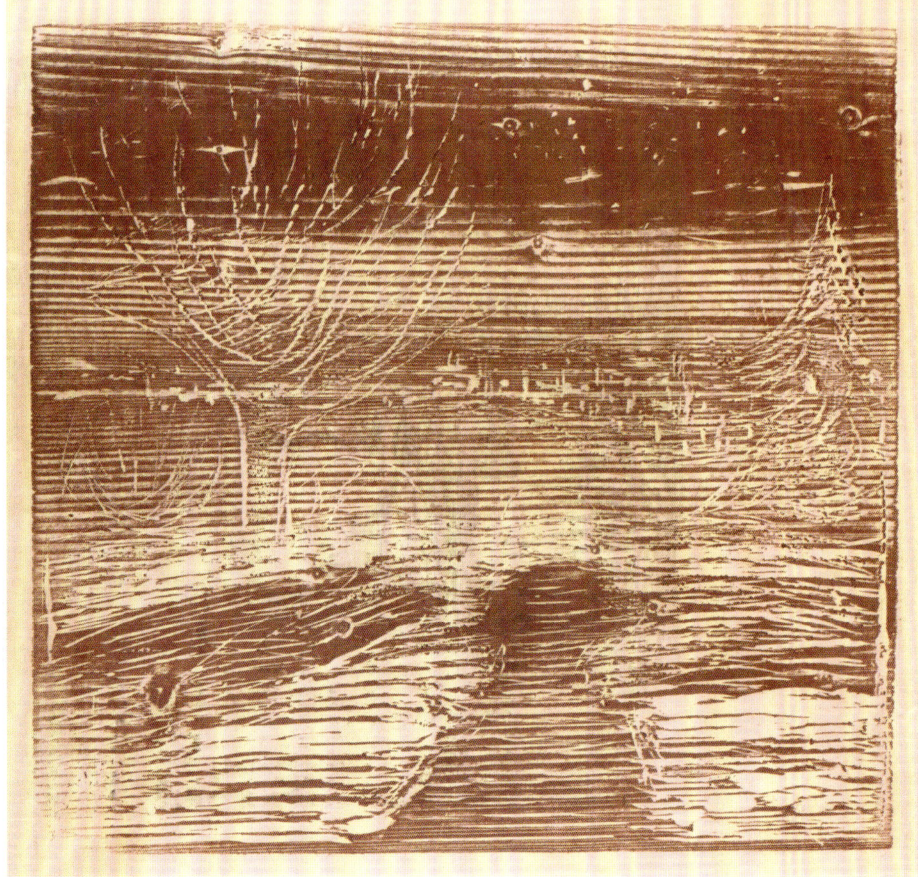

fig. 134 Munch, **Starry Night**, 1930, woodcut, 19⅝ x 20½ in. (50 x 52 cm). Munch Museum

second self-portrait within the same scene that Munch cast against a light patch on the side railing (fig. 136).

This shadow profile may at first be overlooked, but it is more defined than the featureless face of Borkman and should be seen in relation to Munch's embrace of his own strong nose and jutting chin in many of his other self-portraits. A series of photographs from 1930, which Munch took by holding the camera at arm's length, particularly plays up his distinctive features, with some even set against the same porch railing (fig. 137).[191]

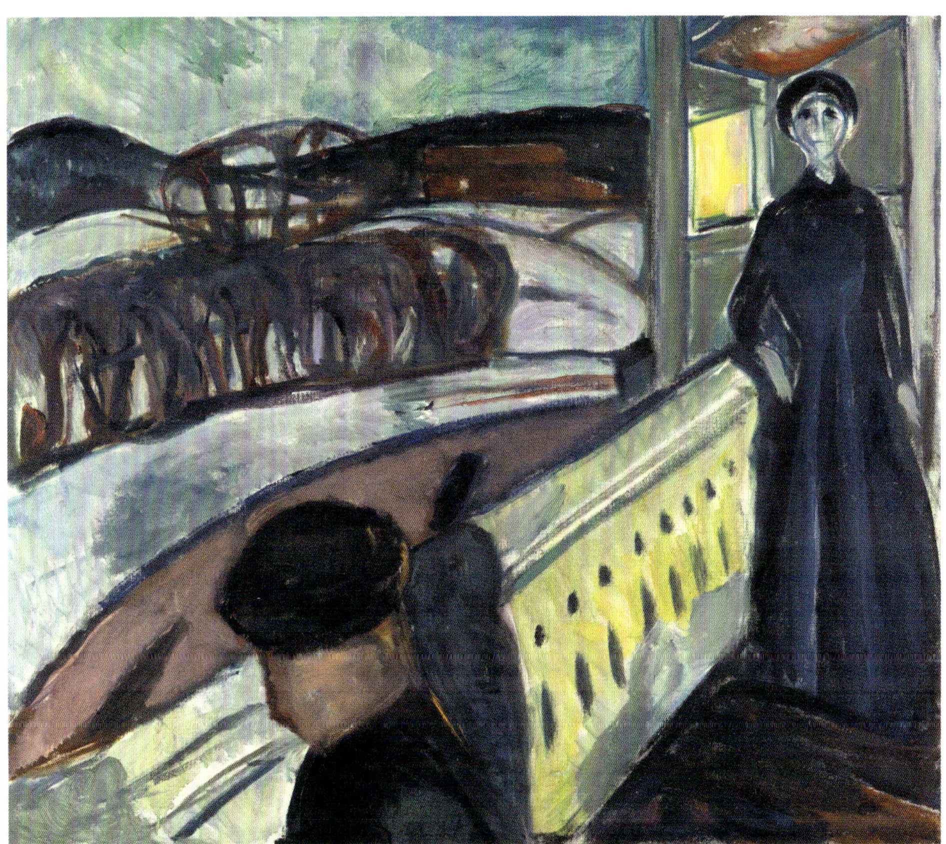

fig. 135 Munch, **On the Veranda Stairs**, 1922–24, oil on canvas, 32 ¼ x 37 ½ in. (82 x 95.5 cm). Munch Museum

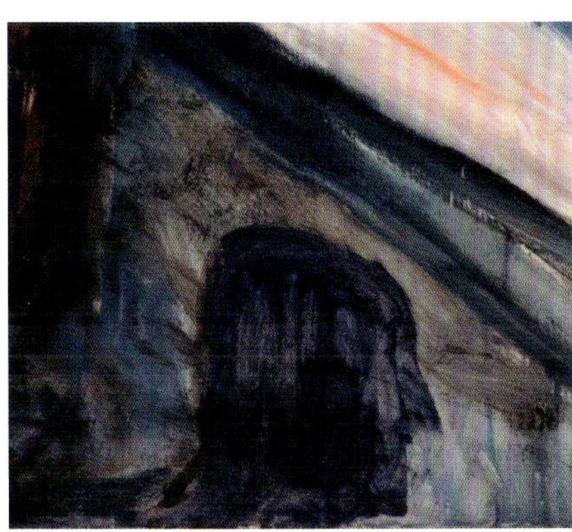

fig. 136 Munch, **Starry Night** (detail), 1922–24

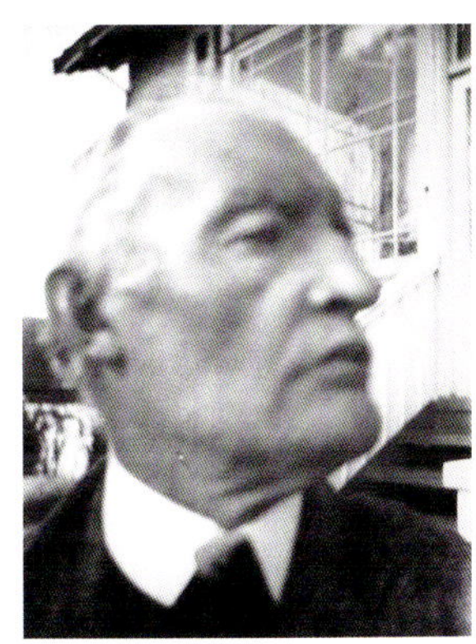

fig. 137 Munch, **Self-portrait in front of veranda steps, Ekely**, 1930, gelatin silver print, 4 ¼ x 3 in. (10.7 X 7.7 cm). Munch Museum

Munch's experiments with photography are a lesser-known side of his work. They were not included in the New York and Washington exhibitions, and the first substantial scholarly treatment was not translated into English until a few years after Johns completed *The Seasons*.[192] They merit attention here for the way they deepen the understanding of Munch's fascination with thresholds between the material and immaterial world—which in turn offers another interpretative angle on Johns's *The Seasons*. Some of Munch's photographs may have served as aids to his paintings, but many more were experiments with the properties of the medium. A full third of them are self-portraits of one type or another, including shadows and "ghosts": images that explore double exposure and transparency. An image of Munch on the beach in Warnemünde, Germany (fig. 138), shows him with his model Rosa Meissner. Munch had instructed her sister, Olga, to take two exposures without advancing the film.[193] The overlap creates a dreamlike effect of dislocation from familiar space and time. The figures' doubles hover over them, simultaneously intruding and taking their leave.

Another image from the same trip seems at first a mistake, showing only the sisters' legs and feet (fig. 139). Munch, however, processed and printed the

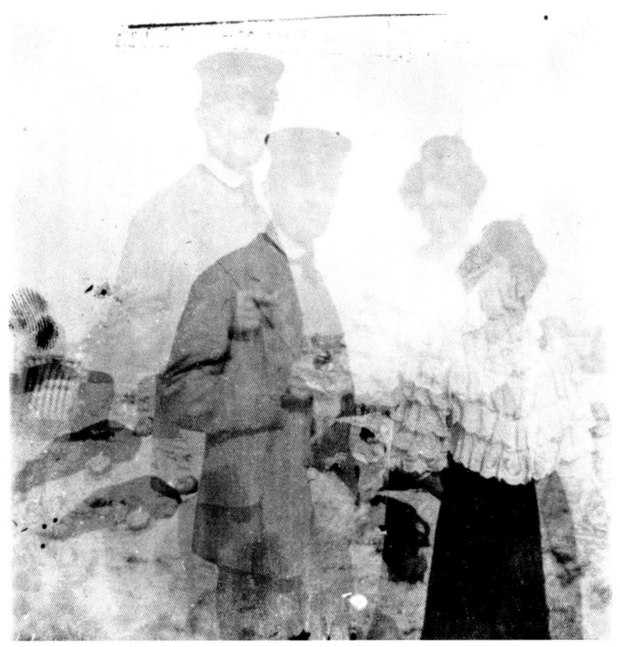

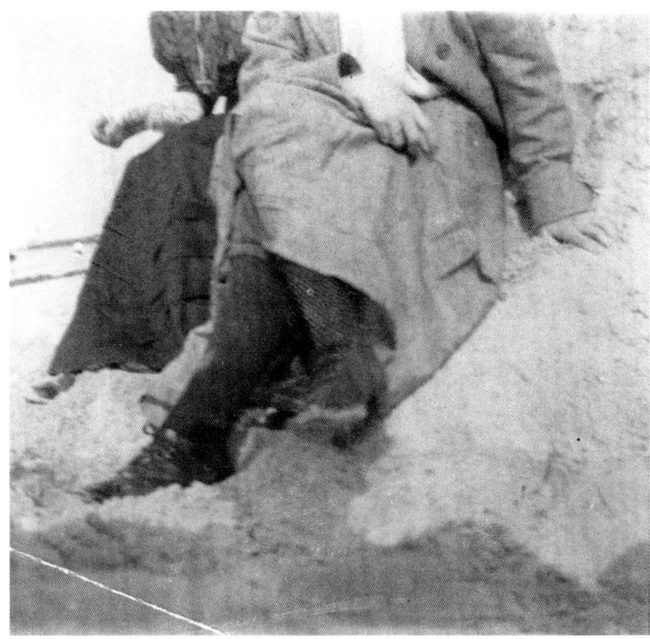

image, and kept it throughout his life.[194] A close examination reveals that the true subject is his large shadow in the foreground, darkening Olga's legs and joining the ephemeral to the corporeal. A later image of Munch's old dog, Fips (fig. 140), further explored this intrusion of the spectral into the everyday world with the artist's shadow sporting a hat and looming in from the right like death coming for the aged, unsuspecting beast.

Many of Munch's photographs belong to a group he called the *Fatal Destiny* portfolio. Produced in 1902–8 during his initial burst of photographic activity, these images furthered his interest in an aesthetic of dematerialization, which first appeared in his paintings of the late 1890s with thinly applied paint and exposure to the elements. The photographs offer some of his earliest explorations of transparency as a metaphor for what lies beyond the visible. As Munch declared, "Why should other beings that are physically less substantial than us not exist, surround us and move around us. The souls of the dead, the souls of our loved ones or of demonic spirits."[195] Munch's images were inspired by his interest in spirit photographs, X-rays, electricity, and radio waves.[196] These varied sciences and

fig. 138 **Edvard Munch with Rosa Meissner on the beach in Warnemünde**, 1907, probably photographed by Olga Meissner, collodion print, 3⅜ x 3⅛ in. (8.5 x 8 cm). Munch Museum

fig. 139 Munch, **Rosa and Olga Meissner on the beach in Warnemünde**, 1907, collodion print, 3½ x 3½ in. (9 x 8.9 cm). Munch Museum

fig. 140 Munch, **Fips**, ca. 1930, gelatin silver print, 3⅛ x 4⅝ in. (8 x 11.7 cm). Munch Museum

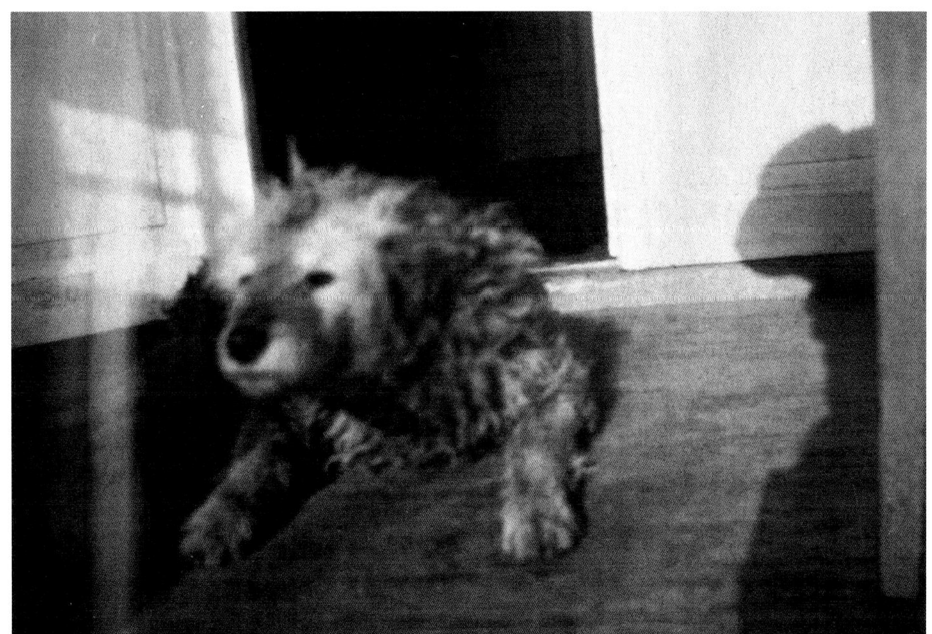

pseudosciences, tapping into unseen worlds, reinforced his preoccupation with life's evanescence and the possibility of existence beyond the material.

In one of his first photographs, Munch is barely visible in the back corner of his room (fig. 141), lying in bed under a white sheet. Blurring shows that he moved in and out of range during exposure,[197] creating a melancholy image that addresses the thin line between presence and absence while underscoring the bed as the site of passage. Some twenty-five years later, during a second burst of photographic activity, Munch again showed himself in a state of diffusion suggesting physical, or metaphysical, transition (fig.142). Eggum surmises that the camera probably lacked an automatic release, so that Munch would have gotten up and looked into the lens at close quarters before ending the exposure, producing the pale, enlarged image of his face that overlaps the painting at the right.[198] The effect is of a spirit escaping the body in a light haze still faintly endowed with the artist's features.

In 1930, Munch suffered from hemorrhaging in his right eye, adding to damage already sustained in his left. In keeping with his deep interest in the mechanics of vision, he produced a number of works, mostly watercolors, exploring the visual impressions caused by the pathological changes.[199] A series of self-portrait photographs from this same time also seem related to his simultaneously fascinated

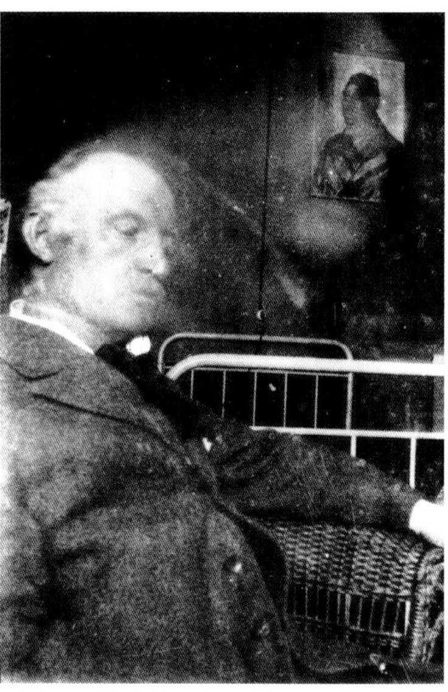

fig. 142 Munch, **Self-portrait in wicker chair by the bed, Ekely,** 1927, photograph. Munch Museum

fig. 141 Munch, **Self-portrait in bed,** ca. 1902, collodion print, 3 ⅞ x 3 ⅝ in. (10 x 9.5 cm). Munch Museum

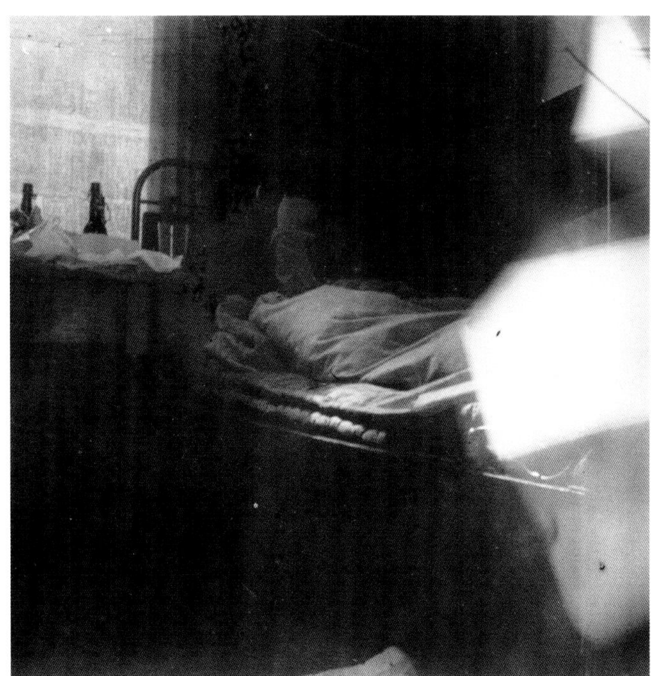

fig. 143 Munch, **Self-portrait in front of two watercolors, Ekely,** ca. 1930, gelatin silver print, 3 ½ x 4 ⅜ in. (8.8 x 11.2 cm). Munch Museum

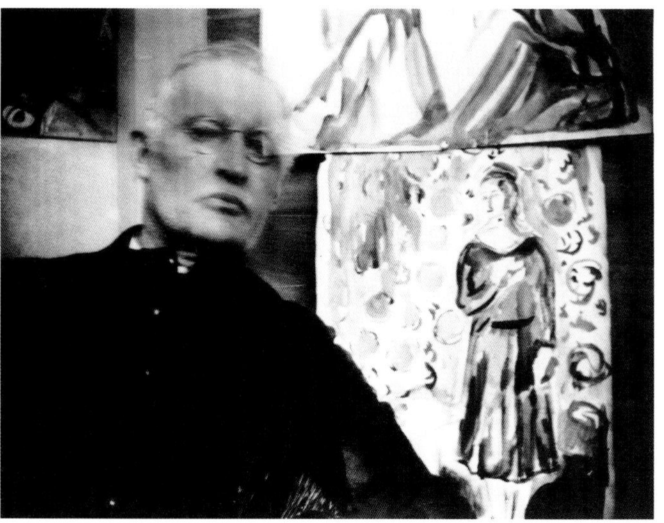

and anxious response to his deteriorating vision. In several of these images (e.g. fig. 143), the corner of paintings strategically align with his eye, drawing attention to his identity as one who sees while also piercing the organ of sight. At the same time, Munch used the effect of transparency to join himself more closely with his work.

One of Munch's last photographs takes the effects of transparency and ghostliness to a heightened level of expressive abstraction. It is from the same sitting as a photograph that shows him stretching his camera arm forward (fig. 144), the blurred and hollowed-out eye sockets creating a morbid presence that recalls the lithograph from a year or two before (fig. 126). For the second, more abstract image (fig. 145), Munch employed overlapping exposures.[200] Now the dark shape rising from the chair replaces the figure entirely, as if capturing pure spirit free of its husk. Fittingly, the barely visible painting on the rear wall is *Metabolism* (fig. 61), one of Munch's great commentaries on the underlying forces of life.

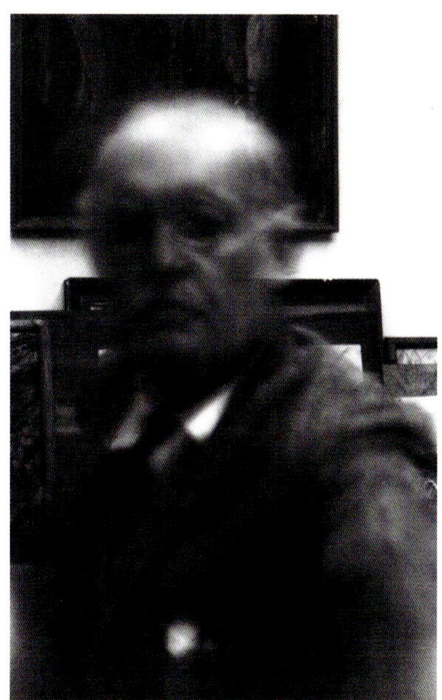

fig. 144 Munch, **Self-portrait in front of** *Metabolism*, **Ekely,** 1931–32, gelatin silver print, 5⅜ x 3⅛ in. (13.5 x 7.8 cm). Munch Museum

fig. 145 Munch, *Metabolism* with **shadow and reflections, Ekely,** 1931–32, gelatin silver print, 5⅝ x 3½ in. (14.5 x 9 cm). Munch Museum

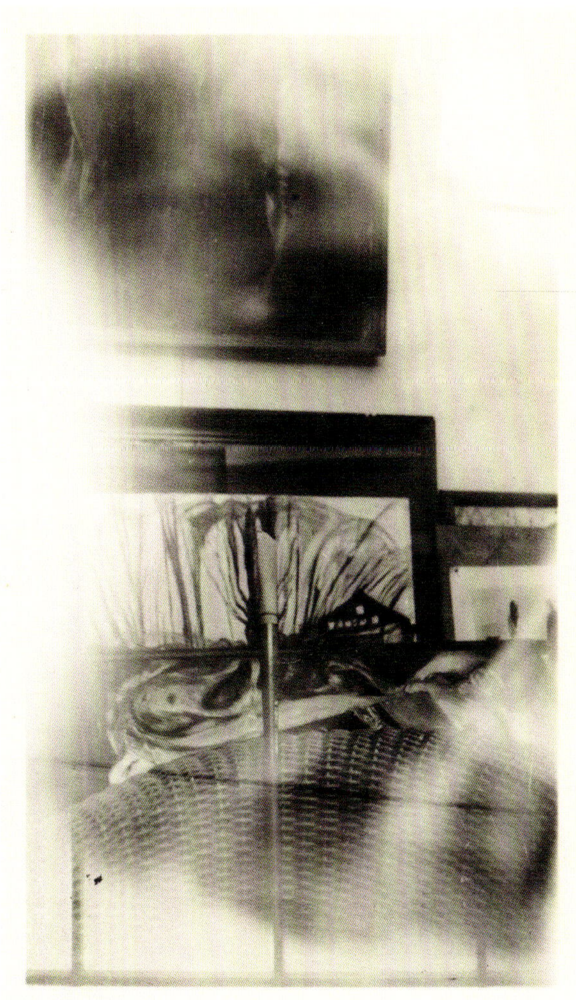

Munch continued to explore the intersection of shadows and ghosts until the end of his life. A *Self-Portrait* from his last years (fig. 146) includes a striking shadow that recalls the profile in the foreground of *Starry Night*. Again framed in a lighter zone, the shadow assumes a quality of independence: its fixity offers a stoic contrast to the flesh and blood artist, whose flushed face, unkempt hair, wild eyes, and slightly parted lips convey panic in the face of the inevitable. This oil was followed by another of Munch's last self-portraits, a small gouache painting that shows him in the no-man's zone between night and morning (fig. 147). Yet he appears erect and alert, as if drawn toward an unseen presence. Yellow light transforms his gaunt features into a cadaverous mask; his shadow seems to stand, semidetached, behind him, portending his demise while also recalling the black angel of death he described as attending him throughout his life.[201]

While shadows are a central motif in Munch's work, he is not alone among modern and contemporary artists in embracing them as an expressive device. In

fig. 146 Munch, **Self-Portrait**, 1940–43, oil on canvas, 22⅗ x 30⅞ in. (57.5 x 78.5 cm). Munch Museum

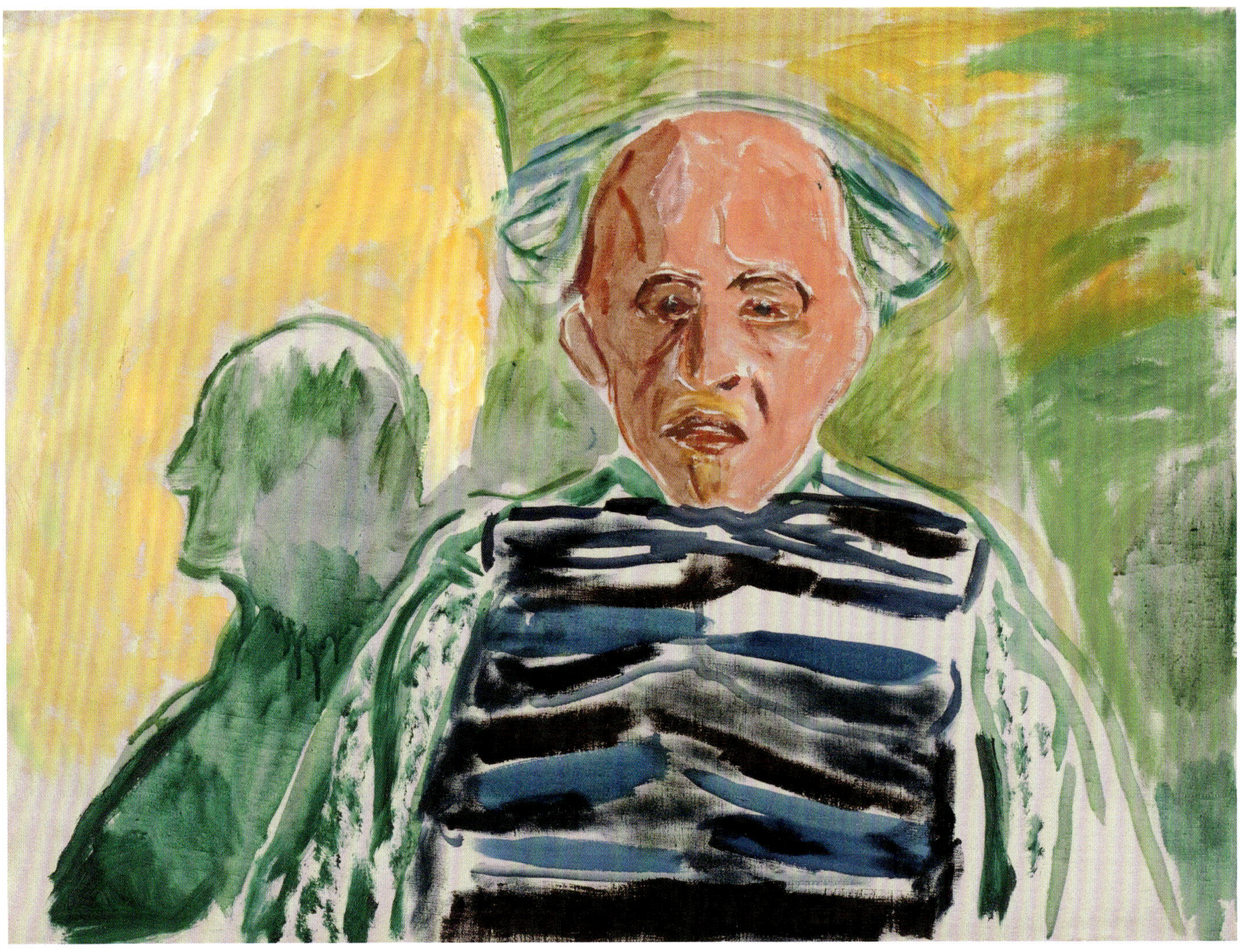

addition to Picasso, other notable examples include Giorgio de Chirico's metaphysical cityscapes; Duchamp's *Tu m'* (Yale University Art Gallery); Magritte's landscapes that confuse day and night and his figurative images such as *The Thought Which Sees,* 1965 (MoMA); and Warhol's *Shadow* series from the late 1970s.[202] An exclusive or one-to-one correspondence is not necessary to allow that a connection between Munch's and Johns's self-portrait shadows may exist. By the mid-1980s, when Johns painted *The Seasons,* he had nearly a decade of engagement with Munch's work. His involvement had progressed from selectively using isolated motifs to internalizing an expanded range of Munch-related themes and motifs. Whether recognizable or hidden, the echoes and allusions are woven into the fabric of Johns's work by his continual reworkings, where they become completely his own while also continuing to resonate with overtones of Munch.

That the shadows in Johns's *The Seasons* are self-portraits, however, is an odd claim when considered further.[203] Although traced from his shadow, their flat, frontal, and

fig. 147 Munch, **Quarter Past Two at Night: Self-Portrait**, 1940–43, gouache and watercolor, 11 7⁄8 x 19 5⁄8 in. (30.2 x 50 cm). Munch Museum

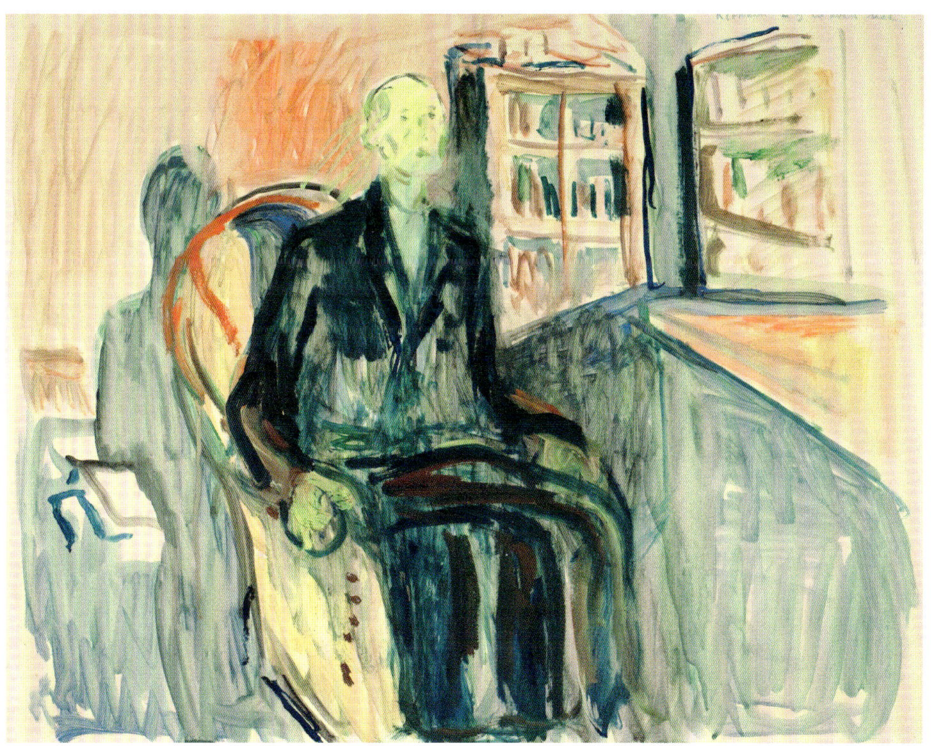

rigid character makes a rather oblique claim to individuality. From antiquity on, it is the profile shadow that represents the sitter, as in many of Munch's self-portraits. In his *Natural History* (ca. 77–79 CE), the Roman author Pliny the Elder located the origin of painting in the story of a girl tracing the shadow of her lover's profile thrown on a wall by lamplight, an act done in anticipation of his departure for war. Thus, painting from its beginning is connected both to the shadow and the theme of presence and absence.[204]

Johns's shadows share in this history to an extent. Like Pliny's story, his images derive not from direct observation of the actual figure but from its projection onto a surface, which reduces its volume to a silhouette—thus, like the flag, crosshatching, and images of *Painted Bronze,* we have another instance of Johns's interest in the representation of a representation. In addition, the rudimentary nature of Johns's shadow seems a reference to beginnings, and in this sense *The Seasons* can be seen as addressing the theme of painting's origins. But, characteristic of Johns, he also

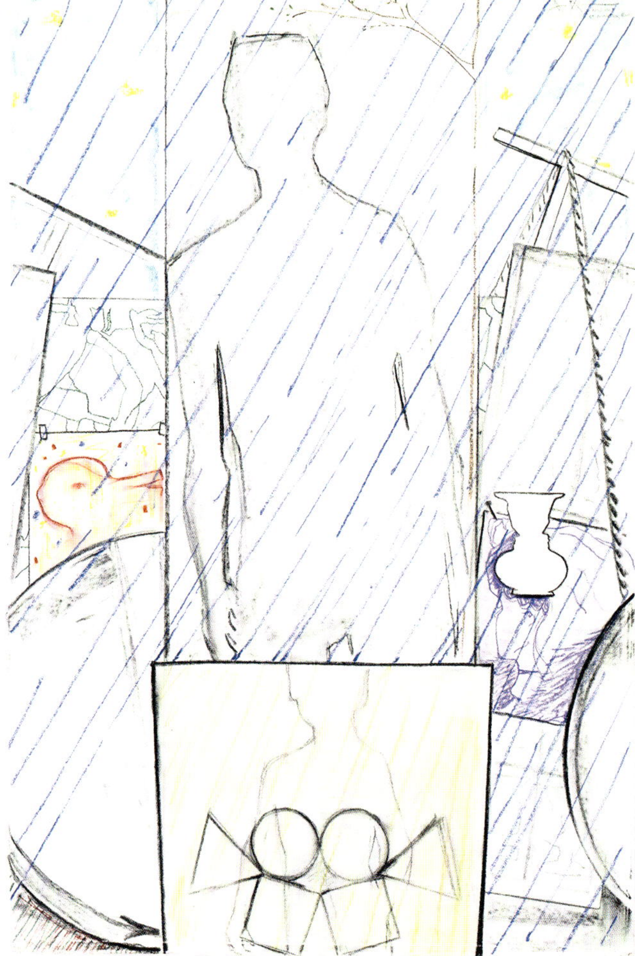

fig. 148 Johns, **Spring**, 1986, pastel and charcoal on paper, 41 ⅝ x 27 ⅞ in. (105.7 x 70.8 cm). Collection of the artist

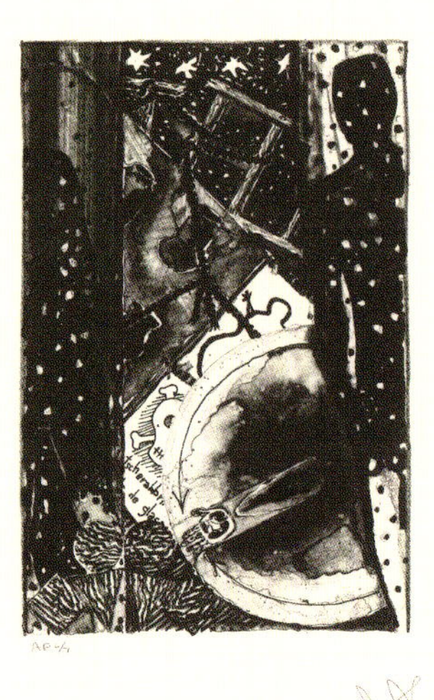

fig. 149 Johns, **Winter**, 1986, intaglio, 16 x 12 in. (40.6 x 30.5 cm). Courtesy Universal Limited Art Editions

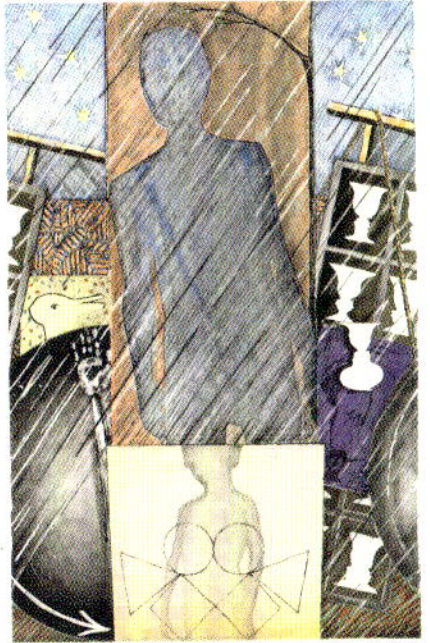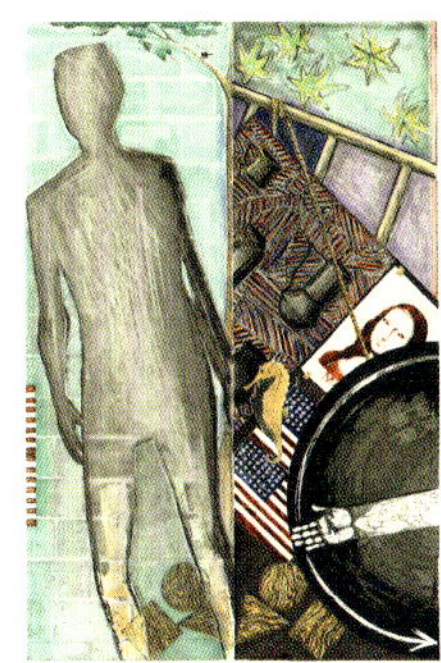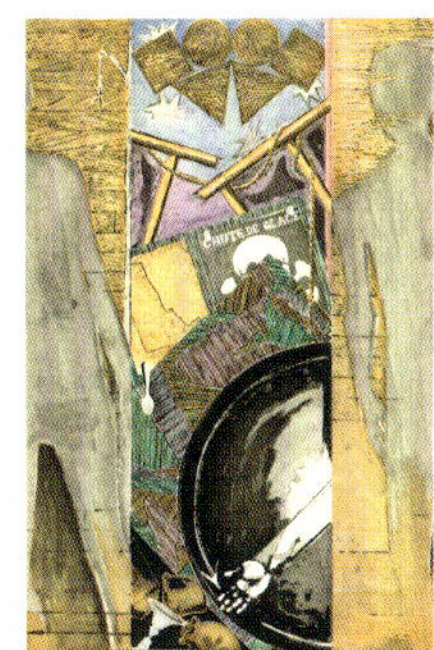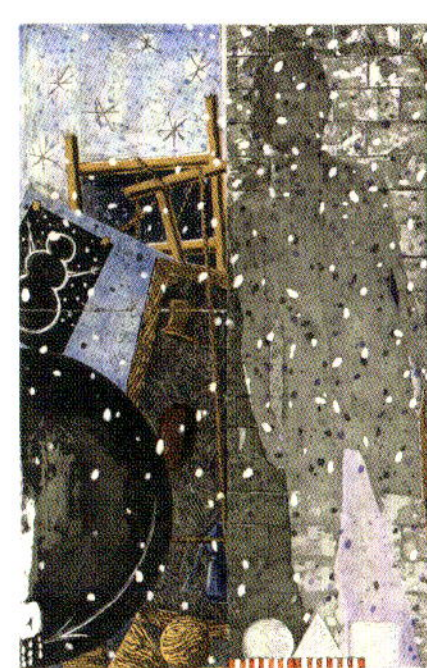

fig. 150 Johns, **The Seasons (Spring, Summer, Fall, Winter)**, 1987, intaglios, 26 x 19 in. (66 x 48.3 cm) each. Courtesy Universal Limited Art Editions

fig. 151 Johns, **The Seasons**, 1989/1990, acrylic over intaglio on paper, 26 ¼ x 57 ³⁄₁₀ in. (66.7 x 146.2 cm). Private collection

refuses this lineage. For the girl who traced her lover's shadow, similitude—and thus the profile—were essential. The shadow was meant as a mnemonic to keep the soon-absent lover present. While Johns has incorporated profile shadows into his work to represent others, when it came to himself, he opted for frontality.[205] Johns's shadows are at once him and not him, traced from his projection but offering very little in their details by which to recognize the subject.

In addition, unlike Munch's expressively distorted shadows, Johns's are nearly unchanged from work to work, except in their surface qualities and position within the image. This fixity is underscored by the illogic of encountering nearly the same density of shadow across seasonally changing conditions of light and weather, conditions that Johns emphasized in several drawing and print versions (figs. 148 and 149).

In contrast to this static quality, Johns also underscored the insubstantiality of the shadows by allowing glimpses of the surfaces behind them (figs. 150 and 151). Using transparency to connect them to their environments, Johns reinforced a sense of his figure as both shadow and ghost, recalling the dual nature of the figures in Munch's paintings and photographs.

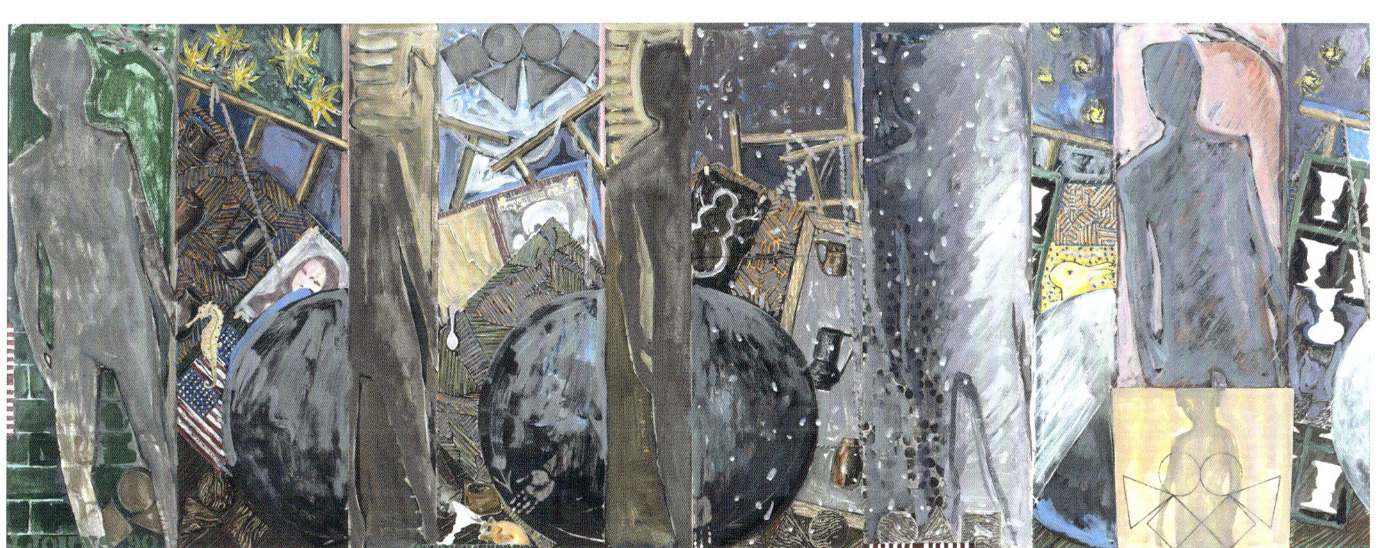

A strange detail that is little discussed, if at all, in the Johns literature is that his shadows appear to have genitals. This incongruous addition connects the figures to the late crosshatch paintings such as *Tantric Details* (figs. 68, 69, and 70). It also marks them as decidedly male, and thus aligned both to Johns as a gendered individual and to his identity as a generative force, endowed with the capacity to create the artistic progeny that surround him in these works.[206] It is worth noting that the shadow on the left side of *Fall* (fig. 117), although echoing the outline of all the other shadows, appears to be facing away from the front, as indicated by faint buttocks lines. It is not simply a split shadow, as usually described, but split and reversed, suggesting a connection of the shadows in *The Seasons* with the *Skin* drawings, in which Johns pressed his naked oiled body against paper and then covered the surface with charcoal. A three-quarters-length work from 1975 (fig. 152) parallels the stiffness and frontality of *The Seasons* shadows, while two works from 1973 (figs. 153 and 154) show Johns pairing images of his front and back just below the waist.

A final question concerns the shadows' orientation. They read initially as upright figures, but it should be remembered that they were first traced on the ground. And although the surfaces behind the figures read as walls, these originally derived from floors in Johns's various homes and studios. Johns enhanced the impression of recumbency by enclosing the figures within spaces mostly separate from those of the possessions, recalling the box containing the red armprint in the 1981 *Savarin* lithograph. The realism of the possessions contrasts with the shadows. They are substantial, tactile, and detailed, while the shadows are flat, translucent, and generalized—a difference that underscores a discontinuity of place and time. This effect is even more pronounced in several drawings (figs. 155, 156, and 157) in which the figures seem consigned to sepulchral realms remote from the earthly domain of the objects. Beside these remote ghost-shadows, the possessions appear subjected to the kind of kill-or-cure treatment Munch prescribed for his own creations. They are being exposed to the elements, literally seasoned, to withstand the test of time on their own, independent of their creator, or to have their eventual demise resolved all the sooner.

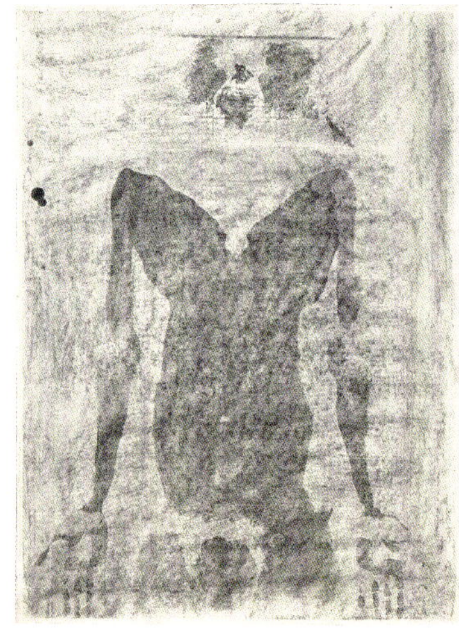

fig. 152 Johns, **Skin**, 1975, charcoal and oil on paper, 41 ¾ x 30 ¾ in. (106.1 x 78.1 cm). Collection of Richard Serra and Clara Weyergraf-Serra

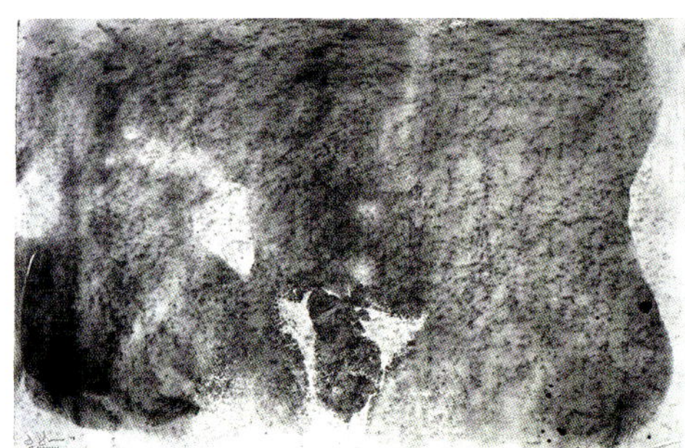

fig. 153 Johns, **Skin I**, 1973, charcoal and oil on paper, 25 ½ x 40 ¼ in. (64.8 x 102.2 cm). Collection of the artist

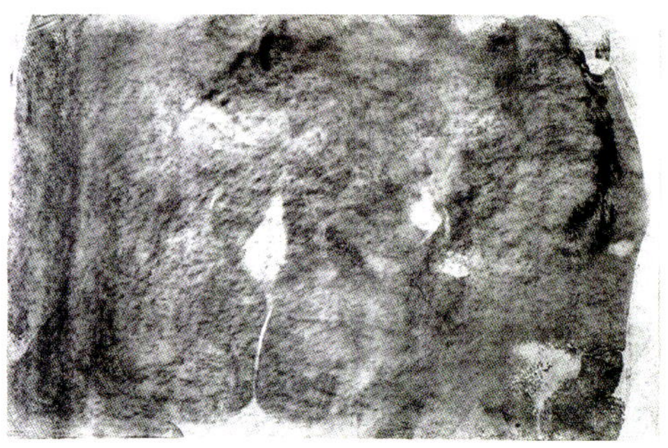

fig. 154 Johns, **Skin II**, 1973, charcoal and oil on paper, 25 ½ x 40 ¼ in. (64.8 x 102.2 cm). Collection of the artist

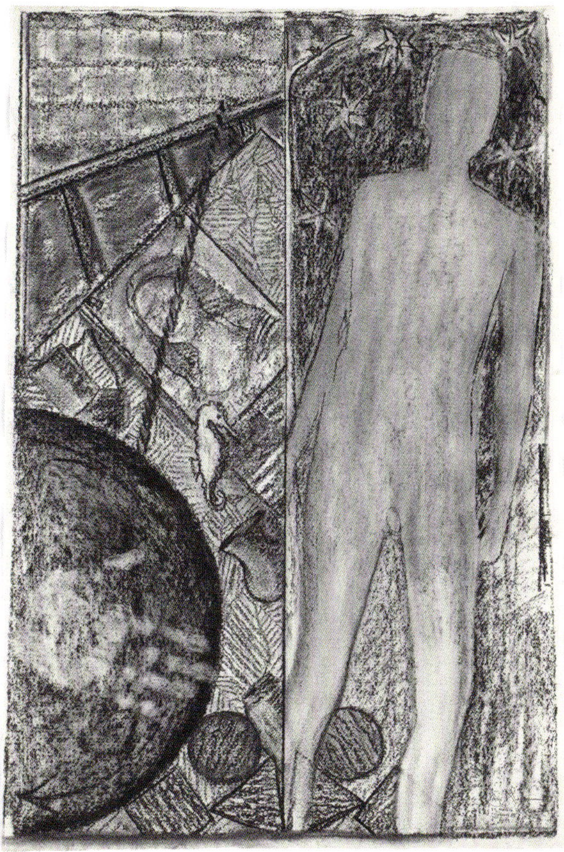

fig. 155 Johns, **Summer**, 1985, charcoal
on paper, 30⅜ x 20⅜ in. (77.2 x 51.8 cm).
Collection of the artist

fig. 156 Johns, **Untitled**, 1988, ink on plastic,
26½ x 19½ in. (67.3 x 49.6 cm). Collection of
the artist

fig. 157 Johns, **Winter**, 1986, charcoal on paper,
42 x 29⅞ in. (106.7 x 75.8 cm). Collection of
Julie and Edward J. Minskoff

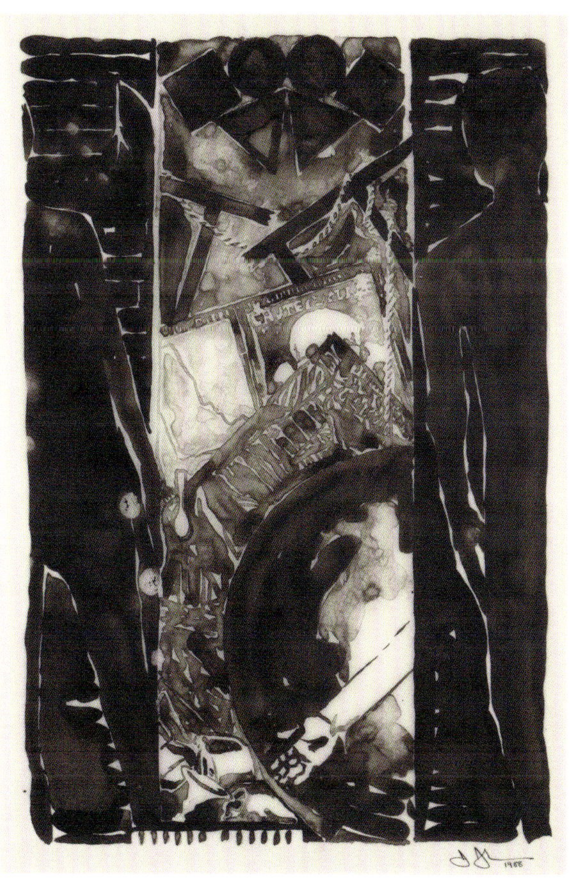

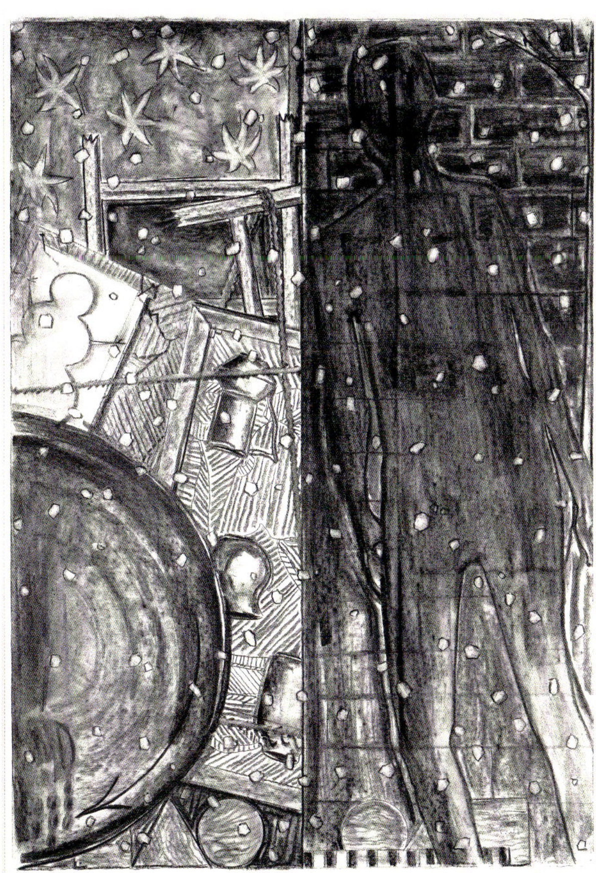

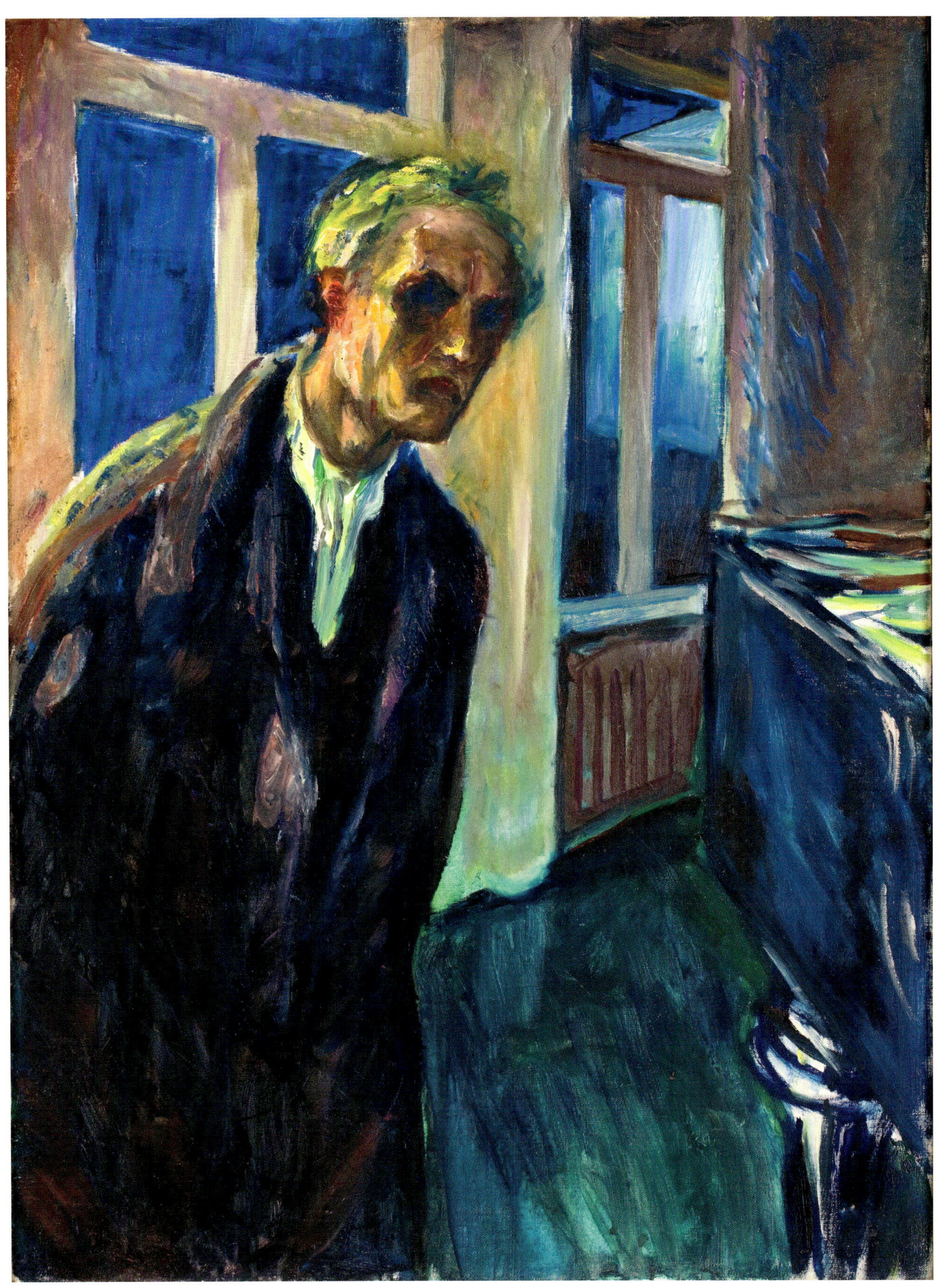

Conclusion

In speaking about the relationship of his *Tantric Detail* works to their source of inspiration, Johns explained,

> Seeing a thing can sometimes trigger the mind to make another thing. In some instances the new work may include, as a sort of subject matter, references to the thing that was seen. And, because works of painting tend to share many aspects, working itself may initiate memories of other works. Naming or pointing to these ghosts sometimes seems a way to stop their nagging.[207]

In a similar way, Munch's work presented Johns with ghosts—particularly nagging ones in their capacity for triggering the mind to make associations that in turn opened doors to new references and connections. Johns pointed to and named these ghosts in any number of ways over nearly a decade, from 1977 to around 1986. At a crossroads in the middle of his career and after a decade of abstraction, they offered him a way forward. While far from the only source that Johns mined during this period, Munch's work provided one important path into the greater personal and expressive content of the 1980s—not just in the most recognized motifs of the red armprint and the late crosshatch paintings bearing Munch's title, but in themes of self-representation, the passage of time, the proximity of death, and the lasting impact of art. Paradoxically, despite early efforts to reject all that was not his, Johns has often borrowed from other artists as a way to find his own voice. It is important to recognize in these borrowings the depth of his engagement with Munch—an artist of seemingly opposite concerns—to fully understand the intuitive, incremental, and often enigmatic nature of Johns's creative process.

fig. 158 Munch, **The Night Wanderer**, 1923–24, oil on canvas, 35 ½ x 26 ¾ in. (90 x 68 cm). Munch Museum

Endnotes

1. There have been a number of exhibitions and publications devoted to Munch's influence on contemporary art. See Maarten Bertheux, *Munch and after Munch* (Amsterdam: Stedelijk Museum; Oslo: Munch Museum, 1996); Christian Gether and Holger Reenberg, eds.; René Lauritsen, trans., *Echoes of the Scream* (Ishøj, Denmark: Arken Museum of Modern Art; Oslo: Munch Museum, 2001); Rosemarie E. Pahlke, ed., *Munch Revisited: Edvard Munch and the Art of Today* (Dortmund, Germany: Museum am Ostwall; Bielefeld, Germany: Kerber 2005); Patricia Berman and Pari Stave, *Munch | Warhol and the Multiple Image* (New York: American-Scandinavian Foundation, 2013); and Tina Yarborough, "The Strange Case of Postmodernism's Appropriation of Edvard Munch," in *Edvard Munch: An Anthology*, ed. Erik Mørstad (Oslo: Unipub forlag/Oslo Academic Press, 2006).

2. For an introduction, see Roberta Bernstein, " 'Seeing a Thing Can Sometimes Trigger the Mind to Make Another Thing,' " in *Jasper Johns: A Retrospective*, ed. Kirk Varnedoe (New York: Museum of Modern Art, 1996).

3. Judith Goldman's untitled text in *Jasper Johns: 17 Monotypes* (West Islip, New York: Universal Limited Art Editions, 1982) is a notable exception and contains the most substantial discussion of Johns and Munch prior to this publication. See also Mark Rosenthal, *Jasper Johns: Work Since 1974* (New York: Thames and Hudson; Philadelphia: Philadelphia Museum of Art, 1988), 50–54; Bernstein, " 'Seeing a Thing,' " 50; Nan Rosenthal and Ruth E. Fine, *The Drawings of Jasper Johns* (Washington, DC: National Gallery of Art, 1990), 260; and Yarborough, "Strange Case."

4. The major works with direct reference include the two 1978 *Savarin* monotypes with skeleton arms; the 1981 *Savarin* monotype with the red arm; the seventeen *Savarin* monotypes from 1982; and the three large *Between the Clock and the Bed* paintings from 1981–83. Indirect references include the Whitney poster and related prints with wood grain, as well as the numerous other works with more tangential connections discussed in the essay. Secondary works with direct references include all the drawings and prints related to *Between the Clock and the Bed*; see fn. 139.

5. *The More Things Change: An Interview with Jasper Johns,* May 30th, 2014; http://www. aperture.org/blog/jasper-johns-interview/. See also Christophe Cherix and Anne Temkin, *Jasper Johns: Regrets* (New York: MoMA, 2014), 17.

6. While living primarily in Berlin during these years, he traveled extensively in Europe and often returned to Norway.

7. Prior to another peak of emotive painting by American and European Neo-Expressionists in the early 1980s.

8. Johns first arrived in New York from South Carolina in 1948. After serving in the army he returned to New York for good in 1953.

9. Quoted in Vivien Raynor, "Jasper Johns: 'I have attempted to develop my thinking in such a way that the work I've done is not me,' " 1973, in *Jasper Johns: Writings, Sketchbook Notes, Interviews,* ed. Kirk Varnedoe (New York: MoMA, 1996), 145.

10. Quoted in "His Heart Belongs to Dada," 1959, and Edmund White, "Enigmas and Double Visions," 1977, in ibid., 82, 154.

11. See ibid., 52.

12. Quoted in Peter Fuller, "Jasper Johns Interviewed Part II," 1978, ibid., 187.

13. Ragna Stang, *Edvard Munch: The Man and His Art* (New York: Abbeville, 1979), 11.

14. Ibid., 22.

15. Ibid., 11.

16. *Edvard Munch,* organized by the Fogg Art Museum, Harvard University, Cambridge, Massachusetts, with the Institute of Contemporary Art, Boston, traveled extensively within the United States, including MoMA, June 30–August 13, 1950. In " 'Seeing a Thing,' " fn. 60, Bernstein notes that Johns saw the exhibition, and Johns confirmed this in conversation with the author, May 5, 2013. The first solo exhibition of Munch's work in the United States took place seven years earlier—during Munch's lifetime. It was not a career survey but rather consisted of thirty-four prints curated by Una E. Johnson and shown at the Brooklyn Museum of Art, December 18, 1942–February 22, 1943.

17. See Øivind Storm Bjerke, "Munch's Chinese Box: Setting up Munch as a World Artist," in *Edvard Munch: 1863–1944*, ed. Mai Britt Guleng et al. (Milan: Skira; Oslo: National Museum of Art, Architecture and Design and Munch Museum, 2013).

18. "I probably didn't know the work at all. That's probably what drew me to see it." In conversation with the author, June 20, 2014.

19. Ibid. The exhibitions were *The Graphic Work of Edvard Munch*, MoMA, February 6–March 3, 1957; *Edvard Munch (Retrospective)*, Guggenheim Museum, October 15, 1965–February 20, 1966; and *The Prints of Edvard Munch*, MoMA, February 13–April 29, 1973.

20. *Jasper Johns: Lithographs,* MoMA, December 22, 1970–May 3, 1971, and *The Prints of Edvard Munch,* MoMA, February 13–April 29, 1973.

21. Davison Art Center, Wesleyan University, Middletown, Connecticut, January 25–March 2, 1975. The catalogue checklist indicates that a Lovis Corinth print hung in between, but Field believes this is incorrect.

22. See Yarborough, "Strange Case," 193–94.

23. See Berman and Stave, *Munch | Warhol*.

24. More accurately described as linear hatching, since the bundles of parallel lines almost never cross, it is usually called crosshatching by popular consensus, including Johns's own. See Annelie Pohlen, "Interview mit Jasper Johns," 1978, in Varnedoe, *Writings,* 172.

25. Michael Crichton, *Jasper Johns*, rev. ed. (New York: Abrams, 1994), 57.

26. Sarah Kent, "Jasper Johns: Strokes of Genius," 1990, in Varnedoe, *Writings,* 259.

27. Varnedoe suggested, in a comment with no citation, that it was in 1971: "He has said he glimpsed such markings on a passing car, and knew immediately (though they only entered his art a year later) that he would use the motif." See "Introduction: A Sense of Life," in Varnedoe, *Retrospective,* 269. Roberta Bernstein says "He had seen it [the pattern on the car] a few years before, so that what appears in the painting is his recollection of the design adapted to his own spectral color scheme (he could not remember the colors of the original)." Roberta Bernstein, *Jasper Johns' Paintings and Sculptures, 1954–1974: "The Changing Focus of the Eye"* (Ann Arbor: UMI Research Press, 1985), 136. In the endnote that closely follows, no. 25, she adds that the stripe pattern is similar to the design of his ceiling in the basement of his East Houston Street house.

28. Rosalind Kraus, "Jasper Johns: The Functions of Irony," *October 2* (Summer 1976), 95. One might also view crosshatching as a kind of professional insignia or coat of arms for the abstract painter. Coincidentally, the word "hatchment" is sometimes substituted for the word "achievement," which is the proper term for the full display of heraldry. Also of interest is that hatchment is now almost exclusively used in a funerary context.

29. He then had to recreate the pattern from memory, as he could not relocate it once he had decided to use it in a painting, see Crichton, *Jasper Johns,* rev. ed., 52–53.

30. For a detailed analysis of the print, see Richard S. Field, *Jasper Johns: Prints 1970–77* (Middletown, CT: Wesleyan University, 1978), 26–30.

31. See Crichton, *Jasper Johns,* rev. ed., 60.

32. Richard S. Field, "Introduction," in *The Prints of Jasper Johns, 1960–1993, A Catalogue Raisonné,* ed. Universal Limited Art Editions (ULAE) (West Islip, NY: ULAE, 1994), unpaginated.

33. Ibid.

34. Johns says he first thought to name his painting *Scent* and then reconsidered, to avoid making a connection with the Pollock painting, which he knew well. In the end, he decided to use the title but states that he did not consider the two works related. See David Bourdon, "Jasper Johns: 'I Never Sensed Myself as Being Static,'" 1977, in Varnedoe, *Writings,* 155–56. Nonetheless, there is substantial literature on Johns's interest in Pollock and on this painting as a particular connector. See, for example, Fred Orton, *Figuring Jasper Johns* (London: Reaktion, 1994), 78.

35. Kraus, "Functions of Irony," 98.

36. See, for example, the pairing of *Jubilee,* 1959 (private collection) and *False Start,* 1959 (private collection), or *Two Flags,* 1959 (Museum of Modern Art Ludwig Foundation, Vienna).

37. Johns's use of everyday things as subjects for sculpture underscored his interest in the readymades of Marcel Duchamp—although unlike Duchamp, Johns generally made his works by hand with art materials rather than appropriating commercially manufactured items. Roni

Feinstein notes a further connection to Duchamp in Johns's choice of the Savarin coffee brand, which she relates to Duchamp's *Apolinère Enameled* of 1916–17. Duchamp altered the lettering of a painted tin advertisement for Sapolin enamel paints intentionally to misspell the name of his friend, the poet Guillaume Apollinaire. "New Thoughts for Jasper Johns' Sculpture," *Arts* 54, no. 8 (April 1980), 139–45.

38. One of only two sculptures treated this way. The other, also called *Painted Bronze* (Kunstmuseum Basel), presents two Ballantine Ale cans that are also life-size but more evidently painted bronze. Many authors have written about this deliberate confusion. See, for example, Max Kozloff, *Jasper Johns* (New York: Abrams, 1967), 31.

39. February 13–April 12, 1964, curated by Alan R. Solomon.

40. For a related notion of the Savarin motif as personification, see Orton, *Figuring Jasper Johns*, chap. 3. Also see Goldman, *17 Monotypes,* unpaginated, who notes that Johns treats the motif of the Savarin can and brushes differently than most of his other motifs—never fragmented or seen from the back or sides, and mostly centered.

41. According to Field in "Introduction," unpaginated.

42. Or, as Field describes it, "concept vs. illusion," in ibid.

43. The elements that link this print to Munch's 1895 *Self-Portrait* are already here—the can as surrogate self-portrait set against a dark ground and above the armlike stroke—tempting speculation that Johns may have already recognized the connection at this early date. It should be noted that between 1969 and 1977, the Savarin motif makes an appearance, faintly, at the bottom of *Decoy*—a painting (Museum Ludwig, Cologne) and print, both 1971.

44. *Jasper Johns,* October 17, 1977–January 22, 1978, curated by David Whitney.

45. In conversation with the author, June 20, 2014, and in Christian Geelhaar, "Interview mit Jasper Johns/Interview with Jasper Johns," 1978, in Varnedoe, *Writings,* 192.

46. In conversation with the author, June 20, 2014, Johns confirmed that the Gund drawing came before the ink wash drawing, which is dated January 30, 1977, according to MoMA records.

47. It conforms most closely to the *Corpse and Mirror* paintings, but is not an exact match and has occasioned a variety of identifications: see Riva Castleman, *Jasper Johns: A Print Retrospective* (New York: MoMA, 1986), 44; Field, *Prints 1970–1977,* 51; Charles W. Haxthausen, "Translation and Transformation in *Target with Four Faces:* The Painting, the Drawing, and the Etching," in *Jasper Johns: Printed Symbols* (Minneapolis: Walker Art Center, 1990), 72; Rosenthal and Fine, *Drawings,* 150; and Goldman, *17 Monotypes,* unpaginated. Johns, however, confirmed the identification with the paintings by giving the title *Savarin 5 (Corpse and Mirror)* to a subsequent print whose background pattern resembles the other Savarin prints.

48. See, for example, Leo Steinberg, "Jasper Johns: the First Seven Years of His Art," in *Other Criteria: Confrontations with Twentieth-Century Art* (Chicago: University of Chicago Press, 2007).

49. See Orton, *Figuring Jasper Johns,* chap. 3.

50. In wood color, printed with the letterpress printer, according to Bill Goldston, in conversation with the author, December 1, 2014.

51. A fragment that, unlike the poster, does not seem based on the *Corpse and Mirror* paintings. Although bearing some resemblance to the left panel of *Untitled,* 1972, it may be an independent pattern that stands for crosshatching in general.

52. Goldston recalled that they were working on all three prints at the same time, although the Whitney poster came first, and that "a lot of work was going on then," with Johns "in the print studio two to three times a week." In conversation with the author, December 1, 2014.

53. I mean to emphasize here the representation of wood grain—as opposed to real wood, which Johns has incorporated from time to time into his work from the beginning of his career, as in *Construction with Toy Piano,* 1954 (Kunstmuseum Basel); *Target with Plaster Casts,* 1955 (collection of David Geffen); and *Target with Four Faces,* 1955 (MoMA). Note that a faint wood-grain pattern appears on the front of the pedestal in the photoengraved image in *1st Etchings (Savarin),* 1968 (fig. 12), an an inherent part of the wood plinth. This, too, may have provided a source of inspiration for the wood grain beneath the Savarin can in the Whitney poster.

54. Email from Johns studio to author, December 16, 2014.

55. Samuel Beckett and Jasper Johns, *Foirades/Fizzles* (London: Petersburg Press, 1976).

56. For a detailed account, see Richard Field, "The Making of Foirades/Fizzles," in *Foirades/Fizzles: Echo and Allusion in the Art of Jasper Johns* (Los Angeles: Wight Art Gallery, University of California, 1987), 114–15.

57. Suggested by Goldston in conversation with the author, December 1, 2014.

58. Email from Johns's office, December 16, 2014. At the same time, one needs to reckon with the undated photograph that appears in Richard Francis, *Jasper Johns* (New York: Abbeville, 1984), 115, showing Johns taking a rubbing from a strip of wood. The dimensions of the strip, however, match the ledge just beneath the can but not the vertical plank beneath that; this rubbing likely makes its first appearance in the 1978 lithograph *Savarin 5 (Corpse and Mirror)* (fig. 41).

59. In conversation with the author, June 20, 2014.

60. Bill Goldston confirms that "Munch was being thought about" at ULAE at the time and that Grosman was "very aware" of his work; in conversation with the author, December 1, 2014.

61. Johns recalls that Castleman took him to art dealers around the time he was working on the *Savarin* prints. Although he is not sure why, he did not end up buying the Munch; in conversation with the author, May 5, 2013. Johns does not know if he saw the Davison Art Center exhibition (in conversation with the author, June 20, 2014), but Field remembers speaking with him about it; in conversation with the author, June 10, 2014.

62. For one account of the variations, see Elizabeth Prelinger and Andrew Robison, *Edvard Munch: Master Prints* (Washington, DC: National Gallery of Art; New York: DelMonico Books, Prestel, 2010), 26–37.

63. Quoted in Sue Prideaux, *Edvard Munch: Behind the Scream* (New Haven and London: Yale University Press, 2005), 150–51. According to Prideaux, what appears to be a bridge or road was in fact a path with a safety railing.

64. Ute Kuhlemann Falck, "Idea and Reality: Edvard Munch and the Woodcut Technique," unpublished essay. Falck further describes how black-line woodcut technique requires cutting away the wood around the line; thus the printed line in the image is artificially created—a representation of a line rather than the actual mark left by the artist's gouging of the wood matrix.

65. In conversation with the author, June 20, 2014.

66. Recalling the direction of the pattern of *Corpse and Mirror II* and related Savarin images—see Rosenthal and Fine, *Drawings,* 152.

67. For additional discussion of crosshatching and handprints, see James Cuno, "Voices and Mirrors/Echoes and Allusions: Jasper Johns's *Untitled,* 1972," in Beckett and Johns, *Foirades/Fizzles,* 205.

68. Rosenthal and Fine, *Drawings,* 234.

69. A cast of a hand, rather than an imprint, appeared as early as *Target with Plaster Casts,* 1955, and Jill Johnston says the first painted handprint is in *Spanked Child* (location unknown), 1952: see Johnston, *Jasper Johns: Privileged Information* (New York: Thames and Hudson, 1996), 229.

70. See also *Diver,* 1962 (collection of Norman and Irma Braman); *Diver,* 1963 (MoMA); *Land's End,* 1963 (San Francisco Museum of Modern Art); and *Periscope (Hart Crane),* 1963 (Menil Collection).

71. On the symbolic potency of Johns's handprint see Johnston, *Privileged Information,* 228–29, and on the relationship of handprints to touch and voice, see Cuno, "Voices and Mirrors," 222–25. Note, too, a work not mentioned in the Johns literature as an example of other prominent handprints in paintings: Willem de Kooning's *Lisbeth's Painting,* 1958 (Virginia Museum of Fine Arts), which features those of his daughter.

72. Email from the Johns office, December 16, 2014.

73. In contrast, Trygve Nergaard reads it as a declaration of triumph, of the spirit over the body and idea over technique. See Nergaard, "Despair," in National Gallery of Art, *Edvard Munch: Symbols & Images* (Washington, DC: National Gallery of Art, 1978), 135.

74. The prints were made in the first few months of 1978 and published in May of that year; email from Goldston, December 18, 2014.

75. Johns's "bloody" handprint makes an interesting parallel with the image of a damaged hand that Munch created for use as a kind of personal emblem of physical and emotional trauma—connected to the wound he received from a gunshot during an argument with his fiancé, Tulla Larsen, in 1902. He called it "the bloody hand" and "the fatal hand." It appears in his letters and in a catalogue of his graphic work. See Brevs. 604 (PN 707), s. 1. Nasjonalbiblioteket. Brev til Jappe Nilssen. Datert 23.12.1906 at website *eMunch, Edvard Munch's Writings* (http://www.emunch.no/listOfDrawings_images.xhtml#.VY2PyetN30c). Thanks to Sivert Thue for bringing this to my attention. See also Sarah G. Epstein, *The Prints of Edvard Munch: Mirror of His Life* (Oberlin, Ohio: Allen Memorial Art Museum, 1983), 133. The row of light, pebblelike shapes at the bottom of the can be imagined as lending a further allusion to Munch and mortality, given their uncanny resemblance to a skull's upper row of teeth.

76. November 11, 1978–March 4, 1979. Johns confirmed his visit but did not recall the circumstances; in conversation with the author, June 20, 2014.

77. Ibid. Goldston also recalls that Johns had made a drawing on mylar—the Gund drawing—to use in preparing the lithographic plate for the 1977 Whitney poster, but that the drawing did not have enough substance to produce good detail and the plate went unused; in conversation with the author, December 1, 2014.

78. Johns's inclusion of Munch's initials recalls his inclusion of Duchamp's initials ten years earlier, stenciled onto the lithograph *Fragment—According to What—Hinged Canvas,* 1971. See Castleman, *Print Retrospective,* 44.

79. Suggested to the author by Goldston. Curiously, the 1981 Savarin print was produced on the offset lithographic press, which does not reverse images during the printing process—so that the letters would have appeared to Johns exactly as they appear on the final image. Nonetheless, one is tempted to consider this a sophisticated "un-reversal" that may have entered Johns's consciousness as a result of his deep familiarity with all facets of printmaking and the central role of reversal in his work. Note that from the beginning of Johns's work, arm- and handprints have served as vehicles to incorporate other voices, allowing Johns to navigate his relationship to predecessors. See Cuno, "Voices and Mirrors," 209–25.

80. Michael Crichton, *Jasper Johns,* 1st ed. (New York: Abrams; Whitney Museum of Art, 1977), 62. Crichton presumably completed the text in 1976 since he dated his acknowledgements January 1977.

81. Varnedoe, *Retrospective,* 301.

82. Ibid., 28. See also diagram in Rosenthal, *Work Since 1974,* 34.

83. Varnedoe, *Retrospective,* 269.

84. Earlier crosshatch paintings had similarly used the titles to inflect abstract compositions with emotive and physical associations—*Corpse and Mirror* suggests the macabre and the hybrid monsters of the Surrealist game; *The Dutch Wives,* 1975 (collection of the artist), hints at surrogate sexuality by recalling the board with a hole that sailors were said to use for relieving pent-up sexual tension; and *Weeping Women,* 1975 (collection of David Geffen), conjures Picasso's images of his distressed mistress Dora Maar. In *17 Monotypes,* Goldman says this last title also refers to Munch's *Weeping Woman,* but Johns has said this isn't the case; in conversation with the author, June 20, 2014.

85. For detailed descriptions of the drawing, see Rosenthal and Fine, *Drawings,* 247–48, and Peter C. Marzio et. al., *American Art and Philanthropy: Twenty Years of Collecting at the Museum of Fine Arts, Houston* (Houston: Museum of Fine Arts, 2010), 335–36.

86. Ajit Mookerjee, *Tantra Art: Its Philosophy and Physics* (New Delhi, New York, Paris: Kumar Gallery, 1966; repr., Basel: Ravi Kumar, 1971).

87. The drawing is dated June 1979 in the lower right corner. The article on the Pope's visit to Auschwitz appeared on June 8, 1979. Six major new paintings by Johns were included in the *36th Biennial Exhibition of Contemporary American Painting* at the Corcoran Gallery of Art, Washington, DC, February 23–April 8, 1979, and Johns would likely have gone for the opening or sometime during the course of the show, perhaps combining the trip with a visit to the National Gallery of Art.

88. See, for example, Patricia G. Berman, "Edvard Munch's 'Modern Life of the Soul,'" in *Edvard Munch, The Modern Life of the Soul,* ed. Kynaston McShine et al. (New York: MoMA, 2006), 39.

89. Quoted in Arne Eggum, *Edvard Munch: Paintings, Sketches, and Studies* (New York: Clarkson N. Potter, 1984), 116.

90. This is the second of three paintings with same title; it was painted in 1980 and the frame completed in 1981.

91. Munch's drawing was first published in Magne Bruteig and Ute Kuhlemann Falck, eds., *Edvard Munch: Works on Paper* (Brussels: Mercatorfonds; Oslo: Munch Museum, 2013), 18, and first exhibited in the United States in 2016, in connection with the exhibition that this current publication accompanied.

92. For additional discussion about Johns and O'Hara, and the role of cutlery in Johns's work, see Bernstein, *Paintings and Sculptures,* 79–80; Orton, *Figuring Jasper Johns,* 61–73; and Cuno, "Voices and Mirrors," 218–21.

93. Fine and Rosenthal, "Interview with Jasper Johns," in Rosenthal and Fine, *Drawings,* 88.

94. In 1943, Munch wrote to Christian Gierløff: "I'm very much looking forward to the enormous cod, both the one with the magnificent head and the lightly-salted one with the ivory flesh," suggesting a later date for the painting. Quoted in Stang, *Edvard Munch,* 26.

95. See Frank Høifødt, "Edvard Munch—Style and Theme around the Year 1900," in Klaus Albrecht Schröder and Antonia Hoerschelmann, eds., *Edvard Munch: Theme and Variation* (Ostfildern-Ruit: Hatje Cantz; Vienna: Albertina, 2003), 54.

96. Quoted in McShine et al., *Modern Life of the Soul*, 212.

97. Arne Eggum identified the city as Oslo, at the time called Kristiania. See Eggum, "The Theme of Death," in National Gallery of Art, *Symbols & Images*, 179.

98. Both quoted in Stang, *Edvard Munch,* 26.

99. John Russell likened the central form of the god to Cunningham himself, noting that "one of the names of Siva (to whom Samvara is related) is the Lord of the Dance." "People Either Get the Point Or They Don't," *New York Times,* November 19, 1989. For further connections to Cunningham and his troupe, see Johnston, *Privileged Information,* 269–74.

100. See Bernstein, " 'Seeing a Thing,' " 50.

101. Rosenthal, *Work Since 1974,* 44.

102. Unlike, say, Hans Baldung, and the usual motif in which the maiden recoils in horror at the unexpected substitution of death for her lover.

103. McShine et al., *Modern Life of the Soul*, 213.

104. On the relationship between the drawing and paintings, see Rosenthal and Fine, *Drawings*, 255–56.

105. David Shapiro, *Jasper Johns Drawings, 1954–1984* (New York: Abrams, 1984), 39.

106. Rosenthal established with Johns that this work came first, *Work Since 1974,* 50.

107. Ibid.

108. For details about the making of the work and an image of the back, see James Rondeau, "Jasper Johns: Gray," in *Jasper Johns: Gray* (New Haven and London: Yale University Press; Chicago: Art Institute of Chicago, 2007), 60.

109. Note that encaustic was used for Fayoum mummy portrait paintings, and beeswax, the principal ingredient of encaustic, is associated with traditional embalming processes.

110. The winter studio remains and has been restored, but the main house and other buildings were torn down in 1960 to make room for artists' residences and studios.

111. Given the lack of hands on the clock, the symbolism is sometimes described more specifically as the end of time.

112. Frederick B. Deknatel, *Edvard Munch* (New York: Chanticleer Press; MoMA; Boston: Institute of Contemporary Art, 1950), 63.

113. Eggum, "Munch's Self-Portraits," in National Gallery of Art, *Symbols & Images,* 29.

114. Stang, *Edvard Munch,* 85.

115. Iris Müller-Westermann, "A Modern Eye: Edvard Munch's Self-Portraits after 1908," in *Edvard Munch: The Modern Eye*, ed. Angela Lampe et al. (London: Tate, 2012), 289.

116. Steihaug, "Edvard Munch's Performative Self-Portraits," in Guleng et al., *Edvard Munch: 1863–1944,* 22.

117. Ibid.

118. Ingebjørg Ydstie, "The Cinema-Art Galleries of Halfdan Nobel Roede," in Lampe et al., *Modern Eye,* 181.

119. Reinhold Heller suggested that Munch was staging a memento mori image on the occasion of his birthday: "Who Is/Was Edvard Munch" (paper presented at "Edvard Munch and/in Modernism," Oslo, September 18, 2013).

120. The similarity to the painting is also noted by Arne Eggum, *Munch and Photography* (New Haven and London: Yale University Press, 1989), 193. Eggum suggests that Munch also used a mirror for the painting, which he identifies as on the floor behind Munch in the image on page 194.

121. The only known photograph of Munch's house with a grandfather clock—serendipitously mirrored behind Munch's head—locates it in a different room (fig. 158), but comparison with the sketch and painting shows that it is the same clock in every detail; Munch likely had it moved as he consolidated rooms within the house.

122. Note, however, that Munch included a grandfather clock in his set-design sketches for Max Reinhardt's 1906 production of Ibsen's *Ghosts* in Berlin. Joan Templeton describes this both as a symbolic presence and as a reference to the actual clock that Munch grew up with and kept to the end of his life. Templeton, *Munch's Ibsen: A Painter's Visions of a Playwright* (Seattle: University of Washington Press, 2008), 45.

123. The notion of this shape as a sculpture was suggested by Clarence Burton Sheffield, Jr. However, he considers it the profile of a head that Munch never made, though it resonates with the profile head in *Starry Night II,* 1922–24 (fig. 129), and *Self-Portrait* (with the striped sweater), 1940–43 (fig. 146). Sheffield, "The Unsung Role of Sculpture in Edvard Munch's Creative Process and Public Persona" (paper presented at "Edvard Munch and/ in Modernism," Oslo, September 20, 2013.) In the same paper, Sheffield proposed dates for *Workers in the Snow;* an early version of the sculpture, most likely executed in plastilin in 1910, served as the basis for a plaster cast in 1914 and a subsequent bronze cast in 1932.

124. Müller-Westermann, "Self-Portraits after 1908," 289.

125. See Eggum, *Munch and Photography,* 194, and Elizabeth Prelinger, *After* The Scream: *The Late Paintings of Edvard Munch* (Atlanta: High Museum of Art; New Haven and London: Yale University Press, 2002), 156.

126. Little is known about the origins of the bedspread. Arne Eggum, in conversation with Jon-Ove Steihaug, related it to the textile that Ingse Vibe can be seen making in the image reproduced in illustration 177 of *Munch and Photography*. He noted that Ingse, a Norwegian actress, and Edvard had a long, close friendship, and suggested that the bedspread was a token of her love and thus included by Munch in his self-portrait. But the textile she is making appears to be a crocheted piece with a different kind of pattern. What is known is that Munch's sister, Inger, inherited the original bedspread from her brother and gave it to the person who looked after her in her old age, Marit Valde. The Friends of the Munch Museum purchased the bedspread from Valde's niece, Guri Haaland, and donated it to the museum in 1997.

127. Eggum, *Munch and Photography,* 194.

128. Crichton, *Jasper Johns,* rev. ed., 63.

129. Presumably because the authors noticed that several drawings from 1980 were also titled *Between the Clock and the Bed* (see below in my essay, and Rosenthal and Fine, *Drawings,* 258–61).

130. In conversation with the author, June 20, 2014.

131. In conversation with the author, June 12, 2013, and October 16, 2013. Katz established with some conviction that he sent the card in 1974, not 1980 or 1981. He believes he sent it from Paris when he and writer Willy Eisenhart visited the exhibition *Edvard Munch: 1863–1944,* Musée National d'Art Moderne, March 22–May 12, 1974. He has the exhibition catalogue in his library. This would have been quite early in Johns's crosshatching period, but Katz was a close friend and would have been familiar with his newest work. He recalls thinking, "There's a single man standing by something that looks like it could be a Jasper Johns sketch."

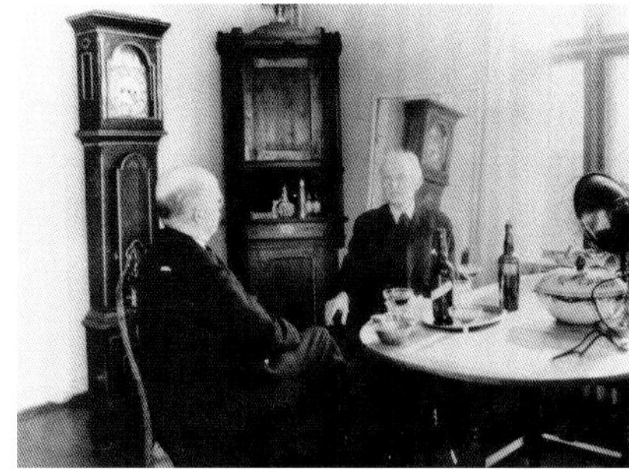

fig. 159 **Munch being interviewed by the Swedish Weekly** *Veckojournalen* **at Ekely**, 1937, photographed by Anders B. Wilse. Munch Museum Archives

132. Johns's office reports that currently "there are a dozen or more 'Munch' books of assorted types" in Johns's library. Email to the author, September 29, 2015.

133. The work is double dated because Johns reworked it in 1988 to address fading.

134. Francis, *Jasper Johns,* 100.

135. Rosenthal, *Work Since 1974,* 54, fn. 109.

136. Crichton, *Jasper Johns,* rev. ed., 63. Note that in this exchange Johns evidently understood the title of Munch's painting to be simply *Between the Clock and the Bed.* Johns has further commented: "I would say I attempted to give some sense of *Between the Clock and the Bed . . .* an existence between two other existences." In conversation with the author, June 20, 2014.

137. The motif itself derives from an earlier painting, *Studio II*, 1966 (Whitney Museum of American Art), and recalls the inclusion of reversed paintings in several other works, such as *According to What,* 1964 (private collection), and *Souvenir II,* 1964 (collection of Barbara and Richard S. Lane).

138. In conversation with the author, June 20, 2014.

139. There are a number of other drawings and prints related to *Between the Clock and the Bed*, some titled, some not. See Rosenthal and Fine, *Drawings,* 258–67; Shapiro, *Drawings,* 1954–1984, cat. 139, 140, 145, 146; ULAE Catalogue Raisonné, prints 245 and 246; and a 1988 drawing (Ryobi Foundation, DBA Powers Art Center).

140. See Rosenthal and Fine, *Drawings,* 260.

141. The claim appears as follows: "In 1981, the art historian Per Hovdenakk sent Johns a postcard in which he drew Johns' attention to the similarity between the cross-hatched images and the picture on the postcard. This postcard bore the image of Edvard Munch's *Self-Portrait. Between the Clock and the Bed.*" Holger Reenberg, "Echoes of the Scream," in Gether and Reenberg, *Echoes of the Scream*, 64. Doubt is cast, however, as Johns did not mention this instance when asked by the author about who sent the card (June 20, 2014). Furthermore, although Hovdenakk has said he toured Johns around the Munch Museum in 1973 and showed him *Between the Clock and the Bed* (see Berman and Stave, *Munch | Warhol*, 41), Johns has actually never visited Oslo (email to the author, July 2, 2013, and confirmed in Johns's edits to catalogue manuscript).

142. See fn. 5.

143. Goldston, in conversation with author, December 1, 2014. See also Goldman, *17 Monotypes,* unpaginated.

144. These yielded a total of thirty-three prints, as some of the images were printed up to four times in variable editions. Six are unique monotypes printed on blank paper, one of which is a counterproof, pulled from another monotype rather than from a new painting on Plexiglas. Eleven of the prints were made using the lithograph as a structure and are described as "monotypes with lithograph."

145. The oval frame in these 1982 prints also recalls the motif of the number zero in Johns's number works, in particular the lithograph *Figure 0,* 1969 (ULAE 59).

146. Wood grain also continues beyond these years, opening onto new themes and associations, as in several untitled prints from 1992–93 that follow the last of *The Seasons* prints.

147. On the relationship of the drawings to the painting, see Rosenthal and Fine, *Drawings,* 282–85.

148. Meriting further consideration is the relationship of both these paintings to Matisse's *Red Studio,* 1911 (MoMA): the shallow space, the play between flatness and illusion, the trapezoidal shape of the table projecting into the space, and the frames and canvases at the rear leaning against the wall—deliberate confusions between representation and representation of representation, and the showcasing of one's own art, among other shared themes. Another felicitous parallel is the grandfather clocks in both the Matisse and Munch paintings.

149. Crichton identifies these as *Between the Clock and the Bed* drawings, *Jasper Johns,* rev. ed., 63. Yet they show two-panel works, not three, as seen when appearing whole in *Perilous Night*, 1982, and the horizontal divisions do not occur in *Between the Clock and the Bed.* Rosenthal and Fine identify the images as the top part of an untitled 1982 ink on plastic drawing; see *Drawings,* 280.

150. The Norwegian word that Munch used, according to his biographers, was "hestekur," which translates as "horse cure."

151. Quoted in Dieter Buchhart, "The Duality of a Material-based Modernity," in *Edvard Munch: Signs of Modern Art* (Basel: Fondation Beyeler; Schwäbisch Hall, Germany: Kunsthalle Würth, 2007), 11. Recent scholarship has questioned the extent of Munch's intentionality in exposing his works to the elements and other harsh treatment, for example Mille Stein, "Kill or Cure Treatment as a Modernistic Instrument" (paper presented at *Edvard Munch and/in Modernism,* Oslo, September 20, 2013).

152. Buchhart, "Duality," 11.

153. Buchhart, "Disappearance—Experiments with Materials and Motifs," in Schröder and Hoerschelmann, *Theme and Variation,* 25.

154. See Ibid., 21.

155. See Rosenthal and Fine, *Drawings,* 280.

156. The strips of wood in both *In the Studio* and *Perilous Night* are similar to the strip in *Savarin 5 (Corpse and Mirror),* 1978 (see n. 58).

157. See, for example, Nan Rosenthal, "Drawing as Rereading," in Rosenthal and Fine, *Drawings,* 36–39; Rosenthal, *Work Since 1974,* 65–72; and Johnston, *Privileged Information,* 33–34, 47–48.

158. Fine and Rosenthal, "Interview with Jasper Johns," 82; Johnston, *Privileged Information,* 36.

159. Fine and Rosenthal, "Interview with Jasper Johns," 82.

160. Now in the Musée Unterlinden in Colmar, Alsace, where Johns saw it. See Rosenthal, "Drawing as Rereading," 36–39.

161. Quoted in Johnston, *Privileged Information,* 283.

162. Rosenthal and Fine, *Drawings,* 280

163. See Johnston, who calls it an Irish folktale in *Privileged Information,* 118. Recordings can be found online of Campbell describing the story of the perilous bed as an Arthurian tale concerning the Isle of Women and the knight Gawain. Perhaps also of interest to Johns, the floor is made of the polished stone called jasper.

164. David Revill, *The Roaring Silence: John Cage, A Life* (New York: Arcade, 1993), 85.

165. For details about the sign, see Rosenthal and Fine, *Drawings,* 288.

166. Published in *Puck* as "My Wife and My Mother-in-Law" in 1915 by the cartoonist W. E. Hill, though apparently it had already existed for decades as a popular image in Germany.

167. For further analysis, see Rosenthal, *Work Since 1974,* 76–84.

168. See especially Lampe et al., *Modern Eye,* and Guleng et al., *Edvard Munch: 1863–1944.*

169. Stang, *Edvard Munch,* 31.

170. See Patricia G. Berman and Jane Van Nimmen, *Munch and Women: Image and Myth* (Alexandria, Virginia: Art Services International, 1997), 92.

171. There is extensive discussion of the role of repetition in Munch's work. See, for example, Berman and Stave, *Munch|Warhol*; Jay A. Clarke, "Art Equals Life? Munch and the Problem of Biography," in Guleng et al., *Edvard Munch: 1863–1944*; Trine Nordkvelle, "Reading the Repeated *Kiss.* A Narratological Experiment," in Guleng et al., *Edvard Munch: 1863–1944*; Eggum, "The Theme of Death," in National Gallery of Art, *Symbols & Images*; and Antonia Hoerschelmann, "Crossover—Munch and Modernity" in Schröder and Hoerschelmann, *Theme and Variation,* and "Dislocated Motifs: Munch's Tendency toward Repetition," in Lampe et al., *Modern Eye.*

172. See Templeton, *Munch's Ibsen,* 45.

173. Steihaug, "Performative Self-Portraits," 20.

174. Quoted in Müller-Westermann, "Self-Portraits after 1908," 285.

175. April Bernard and Mimi Thompson, "Johns on . . . ," 1984, in Varnedoe, *Writings,* 217.

176. "I wanted something that would be literal. It is less literal than I intended it to be, but nevertheless it started out as a literal tracing. I stood in the sunlight and there was a piece of paper on the ground and someone drew my shadow. I used that in the painting." Deborah Solomon, "The Unflagging Artistry of Jasper Johns," *New York Times,* June 19, 1988.

177. Barbara Rose was the first to propose these identifications in "Jasper Johns: The Seasons," *Vogue,* January 1987, 259–60. They have been repeated by other authors in subsequent

publications, although the similar size, shape, and pattern of these surfaces in *Spring, Summer,* and *Winter* somewhat undercuts the argument.

178. On the sequence of transitions, see Judith Goldman, *Jasper Johns: The Seasons* (New York: Leo Castelli Gallery, 1987), unpaginated; Rose, "Seasons," 199; Rosenthal, *Work Since 1974,* 89; and Johns in Paul Taylor, "Jasper Johns," 1990, in Varnedoe, *Writings,* 251.

179. On the relationship of *The Seasons* to Picasso, see Goldman, *Seasons*; Rose, "Seasons"; Rosenthal, *Work Since 1974,* 89; Bernstein, " 'Seeing a Thing,' "; and Johnston, *Privileged Information,* 28–30.

180. See, for example, Johnston, *Privileged Information,* 26. The term "whole" should be qualified in any case as the shadows end at the ankles. Their placement at the bottom of the canvas is a convenient way to cover the missing feet; it also joins pictorial space to real space, as if the shadow were being cast in real time by the artist or the viewer. For a related image of Johns's shadow projected onto a work in progress, see Victor I. Stoichita, "Three Academic Ideas," in *Past Things and Present: Jasper Johns since 1983* (Minneapolis: Walker Art Center, 2003), 46.

181. For recent interpretations of these much-discussed works, see Steihaug, "Performative Self-Portraits," 18–19.

182. The image was inspired in part by a prose poem Munch wrote about his affair with an older married woman: "They walked across the room to the open window, and leaning out looked down into the garden . . . it was chilly out there—The trees stood like big dark masses against the air—and up there is the moon—one is barely aware of it—it will emerge later—it is so mysterious." McShine et al., *Modern Life of the Soul,* 206.

183. For a study of Munch's *Starry Night* works, see Louise Lippincott, *Starry Night* (Malibu, California: Getty Museum Studies on Art, 1988). Also see Templeton, *Munch's Ibsen,* 147–50. On *Attraction,* see Schröder and Hoerschelmann, *Theme and Variation,* 158.

184. Templeton, *Munch's Ibsen,* 150.

185. It is often considered the middle of three closely related paintings from 1922–24.

186. The name change from Kristiania to Oslo occurred in 1924, the same year the painting was completed.

187. Two years later, in 1926, Munch positioned himself beside the post and ball for a photograph by his sister, Inger, again underscoring the anthropomorphic qualities of the distinctive architectural feature. Munch may also have drawn inspiration from the even more substantial posts and balls on the railing of the still-extant winter studio, which are larger than life size, as can be seen in vintage photographs by Ragnvald Vaering from 1933. See also stills from the last of four short films Munch produced in 1927, in which he places his head directly in front of the newel post ball and then beside it; reproduced in Eggum, *Munch and Photography,* 169.

188. Quoted in Templeton, *Munch's Ibsen,* 134.

189. Ibid., 145.

190. Ibid.

191. Holding the camera at arm's length is a common practice today, but Munch's image is quite likely the first known instance in photography. See Clément Chéroux, " 'Write Your life!': Photograph and Autobiography," in Lampe et al., *Modern Eye.* Chéroux notes that Munch turned the camera on himself like a mirror to capture aspects of his features that he couldn't otherwise see in his reflection.

192. Eggum, *Munch and Photography.* Also see Chéroux, "Photograph and Autobiography," and Cecilie Tyri Holt, *Edvard Munch. Fotografier* (Oslo: Forlaget Press, 2013).

193. Eggum, *Munch and Photography,* 128.

194. Ibid., 130. Also see Chéroux, "Photograph and Autobiography," 61.

195. Quoted in Pascal Rousseau, "Radiation: Metabolising the 'new rays,' " in Lampe et al., *Modern Eye,* 165.

196. Sue Prideaux, *Edvard Munch: Behind the Scream*, 2nd ed. (New Haven and London: Yale University Press, 2007), 255. See also Rousseau, "Radiation," for a fuller account of his interest in these phenomena.

197. Eggum, *Munch and Photography,* 104–5.

198. Ibid., 164. The painting is *African with Green Scarf,* 1916.

199. See Philippe Lanthony, "The Entopic Vision of Edvard Munch," and Ingebjørg Ydstie, "'Painting is what the brain perceives through the filter of the eye,'" both in Lampe et al., *Modern Eye.*

200. The image is possibly a triple exposure, according to Eggum, *Munch and Photography,* 183.

201. Eggum relates the image to Plato's Allegory of the Cave: "he seems to portray himself in the moment he 'breaks the chains' and 'directs his soul towards that which is the source of light, leaving behind him shadows and reflections.'" *Munch and Photography,* 195.

202. See Victor I. Stoichita, *A Short History of the Shadow* (London: Reaktion, 1997), ch. 7.

203. Besides the surrogate image of the Savarin can and brushes, with its clear connections to Munch, instances of self-portraiture in Johns's work were previously limited to the inclusion of his face on a Japanese tourist plate that appears in the 1964 paintings *Souvenir* (collection of the artist) and *Souvenir 2* (private collection) and related drawings and prints, and to impressions of his face in the various *Skin* drawings and prints, such as discussed below.

204. See Stoichita, *Short History of the Shadow,* ch. 1.

205. A double portrait of Picasso appears in the early 1970s in print versions of *Cup 2 Picasso* and *Cups 4 Picasso.* These relate to Johns's profile of Duchamp in *According to What,* 1964 (private collection), which is based on Duchamp's shadowy *Self-Portrait in Profile,* 1958. In two of *The Seasons* paintings, especially *Spring,* Johns contrasts his frontal shadow with a number of shadow profiles rendered, like the Picasso portrait, as double-images that flip between faces and a vase, in reference to the "ambiguous vase" illusion devised by Edgar Rubin. These are based on a porcelain vase with the profiles of Queen Elizabeth and Prince Philip produced for her Silver Jubilee in 1977 (see Francis, *Jasper Johns,* 106).

206. Rose appears to be the first to mention that the seahorse in *Summer* refers not only to the pregnant horse in Picasso's painting—itself a reference to Picasso's mistress Marie Thérèse Walther—but also to Johns: seahorses are one of the few species in which the male bears offspring. Johns's "offspring" are his creative endeavors, the works that surround him; see Rose, "Seasons," 259. Stoichita also notes that the Archangel Gabriel tells Mary that the Holy Spirit will "overshadow thee," that is, impregnate her, suggesting the fertilizing power of the shadow and its long history of magical attributes; see *History of the Shadow*, 67–68.

207. Francis, *Jasper Johns,* 98.

Reader's Note:

Dimensions are height x width x depth. Works on paper are sheet size. The medium and dimensions are unknown for some Munch-related photographs. Works displayed in one venue only are indicated below.

Exhibition Checklist

Edvard Munch

Norwegian, 1863–1944

Paintings

Stanislaw Przybyszewski, 1894, casein and distemper on canvas, 29 1/2 x 23 5/8 in. (75 x 60 cm). Munch Museum (fig. 99)

Despair, 1894, oil on canvas, 36 1/4 x 28 1/2 in. (92 x 72.5 cm). Munch Museum (fig. 98)

Death and Life, 1894, oil on canvas, 50 3/8 x 33 7/8 in. (128 x 86 cm). Munch Museum **(Oslo only)**

Madonna, 1895–97?, oil on canvas, 39 3/4 x 27 3/4 in. (101 x 70.5 cm). Collection of Nelson Blitz, Jr. and Catherine Woodard **(Richmond only)** (fig. 51)

Inheritance, 1897–99, oil on canvas, 55 1/2 x 47 1/4 in. (141 x 120 cm). Munch Museum (fig. 111)

Hospital Ward, 1897–99, oil on unprimed canvas, 31 1/2 x 55 1/8 in. (80 x 140 cm). Munch Museum (fig. 110)

Metabolism, 1898–99, oil on canvas with carved wooden frame, 68 7/8 x 56 5/16 in. (175 x 143 cm), painting dimensions. Munch Museum **(Oslo only)** (fig. 61)

Self-Portrait in Hell, 1903, oil on canvas, 32 1/4 x 26 in. (82 x 66 cm). Munch Museum (fig. 122)

Self-Portrait with Brushes, 1904, oil on canvas, 77 1/2 x 35 3/4 in. (197 x 91 cm). Munch Museum (fig. 15)

On the Veranda Stairs, 1922–24, oil on canvas, 32 1/4 x 37 1/2 in. (82 x 95.5 cm). Munch Museum (fig. 135)

Starry Night II, 1922–24, oil on canvas, 47 1/2 x 39 1/3 in. (120.5 x 100 cm). Munch Museum (fig. 129)

The Night Wanderer, 1923–24, oil on canvas, 35 1/2 x 26 3/4 in. (90 x 68 cm). Munch Museum (page 106)

The Dance of Life, 1925, oil on canvas, 56 1/4 x 81 7/8 in. (143 x 208 cm). Munch Museum (fig. 66)

Self-Portrait, with a Cod's Head on a Plate, 1940–42, oil on wooden panel, 21 5/8 x 17 7/8 in. (55 x 45.5 cm). Munch Museum (fig. 60)

Self-Portrait between the Clock and the Bed, 1940–43, oil on canvas, 58 7/8 x 47 1/2 in. (149.5 x 120.5 cm). Munch Museum (fig. 75)

Self-Portrait, 1940–43, oil on canvas, 22 3/5 x 30 7/8 in. (57.5 x 78.5 cm). Munch Museum (fig. 146)

Drawings

Self-Portrait in Profile, ca. 1910, pencil in sketchbook, 16 3/4 x 10 5/8 in. (42.5 x 27.1 cm). Munch Museum **(Richmond only)** (fig. 124)

Sketch of a Vulva, ca. 1915–30?, charcoal and pencil on paper, 21 1/2 x 26 5/8 in. (53.7 x 67.6 cm). Munch Museum (fig. 57)

Bent-over Man Looking at His Mirror Image, 1919, crayon in sketchbook, 5 x 7 in. (12.8 x 17.8 cm). Munch Museum (page x)

Self-Portrait in Wicker Chair (Spanish Flu), 1919, crayon on paper, 11 3/8 x 8 3/4 in. (29 x 22.3 cm). Munch Museum (Richmond only) (fig. 113)

Woman between the Veranda and Studio at Ekely, 1922, crayon in sketchbook, 10 3/8 x 8 1/8 in. (26.5 x 20.6 cm). Munch Museum (fig. 131)

Munch Seated, ca. 1936, pen and ink on paper, 10 3/4 x 8 1/2 in. (27.5 x 21.6 cm). Munch Museum **(Oslo only)**

Starry Night, 1922–24, charcoal on paper, 27 5/8 x 24 5/8 in. (70 x 62.5 cm). Munch Museum (fig. 132)

Variation of The Night Wanderer, 1925–26, pencil in sketchbook, 8 x 6 7/8 in. (20.5 x 17.6 cm). Munch Museum

Prints

Death and the Maiden, 1894, drypoint, 20 1/8 x 13 3/4 in. (51 x 35 cm). Munch Museum **(Richmond only)** (fig. 65)

Madonna, 1894, drypoint,
25 $^7/_8$ x 19 $^3/_4$ in. (65.9 x 50 cm).
Munch Museum (fig. 52)

The Scream, 1895, lithograph,
20 $^{11}/_{16}$ x 15 $^7/_8$ in. (52.5 x 40).
The Museum of Modern Art,
New York, Matthew T. Mellon
Fund **(Richmond only)**

The Scream, 1895, lithograph,
18 $^3/_8$ x 13 $^5/_8$ in. (46.5 x 34.5 cm).
Munch Museum **(Oslo only)** (fig. 30)

Moonlight: Night in Saint-Cloud, 1895,
drypoint, 24 $^5/_8$ x 17 $^5/_8$ in.
(62.6 x 44.7). Munch Museum (fig. 120)

Attraction II, 1895, etching and
drypoint, 14 $^1/_4$ x 18 $^3/_4$ in. (36 x 47.7 cm).
Munch Museum (fig. 127)

Self-Portrait, 1895, lithograph,
18 x 14 $^1/_2$ in. (45.8 x 36.8 cm).
Munch Museum (fig. 44)

Self-Portrait, 1895, lithograph,
25 $^1/_4$ x 19 $^1/_2$ in. (64 x 49.5 cm).
Munch Museum (fig. 45)

Self-Portrait, 1895, lithograph,
17 $^7/_8$ x 12 $^3/_8$ in. (45.5 x 31.5 cm).
Munch Museum (fig. 46)

Madonna, 1895/1902, lithograph,
23 $^5/_8$ x 17 $^3/_8$ in. (60.4 x 44 cm).
Munch Museum (fig. 53)

Madonna, 1895/1902, lithograph,
31 $^1/_2$ x 23 $^5/_8$ in. (80 x 60.2 cm).
Munch Museum (fig. 54)

Angst, 1896, lithograph,
22 $^1/_2$ x 16 $^7/_8$ (57.2 x 43 cm).
Munch Museum (fig. 31)

The Sick Child I, 1896, lithograph,
16 $^3/_8$ x 26 $^1/_8$ in. (41.3 x 66.3 cm).
Munch Museum (fig. 109)

Metabolism, 1897, lithograph,
19 $^3/_4$ x 12 $^7/_8$ in. (50.2 x 32.7 cm).
Munch Museum **(Richmond only)**

The Kiss III, 1898, woodcut,
24 $^7/_8$ x 21 $^7/_8$ in. (63.3 x 55.5 cm).
Munch Museum (fig. 26)

The Kiss IV, 1902, woodcut,
22 $^3/_4$ x 22 $^3/_4$ in. (58 x 58 cm).
Munch Museum (fig. 27)

The Kiss IV, 1902, woodcut,
21 $^7/_8$ x 19 $^7/_8$ in. (55.6 x 50.5 cm).
Munch Museum

Life and Death, 1902(?), etching,
11 $^3/_8$ x 10 $^1/_4$ in. (28.6 x 26).
Munch Museum (fig. 62)

Self-Portrait in Moonlight, 1904–6,
woodcut, 25 $^7/_8$ x 19 $^1/_2$ (65.9 x 49.5).
Munch Museum (fig. 123)

Self-Portrait in Shadow, 1912,
lithograph, 12 1/5 x 10 4/5 in.
(31 x 27.5 cm). Munch Museum

Self-Portrait Facing Right, 1912–13,
woodcut, 20 $^3/_8$ x 16 $^1/_4$ in. (51.8 x 41.1 cm).
Munch Museum (fig. 125)

Dance of Death (II), 1915,
lithograph, 30 $^7/_8$ x 19 $^5/_8$ in.
(78.5 x 49.7 cm). Munch Museum
(Richmond only)

Dance of Death (III), 1915,
lithograph, 21 $^7/_8$ x 14 $^3/_8$ in.
(55.6 x 36.6 cm). Munch Museum (fig. 101)

Metabolism, 1916, lithograph,
31 $^5/_8$ x 22 $^3/_4$ in. (80.6 x 57.9 cm).
Munch Museum (fig. 63)

Starry Night, 1930, woodcut,
19 $^5/_8$ x 20 $^1/_2$ in. (50 x 52 cm).
Munch Museum (fig. 134)

Self-Portrait in Backlight, 1930,
lithograph, 19 $^5/_8$ x 14 $^3/_4$ in.
(50 x 37.7 cm). Munch Museum (fig. 126)

Starry Night: John Gabriel Borkman,
1930, lithograph, 29 $^3/_4$ x 22 in.
(75.8 x 56.1 cm). Munch Museum
(Richmond only) (fig. 133)

Kiss in the Field, 1943, woodcut,
24 $^1/_4$ x 26 $^1/_8$ in. (61.5 x 66.3 cm).
Munch Museum (fig. 28)

Photographs

Self-portrait in bed, ca. 1902,
collodion print (modern copy).
Munch Museum (fig. 141)

**Rosa and Olga Meissner on the
beach in Warnemünde**, 1907,
collodion print (modern copy),
3 $^1/_2$ x 3 $^1/_2$ in. (8.9 x 8.9 cm).
Munch Museum (fig. 139)

**Self-portrait in wicker chair by the
bed, Ekely**, 1927, photograph (modern
copy). Munch Museum (fig. 142)

**Self-portrait in the conservatory
with still life and watercolors, Ekely**,
1932, gelatin silver print, 3 x 3 $^7/_8$ in.
(7.6 x 10 cm), (modern copy).
Munch Museum

**Self-portrait in front of two watercolors,
Ekely**, ca. 1930, gelatin silver print
(modern copy). Munch Museum (fig. 143)

**Self-portrait in front of veranda
steps, Ekely**, 1930, gelatin silver print
(modern copy). Munch Museum (fig. 137)

Fips, ca. 1930, gelatin silver print
(modern copy). Munch Museum (fig. 140)

**Self-portrait in front of *Metabolism*,
Ekely**, 1931–32, gelatin silver print
(modern copy). Munch Museum (fig. 144)

Metabolism with shadow and reflections, Ekely, 1931–32, gelatin silver print (modern copy). Munch Museum (fig. 145)

Munch-related Works

Munch in Herbert Esche's library, Chemnitz, 1905, unknown photographer, (modern copy). Munch Museum Archives (fig. 16)

Edvard Munch with Rosa Meissner on the beach in Warnemünde, 1907, probably photographed by Olga Meissner, collodion print (modern copy). Munch Museum (fig. 138)

Munch in front of the veranda steps at Ekely, 1926, photographed by Inger Munch (modern copy). Munch Museum

Munch in the Winter Studio at Ekely on the occasion of his seventy-fifth birthday, 1938, photographed by Ragnvald Vaering (modern copy). Munch Museum Archives (fig. 78)

Edvard Munch's bedspread, probably early 20th century, cotton applique on linen, 59 x 112 1/2 in. (150 x 286 cm) irregular edge. Munch Museum, donated by The Friends of the Munch Museum, 1997 (fig. 81)

Jasper Johns

American, born 1930

Paintings

Corpse and Mirror II, 1974–75, oil on canvas (four panels), with painted frame, 57 7/8 x 75 1/4 in. (147 x 191.1 cm). Collection of the artist (fig. 8)

Usuyuki, 1977–78, encaustic and collage on canvas (three panels), 35 1/16 x 57 3/8 in. (89.2 x 145.8 cm), framed. The Cleveland Museum of Art, Leonard C. Hanna, Jr. Fund (fig. 48)

Cicada, 1979, oil on canvas, 48 x 36 in. (121.9 x 91.4 cm). The Museum of Fine Arts, Houston, Museum purchase funded by the Caroline Wiess Law Accessions Endowment Fund (fig. 49)

Dancers on a Plane, 1980, oil on canvas with bronze frame, 78 3/8 x 63 3/4 in. (200 x 162 cm), framed. Tate London: Purchased 1981 (fig. 55)

Between the Clock and the Bed, 1981, oil on canvas (three panels), 72 x 126 1/4 in. (182.9 x 320.7 cm). Collection of the artist (fig. 72)

Between the Clock and the Bed, 1981, encaustic on canvas (three panels), 72 1/8 x 126 3/8 in. (183.2 x 321 cm). The Museum of Modern Art, New York, Gift of Agnes Gund **(Richmond only)** (fig. 71)

In the Studio, 1982, encaustic and collage on canvas with objects, 75 x 50 x 5 in. (190.5 x 127 x 12.7). Collection of the artist (fig. 95)

Perilous Night, 1982, encaustic on canvas with objects, 67 1/8 x 96 1/8 x 6 1/4 in. (170.5 x 244.2 x 15.9 cm). National Gallery of Art, Washington, DC, Collection of Robert and Jane Meyerhoff (fig. 102)

Between the Clock and the Bed, 1982–83, encaustic on canvas (three panels), 72 x 126 1/4 in. (182.9 x 320.7 cm). Virginia Museum of Fine Arts, Richmond, Gift of the Sydney and Frances Lewis Foundation (fig. 73)

Untitled, 1984, encaustic on canvas, 50 x 75 in. (127 x 190.5 cm). Collection of the artist (fig. 106)

Summer, 1985, encaustic on canvas, 75 x 50 in. (190.5 x 127 cm). The Museum of Modern Art, New York, Gift of Phillip Johnson (fig. 116)

Spring, 1986, encaustic on canvas, 75 x 50 in. (190.5 x 127 cm). Robert and Jane Meyerhoff Collection (fig. 115)

Fall, 1986, encaustic on canvas, 75 x 50 in. (190.5 x 127 cm). Collection of the artist (fig. 117)

Winter, 1986, encaustic on canvas, 75 x 50 in. (190.5 x 127 cm). Private collection (fig. 118)

Drawings

Handprint, 1964, oil on paper, 20 5/16 x 17 1/4 in. (51.6 x 43.8 cm). Collection of Jack Shear (fig. 37)

Illustration for the book "In Memory of My Feelings," by Frank O'Hara, 1967, graphite and gouache on acetate, 12 7/16 x 19 in. (31.6 x 48.2 cm). The Museum of Modern Art, New York, Gift of the Artist (fig. 59)

Corpse and Mirror, 1975–76, watercolor on paper, 20 x 28 in. (50.8 x 71.1 cm). Private collection (fig. 9)

Savarin, 1977, graphite pencil and crayon on plastic, 37 x 32 1/4 in. (94 x 81.9 cm). Private collection, New York (fig. 17)

Savarin, 1977, ink on plastic, 36 1/4 x 26 1/8 in. (92.1 x 66.4 cm). The Museum of Modern Art, New York, Gift of the Lauder Foundation (fig. 18)

Cicada, 1979, watercolor, graphite pencil, and crayon on paper, 43 x 28 3/4 in. (109.2 x 73 cm). The Museum of Fine Arts, Houston, Museum purchase funded by the Caroline Wiess Law Accessions Endowment Fund (fig. 50)

Tantric Detail, 1980, charcoal on paper, 58 x 41 in. (147.3 x 104.1 cm). Collection of the artist (fig. 67)

Between the Clock and the Bed, 1980, pastel on paper, 27 15/16 x 23 7/16 in. (71.1 x 59.7 cm). Collection of Marsha and Jeffrey Perelman **(Oslo only)** (fig. 84)

Between the Clock and the Bed, 1980/1988, ink and watercolor on plastic, 13 1/4 x 22 1/2 in. (33.7 x 57.2 cm). Private collection (fig. 83)

Untitled, 1982, oil, crayon, and graphite pencil on plastic, 18 7/8 x 12 in. (47.9 x 30.5 cm). Collection of the artist (fig. 96)

Untitled, 1982, pastel and graphite pencil on paper, 17 1/8 x 8 3/8 in. (43.5 x 21.3 cm), sight. Collection of the artist (fig. 97)

Between the Clock and the Bed, 1984, watercolor and graphite pencil on paper, 24 3/8 x 36 1/8 in. (61.9 x 91.8 cm). Robert and Jane Meyerhoff Collection (fig. 85)

Summer, 1985, charcoal on paper, 30 3/8 x 20 3/8 in. (77.2 x 51.8 cm). Collection of the artist (fig. 155)

Winter, 1986, charcoal on paper, 42 x 29 7/8 in. (106.7 x 75.8 cm). Collection of Julie and Edward J. Minskoff (fig. 157)

Spring, 1986, pastel and charcoal on paper, 41 5/8 x 27 7/8 in. (105.7 x 70.8 cm). Collection of the artist (fig. 148)

Spring, 1986, pencil on paper, 24 x 18 3/8 in. (61 x 46.7 cm). The Museum of Modern Art, New York, Gift of Leo Castelli in memory of Toiny Castelli (pg. xii)

Untitled, 1988, ink on plastic, 26 1/2 x 19 1/2 in. (67.3 x 49.6 cm). Collection of the artist (fig. 156)

The Seasons, 1989/1990, acrylic over intaglio on paper, 26 1/4 x 57 3/10 in. (66.7 x 146.2 cm). Private collection (fig. 151)

Prints

Hatteras, 1963, lithograph, 41 x 29 in. (104.1 x 73.7 cm). Ryobi Foundation. (fig. 36)

Skin with O'Hara Poem, 1965, lithograph, 22 x 34 in. (55.9 x 86.4 cm). Ryobi Foundation (fig. 35)

1st Etchings (Savarin), 1968, intaglio, 25 x 20 in. (63.5 x 50.8 cm). Ryobi Foundation (fig. 12)

1st Etchings, 2nd State (Savarin), 1968, intaglio, 25 5/16 x 19 9/16 in. (65.4 x 48.9 cm). Ryobi Foundation (fig. 13)

Four Panels from Untitled 1972, 1974, lithographs with embossing, 40 x 28 1/2 in. (101.6 x 72.4 cm) each. Courtesy of Gemini G.E.L., Los Angeles (fig. 4)

Scent, 1976, lithograph, linocut, and woodcut, 31 1/2 x 47 in. (79.4 x 119.4 cm). Ryobi Foundation (fig. 7)

Corpse and Mirror, 1976, intaglio, 25 1/2 x 19 3/4 in. (64.8 x 50.2 cm). Ryobi Foundation.

Corpse and Mirror, 1976, lithograph, 30 3/4 x 39 3/4 in. (78.1 x 101 cm). Ryobi Foundation.

Untitled, 1977, lithograph, 27 1/2 x 40 in. (69.9 x 101.6 cm). Collection of Stan and Renie Helfgott (fig. 19)

Savarin, 1977, lithograph, 45 x 35 in. (114.3 x 88.9 cm). Collection of Brian Goldston and Peter Balis (fig. 20)

Savarin, 1977, lithograph, 48 x 32 in. (121.9 x 81.3 cm). Courtesy Universal Limited Art Editions (fig. 14)

Savarin, 1981, lithograph, 50 x 38 in. (127 x 96.5). Private Collection (fig. 47)

Savarin 2 (Wash and Line), 1978, lithograph, 26 x 20 1/2 in. (66 x 52.1 cm). Collection of Larissa Goldston (fig. 38)

Savarin 3 (Red), 1978, lithograph, 26 1/16 x 20 1/16 in. (66 x 52.1 cm). Collection of Brian Goldston and Peter Balis (fig. 39)

Savarin 4 (Oval), 1978, lithograph, 26 x 20 1/2 in. (66 x 52.1 cm). Collection of Brian Goldston and Peter Balis (fig. 40)

Savarin 5 (Corpse and Mirror), 1978, lithograph, 26 x 20 1/2 in. (66 x 52.1 cm). Collection of Brian Goldston and Peter Balis (fig. 41)

Savarin, 1978, monotype, 27 1/4 x 19 5/8 in. (69.2 x 49.8 cm). Collection of the artist (fig. 42)

Savarin, 1978, monotype,
26 x 21$\frac{1}{2}$ in. (66 x 54.6 cm).
Private collection (fig. 43)

Usuyuki, 1981, screenprint,
29$\frac{1}{2}$ x 47$\frac{1}{4}$ in. (74.9 x 120 cm).
Ryobi Foundation (fig. 74)

Savarin, 1982, monotype over lithograph,
50$\frac{1}{4}$ x 38$\frac{1}{8}$ in. (127.6 x 96.8 cm).
Whitney Museum of American Art,
New York; Gift of The American
Contemporary Art Foundation, Inc.,
Leonard A. Lauder, President (fig. 87)

Savarin, 1982, monotype, 50 x 38 in.
(127 x 96.5 cm). Whitney Museum of
American Art, New York; Gift of The
American Contemporary Art Foundation,
Inc., Leonard A. Lauder, President (fig. 88)

Savarin, 1982, monotype over lithograph,
50$\frac{1}{4}$ x 38$\frac{1}{8}$ in. (127.6 x 96.8 cm).
Whitney Museum of American Art,
New York; Gift of The American
Contemporary Art Foundation, Inc.,
Leonard A. Lauder, President (fig. 89)

Savarin, 1982, monotype, 50 x 38 in.
(127 x 96.5 cm). Whitney Museum
of American Art, New York;
Gift of The American Contemporary Art
Foundation, Inc., Leonard A. Lauder,
President (fig. 90)

Savarin, 1982, monotype with
hand additions over lithograph,
50$\frac{1}{4}$ x 38$\frac{1}{8}$ in. (127.6 x 96.8 cm).
Whitney Museum of American Art,
New York; Gift of The American
Contemporary Art Foundation, Inc.,
Leonard A. Lauder, President (fig. 91)

Savarin, 1982, monotype over lithograph,
50 x 38$\frac{1}{8}$ in. (127 x 96.8 cm). Whitney
Museum of American Art, New York;
Gift of The American Contemporary Art
Foundation, Inc., Leonard A. Lauder,
President (fig. 92)

Savarin, 1982, monotype,
50 x 38$\frac{1}{8}$ in. (127 x 96.8 cm).
Whitney Museum of American Art,
New York; Gift of The American
Contemporary Art Foundation, Inc.,
Leonard A. Lauder, President (fig. 93)

Savarin, 1982, monotype over lithograph,
49$\frac{3}{4}$ x 38 in. (126.4 x 96.5 cm).
Whitney Museum of American Art,
New York; Gift of The American
Contemporary Art Foundation, Inc.,
Leonard A. Lauder, President (fig. 94)

Winter, 1986, intaglio, 16 x 12 in.
(40.6 x 30.5 cm). Courtesy Universal
Limited Art Editions (fig. 149)

**The Seasons (Spring, Summer, Fall,
Winter)**, 1987, intaglios, 26 x 19 in.
(66 x 48.3 cm) each. Courtesy Universal
Limited Art Editions (fig. 150)

Winter, 1989, lithograph, 15 x 11 in.
(38.1 x 27.9 cm). Courtesy Universal
Limited Art Editions

Index

Photo Credits

Bridgeman Images: figs. 103, 107

Photo © Carl Brunn: fig. 6

Scan Courtesy Cineteca di Bologna: fig. 77

Photo © The Cleveland Museum of Art: fig. 48

Photo: Susan Cole: fig. 86

© O. Vaering Eftf: figs. 78, 100

Photo Maurice Aeschimann Genève © 2015 Estate of Pablo Picasso / Artist Rights Society (ARS), New York: fig. 114

Photo: Børre Høstland © The National Museum of Art, Architecture and Design: figs. 29, 108, 121

© 1974 Jasper Johns and Gemini G.E.L: fig. 4

Photo: Nathan Keay © Museum of Contemporary Art Chicago: fig. 58

Spike Mafford: fig. 151

© Munch Museum: p. x; figs. 15–16, 26–28, 30–31, 44–46, 52–54, 57, 60–63, 65–66, 75–76, 79, 81, 98–99, 101, 109–13, 120, 122–27, 129–47, 148

Digital Image ©The Museum of Modern Art/Licensed by SCALA / Art Resource, NY: p. xii; figs. 1, 18, 59, 71, 116

Image courtesy of the National Gallery of Art, Washington: fig. 72, 115

Photo: © Rheinisches Bildarchiv Köln: fig. 3

© RMN-Grand Palais / Art Resource, NY © 2015 Estate of Pablo Picasso / Artist Rights Society (ARS), New York: fig. 119

© Jamie M. Stukenberg / Professional Graphics Inc., Rockford, Illinois, Courtesy of the Menil Collection, Houston: figs. 9, 155–56

Tate, London / Art Resource, NY: fig. 55

Photo: Jerry L. Thompson, Courtesy of The Menil Collection, Houston: fig. 37

Image courtesy Universal Limited Art Editions: figs. 12–13, 19–20, 22, 35–36, 38–41, 47, 149–50

Universal Limited Art Editions Copyright Jasper Johns / ULAE, 1978 / Licensed by VAGA, New York: fig. 43

Photo: Joshua White/JWPictures.com, Courtesy of The Menil Collection, Houston: fig. 157

Digital Image © Whitney Museum of American Art: figs. 87–94

© Wilse / Norwegian Museum of Cultural History: figs. 80, 158